THE COMPLETE IDIOT'S GUIDE® TO

The Lives of the Saints

by Paul L. Williams, Ph.D.

ALPHA

A Pearson Education Company

International Standard Book Number: 0-02-864211-2
Library of Congress Catalog Card Number: 2001091660

03   02   01   8   7   6   5   4   3   2   1

Interpretation of the printing code: The rightmost number of the first series of numbers is the year of the book's printing; the rightmost number of the second series of numbers is the number of the book's printing. For example, a printing code of 01-1 shows that the first printing occurred in 2001.

Printed in the United States of America

Publisher
Marie Butler-Knight

Senior Acquisitions Editor
Renee Wilmeth

Product Manager
Phil Kitchel

Managing Editor
Jennifer Chisholm

Development Editor
Jennifer Moore

Production Editor
Katherin Bidwell

Copy Editor
Krista Hansing

Illustrator
Jody Schaeffer

Cover Designers
Mike Freeland
Kevin Spear

Book Designers
Scott Cook and Amy Adams of DesignLab

Indexer
Angie Bess

Layout/Proofreading
Angela Calvert
John Etchison

Contents at a Glance

Contents

Part 3: The Middle Ages: When Sainthood Was in Flower — 109

9 White Martyrdom: Confessors Open the Back Door to Heaven — 111

Foreword

Most books on the lives of the saints are disappointments. The authors are really not hagiographers. They merely crack open Alban Butler's classic *Lives of the Saints* and provide readers with a rehash of the stories.

This book by Paul Williams, my friend and former professional colleague, is different, startlingly different. Williams goes beyond Butler to the primary sources—the works of the early Church Fathers, the martyrologies, and primitive ecclesiology—to recount the lives of the Christian heroes and heroines for a distinctly modern audience. The book is amazingly light and fun to read and yet it imparts profundities in a provocative and knowing manner. For example, Williams actually discusses the distinction between the holy and the profane, the physical and the spiritual, so that Christian doctrine becomes clear and understandable. Many often wonder why virginity is such a cardinal virtue for Christians and such a key factor for sainthood. Williams doesn't gloss over this question—he tackles it in a straightforward manner—and, by so doing, provides religious instruction that is sadly missing in many parochial, let alone sectarian, works.

Another factor that makes this work distinctive is its jaunty, journalistic style. Williams, who worked with me in the rough-and-tumble world of newspapers, is a prize-winning journalist who writes to be read not by Patristic scholars but by average readers who wish to be informed and, at the same time, not bored to tears.

Williams is uniquely qualified to deal with this subject. He holds a Ph.D. in medieval theology and served for many years as a college professor and editor of the annual proceedings of The Fellowship of Catholic Scholars. His work on Peter Abelard, which was published by The University Press in 1980, has been hailed as "a definite work" on early scholasticism. Another book, *Everything You Always Wanted to Know About the Catholic Church but Were Afraid to Ask for Fear of Excommunication,* published by Doubleday in 1990, became a text for students of Roman Catholicism.

Many portions of *The Complete Idiot's Guide to the Lives of the Saints* are not only witty but also downright hilarious. This is no mean accomplishment. Williams can treat his subjects with tongue in cheek, while maintaining a necessary measure of reverence and respect. I particularly enjoyed the chapters on the Blessed Virgin Mary and the accounts of her visitations, especially her appearance on Egyptian television.

The book takes readers from the time of the first persecutions to the process of contemporary canonization. It is encyclopedic in content without being an encyclopedia. It is academic without being anemic. It is called *The Complete Idiot's Guide to the Lives of the Saints,* but it is not idiotic. The book, I believe, is a work of immediate importance that will enlighten and engage readers of all religious persuasions.

Mitchell Grochowski

—Mitchell Grochowski is the managing editor of "The Guard," a 104-year-old, continuously published weekly journal, dealing with religion and society, fraternalism, and ethnicity. He is also a professor at the Savanarola Theological Seminary in Scranton, Pennsylvania.

Introduction

I don't mean to brag, but writing this book on the saints has been a cinch for me. Other people would have had to spend countless hours researching thousands of the 10,000 saints, collecting hundreds of anecdotes, and reading volumes of long and tedious books, some in Latin. Others would have had to rewrite paragraphs to make everything flow and gel into an acceptable book. But I knew that my book would be a model of graceful prose, intricate simplicity, great charm, and wonderful wit.

What's more, I knew that I could produce this book without long hours at a desk, facing a blank tablet with a sense of despair. In fact, I knew that I would never be lacking in thought or inspiration. The book would be perfectly structured and completely readable.

I never worried about the reaction of my agents or editors—not even the reaction of my readers—because I knew that this book would sell like hotcakes and become hailed as a new classic of Christian literature. I knew this reaction before I wrote a single word—because I know the saints. I know they possess the power of intercession. They can plead for us before the throne of God and obtain divine favors.

God loves the saints. They are His friends and relations, and, if the saints ask God for something, He most likely will give it to them in the same way that you would provide a favor or some help to your friends and your relatives. This is simple common sense, and it's the way Heaven works. If you experience bad luck, you shouldn't sulk in self-pity. You should turn to St. Agricola of Avignon or St. Cailda, both of whom specialize in bad luck. If you have family problems, you shouldn't sit and stew before a television set. You should call upon St. Baldus or St. Eustace, patron saints for family problems. If you have a bad hair day, you shouldn't scream before the mirror. You should simply turn to St. Martin of Porres, the patron of hairdressers and beauticians.

When it comes to intercession, you have to turn to the right saint for the situation. When perplexed by a problem, most people turn to saints who are besot and besieged with billions of requests, like St. Jude, the saint for lost causes, or St. Joseph, the patron saint of workers, or the Blessed Virgin. But I knew better. I turned to the patron saint of writers, St. Francis de Sales, not overwrought and overworked by pleas and petition.

Most people, sad to say, are unfamiliar with St. Francis de Sales, despite the fact that he is a Doctor of the Church and one of the most influential writers in the history of Christianity. He was frail and bald, and had a long straggly beard. As a saint, he is neither terribly exciting nor terribly attractive. He never performed a mind-boggling miracle such as walking on water or calming a storm. He never killed a dragon or rode a lion. He never cured lepers or raised the dead. When attacked by hungry wolves, St. Francis de Sales did not transform the pack of wolves into a flock of sheep. He simply climbed a tree and stayed there until villagers came to rescue him. St. Francis de Sales is not a bold and brave saint like St. Francis Xavier, nor a warm and fuzzy saint like St. Francis of Assisi.

What's more, St. Francis de Sales is not a national saint like St. Patrick, St. George, St. Andrew, St. David, St. Basil, St. Denis, St. Anthony, or St. Stanislaus. For this reason, he does not receive attention from ethnic groups. No parades or processions are held in his honor. As a member of the heavenly host, St. Francis de Sales keeps a low profile.

St. Francis de Sales is very specialized. He is the patron for writers, editors, and journalists. He is so specialized that standardized prayers are not offered to him. If you want to call upon St. Francis de Sales, you need to make up your own prayer. It can be something straightforward and simple, like my prayer: "O holy St. Francis, please come to my side and help me compose a *Complete Idiot's Guide.*"

I said this prayer, closed my eyes, and waved a sacred relic over a blank page, and words magically appeared. In less than an hour, the entire book was finished without one grammatical, historical, or hagiographical mistake. I simply sent it to the publishers, and they received it with shouts of joyful exaltation.

It was that simple. I knew the right saint for the right problem. If I suffer from an attack of lumbago, I shall turn to St. Lawrence; for gallstones, St. Albinus; for hemorrhoids, St. Fiacre; and for vampire bites, St. Marcel of Paris. (It's important to note that St. Fiacre is great with hemorrhoids but is practically useless when it comes to gallstones.)

Similarly, if you are of Armenian origin and turn to St. Patrick for assistance, the Irish patron saint will club you over the head with his shillelagh because you should be turning to the patron saints of Armenia, St. Bartholomew or St. Gregory the Enlightener.

You should also get to know the saint of your chosen profession, just as I got to know St. Francis de Sales. If you are an accountant, you must place yourself under the protection of St. Matthew. If you are a cook, you'll need to turn to St. Diego Alcala; a construction worker, to St. Thomas; a dancer, to St. Vitus; a dentist, to St. Appollonia; a lawyer, to St. Thomas More; and a teacher, to St. Cassian of Imola. Be careful. If you are a funeral director, you should not call upon St. Magnus of Orkney. St. Magnus is the patron for fishmongers. You should be turning to St. Joseph of Arimathea instead.

What You'll Discover in This Book

This book will guide you from the first saints to the latest. It is divided into five sections:

Part 1, "Eternity 101," is a brief introduction to the saints and a simple guide to the four regions of the afterlife: Heaven, purgatory, limbo, and hell.

Part 2, "A Primer to the Communion of Saints," is an introduction to the very first Christian saints: the holy apostles, the glorious martyrs, and the amazing apologists.

Part 3, "The Middle Ages: When Sainthood Was in Flower," introduces you to the confessors, the Doctors, and the Brides of Christ, all for your enjoyment and edification.

Part 4, "The Queen of Heaven," covers all you'll ever need to know about Mary Ever Virgin, from her humble beginnings on earth to her coronation in Heaven.

Part 5, "Saints in the Twenty-First Century," shows how difficult life has become for saints in the twenty-first century; but if you really want to be a saint, it can be done if you follow the right formula.

Helpful Hints for the Reader

Throughout these pages, you will encounter sidebars that will improve your pilgrimage to the heavenly kingdom.

Divine Revelation

In these boxes, you'll find Scriptural insights into the lives of the saints.

St. Peter Speaks

In these boxes, St. Peter defines terms that you might not be familiar with and clarifies matters of Catholic doctrine and dogma.

Holy Cow!

In these boxes, you'll find interesting trivia and tidbits about the saints and the history of Christianity that you can use to impress your friends.

Hagar the Hagiographer

A *hagiographer* is someone who studies the lives of saints. In these boxes, you'll receive insights and anecdotes about the lives of the saints, plus some prayers you can say to them to ask for their intercession.

Gratitude List

Besides St. Francis de Sales, I would like to thank my wife, Patricia, who is a model of sainthood; my wonderful, virtuous, and beautiful daughter, Katie, who is a gift from God; my sister and spiritual adviser, Judith Schmitt, who safeguards my prose by prayer; my chaste and holy secretary, Mary Riggall, who will receive a great reward in Heaven; and my angelic agents, Sheree Bykofsky and Janet Rosen, who can perform wonders for writers.

Trademarks

All terms mentioned in this book that are known to be or are suspected of being trademarks or service marks have been appropriately capitalized. Alpha Books and Pearson Education, Inc. cannot attest to the accuracy of this information. Use of a term in this book should not be regarded as affecting the validity of any trademark or service mark.

Part 1

Eternity 101

You cannot approach the subject of the saints without knowing who they are, where they live, and what they do.

For starters, the saints are Christian heroes who, for the most part, died hundreds—even thousands—of years ago. They are dead, long dead. And yet, they live in the eternal realm of Heaven.

The saints are alive! They have bodies. They wear clothing. They say prayers. They accomplish wondrous things. And get this: They will answer you when you call them by name.

But, to encounter the saints, you have to enter eternity. You can do this by simply turning the page.

Chapter 1

The Community of Saints

In This Chapter

➤ How saints are different from you and me

➤ How saints can help you out

➤ Why saints are a Catholic thing

➤ Why virginity is crucial to becoming a saint

Saints Be Praised: It All Comes from the Catholics

Let's face it: Saints are a Catholic thing. Only Catholics recite litanies of the saints. Only Catholics have patron saints. Only Catholics pray to the saints. Only Catholics venerate a hank of hair from the saints.

Some people would like to think that it's a Christian thing, but it's not. Oh, sure, Protestants believe in saints, but for them, saints are the heroes of the New Testament. According to Protestants, the four evangelists—Matthew, Mark, Luke, and John—are saints, along with Jesus' 12 apostles (including Matthias, not Judas). Paul is a saint because he is the author of many epistles (the epistles are part of the canon, or body, of the New Testament). And so, say the Protestants, the people who penned the New Testament deserve to be *canonized*.

These few New Testament figures are Protestant saints or holy ones (from the Latin "sanctus," meaning "holy." You can find Protestant churches named after them, most especially after St. Paul.

Indeed, St. Paul would probably be the patron saint of Protestantism, if Protestantism had a patron saint. After all, Paul stood in marked disagreement with Peter, the patron saint of the papacy. But Protestants have no patron saints. They have no lists of the holy ones. They fail to recognize, let alone canonize, saints in the post-apostolic period—that is, the span of time from the New Testament period to the present. No one but Almighty God, Protestants maintain, has the right to acclaim a certain individual as a saint.

St. Peter Speaks

Canonization is the ecclesiastical process of proclaiming a person a saint. You must be dead to be canonized.

Divine Revelation

Throughout the New Testament, believers who affirm that Jesus is the Christ are called saints. St. Paul, for example, addresses his letter to the Romans "to all in Rome who are loved by God and called saints" (Rom. 1:7).

Holy Cow!

In Catholic catechisms or instructional books, Catholics are told to honor the blessed in Heaven and to pray to them.

It's Paganism: Protestants Accuse Catholics of Worshipping Idols

The communion of saints in Protestantism represents not a spiritual group of hallowed figures surrounding the throne of God in Heaven. Rather, it represents the body of Christian believers on earth—that is, the visible church.

Martin Luther denounced the Catholic doctrine of the intercession of saints as a reversion to pagan idolatry. The saints, he said, have no power to intercede for sinners. "There is but one Mediator, Propitiatory, High Priest and Intercessor, namely, Jesus Christ," he wrote.

John Calvin agreed with Luther and condemned the Catholic doctrine of the intercession of the saints as "Satanic." The saints, he said, are the elect, those who have been predestined from all eternity for salvation without regard to their good works or godly character. Calvin, like Luther, defined the communion of saints as the gathering of the faithful. Zwingli, the great Anabaptist reformer, followed suit, stating in his articles that the notion of the saintly intercession is blasphemous and "injurious to Christ."

In the 39 articles of the Anglican Confession, the Invocation of the Saints is rejected as "a fond thing, vainly invented, and grounded upon no warranty of Scripture." It is, the Confession says, a teaching that is "repugnant to the Word of God." This belief is upheld by the following Protestant denominations:

➤ United Methodists

➤ Primitive Methodists

➤ United Baptists

➤ American Baptists

➤ Southern Baptists

➤ Episcopalians

➤ ELCA Lutherans

➤ Missouri Synod Lutherans

➤ Assemblies of God

➤ United Presbyterians

➤ Bible Presbyterians

➤ Evangelical Presbyterians

➤ Quakers

➤ Shakers

➤ Fundamentalists

Holy Cow!

According to a recent *Time/CNN* poll, 79 percent of the American people believe that St. Peter is in Heaven.

Want to Be a Saint? Become a Roman Catholic!

With few exceptions, there are no Protestant saints. There is no St. Martin Luther or St. John Calvin. John Wesley never attained sainthood, nor did Joseph Smith, who, ironically, was the founder of the Church of Latter Day Saints. Dietrich Bonhoeffer, the Protestant cleric who was hanged for opposing the Third Reich, was never pronounced a "servant of Christ." The only Protestants who have been canonized were a number of the 22 martyrs of Uganda, who, as it turned out, were Episcopalians. These Protestant martyrs were canonized by Pope Paul VI in 1964 and represented the Roman Catholic Church's new openness to the so-called "separated brethren."

However, there are a good number of Jewish saints in the Kingdom of Heaven. Abraham, the father of the Judeo-Christian religion, is a saint, along with Isaac, Jacob, and Joseph. King David is a saint, even though he was a great sinner. The major prophets—Isaiah, Jeremiah, and Ezekiel—are saints, along with the minor prophets from Hosea to Malachi. The parents and grandparents of Jesus are saints, along with all the pious Jews (including the twelve apostles) who proclaimed Him as Savior during His earthly ministry. But no Jew who remains outside the Christian tradition has been canonized.

Divine Revelation

Moses, the great Old Testament figure who received the Ten Commandments and knew God face to face, has not been acclaimed as a saint.

There are no Muslim saints and no Hindu saints. Buddha became a saint, but it was by accident (see Chapter 18, "Heavenly Horrors! Saints Get Kicked Out of God's Kingdom," for that wacky story).

There are no secular saints. Abraham Lincoln, Martin Luther King Jr., and John F. Kennedy may be mourned as national martyrs, but they are not canonized saints.

Protestants Protest: It's Not Only Pagan, but It's Unscriptural

Sainthood is a Catholic thing. For Protestants, the Catholic teaching of saints epitomizes false belief—belief based on folklore and "papal superstition." They cannot comprehend why Catholics turn to the saints as mediators and intercessors. They cannot understand why Catholics cherish the images of the saints and venerate their relics. It seems so medieval. It seems so superstitious. It seems so *unscriptural*. And all doctrine, Protestants maintain, must have a basis in the Bible.

To provide a scriptural basis for the communion of saints, Catholic theologians turn to the following passage from the 12th chapter of the Epistle to the Hebrews:

> Therefore, since we are surrounded by such a great cloud of witnesses, let us throw off everything that hinders us, and the sin that so easily entangles, and let us run with perseverance the race marked out for us. (12:1)

Holy Cow!

Martin Luther taught that a belief not based in the Bible must be discarded.

The "cloud of witnesses," Catholics argue, represents the apostles and martyrs, the confessors and desert fathers, the ascetic monks and the holy virgins who lived exemplary Christian lives and who have passed on to their eternal reward. These holy ones have not died. They are alive and well and living in Heaven.

Catholics Rely on the Truth of Tradition

Apart from this vague passage, Catholic scholars concur that no other Biblical text can be used to support the belief in saints as heavenly intercessors between God and man. Such teachings come not from scripture but from tradition. But, for Catholics, that's okay. In Catholicism, the fact that a belief is un-Biblical does not negate its veracity. The dogmas of the Immaculate Conception, the Assumption of Mary, and papal infallibility have little or no basis in scripture. The same can be said about the doctrines of purgatory, limbo, and the Beatific Vision. Nevertheless, according to Catholics, they are true. They insist that sacred teachings, such as the truth of the communion of saints, comes from the following sources:

Divine Revelation

In Catholicism, beliefs can be based on tradition rather than the books of the Bible.

➤ The Old Testament and the New Testament

➤ The writings of the Church Fathers

➤ The pronouncements of the ecumenical or "universal" councils

➤ The proclamations of the popes, who are the successors of St. Peter

The importance of tradition in Catholicism was emphasized by the Second Vatican Council, which declared in 1965:

> Tradition transmits in its entirety the Word of God which has been entrusted to the apostles so that, enlightened by the Spirit of truth, they may faithfully preserve, expound and spread it abroad by their preaching. Thus it comes about that the Church does not draw her certainty about all revealed truth from the holy Scriptures alone.

And so, Protestants say, "It ain't scriptural," while Catholics respond by saying, "So what? It's traditional!"

Let's Cut to Sex

You cannot understand Christianity's condemnation of sexual activity outside the confines of marriage without coming to terms with our make-up as human beings. Sure, we are animals. We possess bodies. We are physical beings. But traditional Christianity teaches that humans are made in the image and likeness of God. Like God, we are spiritual beings. This teaching is substantiated by the fact that we can do things—spiritual things—that other animals cannot do. We can speak. We can think. We can dream. We can plan. We can transcend the limitations of the physical universe. We each possess a soul.

This raises an important question: How is a soul produced? Traditional Christianity teaches that the soul was bestowed upon man by the very breath of God. Genesis 2:7 says: "The Lord God formed the man from the dust of the ground and breathed into his nostrils the breath of life, and man became a living being." This means that man is superior to all other animals. He is above all created things because he possesses a spiritual essence. This essence is passed on from generation to generation by the act of procreation.

Once produced, souls are immortal! For this reason, Christians throughout the ages have issued grave warnings about the terrible spiritual problem of producing souls in a careless or frivolous manner. Once created, souls cannot be cast away in a black hole. They cannot be hauled away to a dumping ground in the hereafter.

Holy Cow!

Medieval theologians taught that the soul is in the sperm and that the egg provides the matter or body. For this reason, they said, men are superior to women.

All discussion of Christian teaching of eternal life is based on the belief that the sexual act is sacred. It is sacred because it produces a sacred product: a soul, an individual, a person. Prominent Christian theologians from St. Thomas Aquinas to Martin Luther taught that the sole purpose of sexual activity is procreation. They maintained that this "truth" is evident by natural law, that is, by the very way that people are made, by their "parts," by the fact that male and female by the act of copulation become "one flesh."

From Sex to Sainthood!

What does all this talk about sex have to do with sainthood? Holiness is related to sexual purity, to chastity, and to virginity. The great female saints were holy virgins. For this reason, the Catholic Church maintains that Mary never had sex with Joseph or any other man, that her hymen remained (and remains) intact.

Divine Revelation

Natural law comes down to a matter of nuts and bolts. It simply means that a part of the male anatomy is meant to join with a part of the female anatomy. Any other way of trying to make the parts fit is unnatural or perverse.

Divine Revelation

Sexual renunciation is a means of obtaining a place of prominence in the Kingdom of Heaven.

Similarly, the great male saints lived lives—in the words of St. Jerome—"as though they did not have bodies." They refused to engage in sexual activities and shunned the wiles of wanton women.

A worldly saint is a contradiction in terms. It is a theological oxymoron. There are no worldly saints, just as there are no saintly sinners. Some saints may have been worldly. But, by definition, they are individuals who have turned from the world, the flesh, and the devil. Very few saints were married—St. Thomas More and St. Elizabeth Ann Seton being notable exceptions. There is a distinction between the physical and the spiritual, the flesh and the spirit, the mortal and the immortal, the holy and the profane that remains embedded in the warp and woof of Christian doctrine. When this distinction is denied, Christian doctrine, as a whole, seems irrational or senseless.

Saints are those who know and uphold the distinction between the sacred and the profane. They separate themselves from the things of this world in order to devote their lives to the eternal, to the transcendent, to the things of the spirit. They pass through human history as wayfarers on a pilgrimage to the Kingdom of God. They have their eyes fixed upon the eternal realm and not the transitory things of this world, not physical pleasure, not fame or gain, not even home and family. For this reason, saints are strange. They do not belong to planet earth. They belong to a different universe. They are, as the Book of Hebrews says, "aliens" (Heb. 11:13).

The Saints Are Alive and Well and Living in Heaven

The saints are not personages from the past. They are alive and well and living in Heaven. The saints are God's closest friends and they are His closest companions. They have access at all times to His throne and they can plead the cases of the living and the dead. They are powerful. They can get things done. They can perform miracles.

What's more, there is a division of labor in Heaven. There are certain saints for certain nations; certain saints for certain professions; certain saints for certain problems; certain saints for certain ailments. In the Kingdom of Heaven, as all *hagiographers* know, it is important to find the right saint for you.

And About Those Halos ...

News flash: Saints don't have halos. Nope. Forget about all those pictures you see of St. Mary, St. Joseph, and St. Francis of Assisi wandering around with shimmering halos hovering above their heads. A halo is a symbol that early Christians took over from the pagans and now is used only by artists to suggest holiness or sainthood. Originally, halos showed a deceased person's relationship to the Roman sun god, Sol. Instead, saints wear crowns of gold.

So if a saint wearing a halo knocks on your door, my advice would be to slam the door shut and drop to your knees in prayer: It's probably the devil in disguise!

Get Ready for a Holy Tour of the Saints' Lives

So now that you know the basics about the saints, you're ready to learn the details—some of them quite gory, most of them bizarre, but all of them utterly fascinating—about God's closest friends. Fasten your seatbelt, grab any saintly relics you might have lying around, and get ready for the holiest roller-coaster ride you've ever been on!

Hagar the Hagiographer

Although you might not have spent much time thinking about the saints, there are some people who have devoted their entire lives to this task. Believe it or not, there is a field of study devoted entirely to the lives of the saints. It is called **hagiology** or **hagiography,** and the people who study this subject are called **hagiographers.**

Divine Revelation

The communion of saints represents the union of the faithful on earth, the blessed in Heaven, and the souls in purgatory.

The Least You Need to Know

➤ Saints are God's closest friends and can intercede on our behalf.

➤ Catholics define saints as a group of hallowed figures surrounding the throne of God in Heaven.

➤ Protestants decry as idolatry praying to the saints in Heaven.

➤ Saints focus on their souls and deny themselves of their bodily desires.

➤ Saints wear golden crowns, not halos.

Chapter 2

Heaven, the Home of the Saints: Eternal Bliss but No Sex, No Pets, and No MTV

In This Chapter

➤ The gated community of Heaven

➤ Heaven as home for the saints

➤ The lay of the land

➤ Why anyone would ever want to go to Heaven

According to Catholic doctrine, there are four distinct regions of the afterlife: Heaven, purgatory, limbo, and hell. These regions are separated by vast chasms of time and space. They are not parts of the same continent—not even continents of the same planet. Rather, each region represents a different plane of existence, a different form of reality, and a different place of being.

Each region is a place—a real place, no less real than where you're sitting now reading this book. And people, real people, *live*—truly and consciously live—in each eternal realm. Some experience eternal bliss; others suffer everlasting horror. Some sleep eternally; others suffer temporarily. As a matter of fact, Christians—both Protestant and Catholic—believe that the dead are more fully alive in the afterlife than they were as flesh-and-blood persons on earth.

You'll get a quick tour of purgatory, limbo, and hell in the next chapter, but in this chapter we'll focus on Heaven, the home of the saints.

St. Peter Speaks

Heaven comes from the Latin word *coelum*, meaning "roof." The ancients thought that Heaven was the roof of the world.

Holy Cow!

In Christian doctrine, God is not part of the universe. He is not at one with creation. God stands apart from creation. Pantheism, the belief that God is in all things, contradicts the teachings of scripture and tradition.

St. Peter Speaks

Everyone ends up in one of the four regions of the afterlife: Heaven, purgatory, limbo, and hell. Catholics have more choices than Protestants, who deny the existence of purgatory and limbo.

Who Has a Home in Heaven

Heaven is the dwelling place of God, of course, but also of several other individuals, including these:

➤ Jesus

➤ Saints

➤ Angels

➤ Singing stones

➤ Four winged beasts that constantly give glory to God

Heaven Is a Gated Community

Based on New Testament teachings, theologians came to discern that the dwelling place of God has carefully defined borders. Hell is not Heaven. Neither is purgatory or limbo. Neither, for that matter, is Portland, Oregon. Heaven is a restricted area in terms of the people who live there and in terms of its geographical borders. In other words, it is a planned community in the manner of an upscale retirement village in Palm Springs.

Heaven Is Inhabited by Real People

Heaven is inhabited by spiritual bodies—real bodies with real shapes—and these bodies belong, in part, to real people with real names. It is not a place of ghostly shapes and phantom forms. And when you call these people by name, they can respond. The names of the human inhabitants of Heaven remain the same as they were at the time of their baptism. Francis Xavier remains Francis Xavier, Ignatius Loyola remains Ignatius Loyola, and Peter Claver remains Peter Claver. These people occupy space. They can be seen. They can be heard. They can be felt. They emit an odor (always pleasing). And, presumably, they can be tasted, if anyone chooses to bite them. The Heaven dwellers are not merged into one great mass. They are not dissolved within the divine essence to form one spiritual body. They retain their individuality.

Because they are real people with real bodies, the residents of Heaven live in real places in Heaven. These places are not humble dwellings, but spacious and luxurious mansions. When Jesus speaks to His disciples about Heaven, He says: "In my Father's house, there are many mansions; if it were not so, I would have told you. I am going there to prepare a place for you." (John 14:2–3).

The Real Skinny on Heaven: It's a Celestial Cube

Inhabited by real people, who live in real houses, Heaven is a real city. The author of Hebrews attests to this belief (11:16). St. Paul claims that he had been transported to this city and that he personally beheld its wonders. But he remains strangely silent about the details:

> I know a man in Christ who fourteen years ago was caught up in the third heaven. Whether it was in the body or out of the body I do not know—God knows. And I know that this man—whether in the body or apart from the body I do not know, but God knows—was caught up to paradise. He heard inexpressible things, things that man is not permitted to tell (2 Corinthians 12:2–4).

St. John, however, who also was granted a view of Heaven, was permitted to tell. He describes the City of God with phantasmagoric language in the book of Revelation, the last book of the New Testament. Heaven, he says, is laid out as a three-dimensional cube, measuring 12,000 stadia, or 1,400 miles, in width and in height. It is surrounded by a colossal wall that is 144 cubits, or 200 feet, thick. For readers who think that many of these claims are incredible, St. John piously states that the measurements of the heavenly city were made not by him, but by an angel who used man-made instruments.

It's Kind of Like the Land of Oz

Besides describing its geometry, St. John records other remarkable things about the City of God. The thick walls, he says, are made of jasper. He neglects

Holy Cow!

Speaking of Heaven in 1950, the young evangelist Billy Graham said: "It is a place as real as Los Angeles, London, Algiers, or Boston. It is 1,600 miles long, 1,600 miles wide, and 1,600 high. Once there, we are going to sit around and have parties, and the angels will wait on us, and we'll drive down the golden streets in a yellow Cadillac convertible."

Divine Revelation

In *A History of Heaven*, scholar Jeffrey Burton Russell writes: "Heaven is not dull; it is not static; it is not monochrome. It is an endless dynamic of joy in which one is ever more oneself as one was meant to be."

to record whether the jasper is colored or remains opaque. If it is colored green, as it was in ancient Israel, then the City of God must appear in the landscape of eternity like the Emerald City in *The Wizard of Oz*.

Heaven itself (or Heaven proper) is fashioned of pure gold. This gold, the prophet tells us, is so pure and so rare that it appears to be translucent. In other words, it looks like glass. The foundations of the massive walls are decorated with every kind of precious stone, including jasper, sapphire, chalcedony, emerald, sardonyx (a kind of onyx), carnelian (a red form of chalcedony), chrysolite, beryl, topaz, chrysoprase (an apple-green form of chalcedony), jacinth, and amethyst. What is jacinth? It obviously is the rarest of all rare stones because, to this day, no one on earth knows what it is.

Hagar the Hagiographer

St. Peter is the patron saint of Heaven. He holds the keys to the pearly gates.

Holy Cow!

Early Christian writers said that Heaven contains not only saints in white robes with harps, but also singing stones!

What About the Pearly Gates?

Twelve gates lead into the celestial city, and each gate, the prophet tells us, is made from a single, gigantic pearl. Don't ask where the pearls came from. It's like reverting to the old question about the chicken and the egg.

Speaking of eggs, if we can believe St. John, Heaven is as ornate as a fabulous Faberge egg (the jeweled eggs that were given as Easter presents to the Czar of Russia). In the midst of the city is a double throne that is occupied by the One and the Lamb of God. The double throne is fronted by a sea of crystal and framed by a rainbow. God and Jesus are served by 24 elders dressed in white and praised eternally by four winged beasts, who "rest not day and night, saying, 'Holy, holy, holy, Lord Almighty, which was, and is, and is to come'" (Revelation 4:8). In attendance are also angels, "ten thousand times ten thousand, and thousands of thousands" (Revelation 5:11).

Is This Place for Real?

Because it seems so completely outlandish, some Christians attempt to give St. John's words an allegorical rather than a literal meaning. They insist that the beloved disciple is using poetic rather than realistic language, that he is merely making Heaven a metaphor for otherworldly perfection. But St. John warns readers in no uncertain terms not to doubt the literal meaning of his report:

> I warn everyone who hears the words of the prophecy of this book: If anyone adds anything to them, God will add to him the plagues described in this book.

And if anyone takes words away from this prophecy, God will take away from him his share in the tree of life and in the holy city described in this book. (Revelation 22:18–20)

Anyone who adds a metaphysical or poetic meaning to St. John's words, after reading this warning, must truly be a nonbeliever, a despiser of religion, or a real idiot.

In God's Kingdom, You Can't Get a Room Without a Reservation

The prophet further says that only the pure can enter the Kingdom of Heaven. Although its gates are never shut, no one who is shameful or deceitful can enter. The Kingdom can be entered only by those whose names are written in the Lamb's Book of Life (Rev. 20:15).

The inhabitants of Heaven are those who died without sin on their souls, without any sin—without even a small or venial sin, let alone a grievous or mortal sin. Moreover, they have been absolved of *original sin*. Original sin, the sin of Adam, the first man, that is passed on from generation to generation, can be absolved or dissolved only by the sacrament of Baptism. This means that saints, of necessity, must be baptized as Christians. Even though St. Anne may not have been sprinkled by water, she received Baptism by intention—that is, by her desire to be baptized and to be united with the Catholic Church, even though no priest was available to officiate.

Hagar the Hagiographer

Speaking of plagues, St. Roch is the patron saint of protection from plagues. He spent his life caring for victims of the bubonic plague that ravaged Italy in the fourteenth century.

St. Peter Speaks

Original sin is the sin of Adam that we all inherit. Because of this sin, we must all endure death, suffering, ignorance, and a strong inclination to actual sin.

The Saints Have Lots of Elbow Room

Because Heaven is open only to those in a state of sanctifying grace, the population of paradise is not great by any standard. Indeed, in terms of population, it ranks much lower than limbo and purgatory, and it is immeasurably smaller than hell. Jesus informed His followers of this fact when He said, "Many are called, but few are chosen" (Matthew 22:14).

The few who enter Heaven are those who have been purged of earthly lusts and desires. They delight in spiritual matters and find perfect peace, happiness, and contentment in the presence of God. This might not seem like fun until you consider that God is perfect joy, perfect love, perfect goodness, and perfect peace. Moreover, He is active, not passive. This means that Heaven is constant activity, constant discovery, constant stimulation, and constant fulfillment. God is perfect being. This means that those who are united with God experience life more abundant than ever before. St. Augustine, the Catholic authority on Heaven, writes:

> The reward of heaven will be God Himself. For when He said by the prophet, "I shall be their God, and they will be my people," He surely meant this: "I shall be their satisfaction; I shall be everything that men can honestly desire: life, health, food, abundance, glory, honor, peace, and all good things." This is the right interpretation of the apostle's words, "That God may be all in all." He will be the end of our desires, and we shall see Him without end, love Him without revulsion, praise Him without weariness. This gift, this emotion, this *activity* will be shared by all, just as life eternal will be the common condition of all.

Divine Revelation

The chief joy of the saints in Heaven is seeing God face to face. This is called the Beatific (or blessed) Vision.

Holy Cow!

According to a recent *Time/CNN* poll, 61 percent of Americans think that they will go straight to Heaven when they die.

Is This a Great Fraternity House, or What?

In Heaven, the blessed are united in love with God and one another. They are united in love—true love, perfect love, everlasting love. They share the same perspective, the same belief, and the same Beatific (or blessed) Vision of God. They possess the truth, the eternal truth—for that reason, they never have disputes or disagreements. They never get bent out of shape; they are in true accord. They form a true brotherhood, a true fellowship, a true community. Christianity, no less than communism, is utopian in outlook. It envisions a rosy ending for true Christians, a place of perfect happiness and contentment. Heaven, according to medieval theologians, is surrounded by nine celestial spheres. It is composed of a substance neither earth, air, fire, nor water but a wonderful "fifth essence"—or, as the word comes down to us, "quintessence."

Yes! But No Toga Parties ...

The pleasures in Heaven are intellectual, not carnal. There is no sex in Heaven, not even connubial bliss. Jesus confirmed this by saying, "The people of this age marry and are given in marriage. But those who are considered worthy of taking part in that age and in the resurrection from the dead will neither marry nor be given in marriage" (Luke 20:34–35). Indeed, anyone who longs for sexual congress is not worthy to enter Heaven. Such a person has not been purified of fleshly desire and must be purged for an extended time in purgatory (a thousand years, at least) before joining the heavenly throng.

What's more, the saints cannot be seduced, not even by a tempting heavenly tart, such as St. Mary Magdalene. They possess the quality of impeccability. This means that they cannot sin. They cannot fall from grace. This is defined as Catholic dogma. After all, if the saints knew that their happiness could come to an end, their happiness would be less than perfect. For this reason, they are confirmed in good. They cannot commit even the slightest venial sin.

No Pets in Paradise

Similarly, there are no pets in the celestial kingdom. The very question in the Catholic scheme of things is absurd. Animals, including educated monkeys and Jack Russell terriers, do not possess immortal souls.

Hagar the Hagiographer

Mary Magdalene, the repentant woman of the streets who washed the feet of Jesus with her tears, is the patron saint of prostitutes. Her feast day is July 22.

What, Then, Are the Specific Joys of Heaven?

The primary joy is God Himself because God is the source of all happiness, and the possession of God assures us, as St. Thomas Aquinas points out, of every other good we may desire. Being with God is the essential beatitude, the greatest of all rewards.

But there are many secondary rewards or, as theologians put it, accidental beatitudes. Here are a few:

➤ Delight in the company of Christ, the angels, and the saints

➤ Joy in the reunion with loved ones

➤ Pleasure in seeing God's new works of creation, including the creation of a new Heaven and a new earth

➤ Bliss in having a painless, spiritual body that can transport you from place to place without going through space

➤ Cheer from having your very own golden crown

No sex. No pets. No booze. If Heaven doesn't seem so heavenly, consider the alternatives: hell or purgatory. I think you'll change your mind.

The Least You Need to Know

➤ Heaven is inhabited by real people.

➤ Heaven is a real city with defined borders.

➤ Only the sinless can enter Heaven.

➤ The greatest joy in Heaven is meeting God.

Chapter 3

Where the Rest of the Poor Souls Go: Purgatory, Limbo, and Hell

---

In This Chapter

➤ Purgatory as a place for less–than–perfect people

➤ What you can do to get out of purgatory

➤ Who rests in eternal limbo

➤ How horrible hell really is

So now that you know where the saints reside, it's time to visit the other parts of the afterlife, where the less-than-saintly of us will end up once we kick the bucket: purgatory, limbo, or hell.

Purgatory

Observing the celestial kingdoms of Heaven and hell, twelfth-century theologians believed that they had discovered a new eternal orb, in much the same manner that eighteenth-century astronomers discovered new planets. This orb was between Heaven and hell and appeared to contain a vast population of unaccounted-for souls. This mysterious realm was neither in Heaven nor in hell, but a separate place between the two eternities. Peter the Chanter, a pious twelfth-century theologian, named this newly discovered place *purgatory*.

A Place for the Average Churchgoer

The name purgatory was apt because this in-between place, the Catholic Church decided, is really a divine penal colony for in-between people—that is, people who are neither holy saints nor grievous sinners.

St. Peter Speaks

Purgatory means a place of purgation or purification.

Holy Cow!

Good news! It's possible to get out of purgatory after you serve your time.

St. Peter Speaks

Extreme unction is the sacrament of last rites. It consists of the anointing of a person with holy oil. This anointing strengthens and purifies the soul.

The souls in purgatory are not in a state of heavenly bliss, nor are they tortured by demons. They are souls that neither have been condemned to eternal confinement in a black pit nor have been approved for eternal bliss in God's Kingdom.

The inhabitants of this middle realm are people who died in a state of venial sin. They are people who died before completing their penance or receiving *extreme unction,* or last rites. They are not people who have committed mortal or serious sins. They are not people who have blasphemed God. They are not people who uphold false or heretical doctrine. They are not fornicators or adulterers. They are not murderers or rapists or people of violence. They are not thieves or charlatans or corruptors of morals (read the section on hell, later in this chapter, for a description of where these folks will end up).

For the most part, the souls sentenced to God's penal colony, the in-between realm, are people who upheld the Commandments, who went to Mass every Sunday and holy day, who honored the precepts of the Church, and who did not lie or cheat or steal. They are people who never committed a serious crime or one of the seven deadly sins. They are people who kept their wedding vows and who raised their children in the fear and admonition of the Lord.

But they are people who were not perfect. They are people who may have had an impure thought, who may have uttered a false oath, and who may have said a curse when they stubbed their toes. In other words, they are good people—honest, God-fearing people who fell short of sainthood.

Naturally, such nice and decent folks do not deserve to burn forever with the really wicked. However, they do not deserve to live like saints in a heavenly mansion. And so, they are sentenced to a stay in purgatory.

It's Bad, but Not So Bad

Being sent to the middle realm is not so bad. After all, you know that someday—usually after thousands of years—you will be allowed to enter Heaven, to see God, and to live among the saints in everlasting happiness. The sure and certain hope of Heaven is before you.

But purgatory is a place of unspeakable suffering. It is a place where you will be punished for your sins until you are purified. How do you purify a soul? How do you cleanse it of all impurities? That's simple. You put it in the purifying fire until it is sterilized.

But This Stuff Is So Medieval!

This theology sounds medieval for a good reason. It *is* medieval. It reflects the feudal notion of fealty, of a vassal's obligations to his overlord. Medieval theologians attempted to calculate the prescribed punishment for each and every offense. By going to confession, a priest could forgive the guilt of sin but not the punishment. The punishment was called *penance*. For penance, a priest might require that you say a certain number of prayers, that you make the Stations of the Cross, that you attend a novena. Serious or mortal sin might require extraordinary penance. The *Cummean Penitential*, the medieval guide for prescribing acts of penance, said that homosexual acts must be punished by a period of four to seven years of fasting and prayer. Almost all men and women die before they can fulfill their penance. Therefore, they must finish serving their penance in the Afterlife.

Throughout the thirteenth century, the doctrine of purgatory continued to be developed and refined. Theologians began to say that the time of a dearly departed person's stay in purgatory could be shortened by suffrage. Suffrage means a short intercessory prayer. Every short prayer could shorten the sentence of a loved one by months or even years. St. Thomas Aquinas said that many good works of the living could be offered to shorten the

Holy Cow!

Catholics believe that when they die, most good Christians don't go straight to Heaven according to Christian doctrine. They rather end up serving thousands of years of hard time in purgatory.

St. Peter Speaks

Penance means punishment. When you go to Confession, a priest absolves you of the guilt (the *culpa*) of sin and prescribes the punishment (the *poena*).

Hagar the Hagiographer

St. Bonaventure said that the punishment of souls in purgatory is much more severe than any punishment that can be given to someone on earth.

time of a suffering soul in God's penal colony. These good works, he said, could consist of such things as gifts to the poor, the celebration of the Mass, and contributions to the Church.

How to Get a Pal out of Purgatory

The idea developed that the merits of Christ and the saints could be applied to the suffering souls in purgatory. These merits, the Church taught, were contained in a treasure chest in Heaven. God placed this treasure chest in the hands of the Vicar of Christ on earth, the Bishop of Rome, to use at his discretion.

By the time of the Protestant reformation in the sixteenth century, it was believed that the pope could draw from the treasure chest of merits to cancel out all or part of a person's unperformed penance. The application of the merits of Christ and the saints for the remission of the penalty of sin is called an indulgence.

Indulgences can be granted only by the pope because he holds the treasure chest. He can apply enough merits for a partial indulgence—that is, for the remission of some of the necessary penance—or he can apply enough merits for a plenary or full indulgence—that is, for the remission of all of the penalty of sin.

The Church taught that these indulgences are not only helpful for the living (who might have received a stiff penance from a priest in the confessional) but also for the souls in purgatory.

Naturally, people were more than willing to do what they could to get their loved ones out of purgatory. So, they performed good works to obtain divine favor, such as making pilgrimages, building churches, and performing acts of charity. They also sought to make substantial contributions of cash to the Church.

Holy Cow!

According to a recent *Time/CNN* survey, only 15 percent of Americans expect to be sentenced to purgatory.

Hagar the Hagiographer

St. Nicholas of Tolentino (1245–1305) is the patron saint of souls in purgatory. He ministered to outcasts and criminals during his life. Pope Eugene IV canonized him in 1449, and his relics were rediscovered in 1926 at a chapel in Tolentino.

Indulgences! Merits! Purgatory! It's Enough to Drive a Protestant Crazy!

The trouble with indulgences, purgatory, and the treasure box of saintly merits came during the pontificate of Pope Boniface IX (1389-1404), who declared 1400 to be a banner year. In keeping with tradition, Boniface said that any good member of the Church could obtain a plenary or full indulgence by making a pilgrimage to Rome and praying at one of the sacred shrines to the saints. However, he added, those who could not make the pilgrimage could still obtain a full indulgence for themselves or their loved ones in purgatory simply by saying a series of prayers in a local church and paying a fixed amount of money to a duly appointed *pardoner* of the Church.

For the next 200 years, pardoners traveled throughout Christendom selling indulgences. One pardoner named Tetzel appeared in Wittenberg, Germany. He had a good sales gimmick. He appealed to the faithful by singing this little jingle: "As soon as the money in the coffer rings/A soul from purgatory instantly springs." An Augustinian friar was outraged by the pardoner's remarks and nailed a letter of protest to the door of the Wittenberg Cathedral. The name of the friar was Martin Luther. The letter of protest sparked the Protestant Reformation.

Although there is no mention of purgatory in the Bible, Catholics insist that the doctrine of purgatory is based on the teachings of tradition—most especially, the ancient Christian practice of saying prayers for the dead. The saints in Heaven don't need our prayers, and the damned in hell can't be saved by our prayers. Such prayers can only be beneficial to those who are between Heaven and hell, a place of purification.

St. Peter Speaks

Pardoners were papal emissaries who went from church to church to sell officially sealed letters of indulgence.

Holy Cow!

Martin Luther and John Calvin maintained that Christian teaching must be based on scripture alone. The rallying cry of the Protestant Reformation was the Latin slogan "sola scriptura."

In Limbo-Land

Okay, you're thinking, I get the notion of purgatory. I know how such a doctrine could develop from the practice of praying for the dead. I understand the logic of a penal colony in the afterlife. I comprehend the notion of performing good works and saying prayers to help shorten the stay of individuals in purgatory. I even grasp the concept of a treasure chest of merits earned by Jesus and the saints and the notion that these merits can be applied to the suffering souls in God's penal colony. It may not be Biblical, but it does make sense. But *limbo*? Come on, this is a teaching that makes no sense.

St. Peter Speaks

Limbo, according to St. Thomas Aquinas, is a place of neither reward nor punishment.

But, logically, according to Catholic theologians, the doctrine of limbo does make sense. The doctrine developed from speculation about the souls of infants who died before receiving the sacrament of Baptism and righteous men and women who were born before the Incarnation and had no saving knowledge of Jesus Christ.

A Place for Unbaptized Babies

What happens when an infant dies? If it has not been washed of original sin by the waters of Baptism, what will happen to it? It cannot be sent to Heaven because all those who enter Heaven must be in a state of sanctifying grace—that is, they must be people who have been cleansed of all sin, original and actual. If this is the case, will the infants be sent to hell to burn for all eternity with the wicked? This doesn't seem right. After all, God is good, perfectly good, and He wouldn't permit innocent babies to suffer for sins they did not commit. What's the answer?

Medieval thinkers, including the great rationalist Peter Abelard, came up with an answer. They said that God places unbaptized babies in a special place where they suffer no pain or torment. The medievalists called this place limbo, believing that it must be located somewhere between the edge of Heaven and the edge of hell. Limbo comes from the Latin word *limbus,* meaning "edge."

Sanctified Sleep Spells Pure Contentment

In limbo, the babies suffer no pain or discomfort, not even an awareness of their separation from God. They remain in a sleep from which they will never awake.

In their sleep, the babies do not experience any discontent. Indeed, they are perfectly happy and snug and comfortable. They are as happy as the healthiest babies at rest in a modern nursery. St. Thomas Aquinas said that the infants in limbo are not merely in a negative state of immunity from suffering and sorrow, but in a positive state of contentment.

Holy Cow!

The real day that "the saints came marching in" was the day of the Ascension of Jesus Christ into Heaven.

But this eternal land of Nod is not restricted to infants. It was also the temporary abode of the patriarchs and prophets of the Old Testament. When Abraham died, he did not ascend into Heaven. Abraham was born before the Ascension of Christ into Heaven. Until this event occurred, no one could enter, not even the most faithful believer. Moses could not enter Heaven. David could not enter Heaven. Isaiah and Jeremiah could not enter Heaven. Daniel could not enter Heaven. St. Ann and St. Joachim, the maternal grandparents of Jesus, could not enter Heaven. Not even St. Joseph, the father of Jesus, could enter Heaven. They all had to wait, and the perfect waiting place was the realm of limbo. The waiting was necessary because the Beatific Vision, the vision of salvation, was not complete until Jesus Christ assumed His throne at the right hand of God. Without Christ on the throne, Heaven would not be a place of perfect happiness.

Keep Knockin', but You Can't Come In

Limbo is the one area of the afterlife that you cannot enter by your own free will. You can get to Heaven by living a saintly life. You can get to purgatory by living a nearly saintly life. You can get to hell by living an unsaintly life. But you cannot get to limbo, no matter what you do.

As a matter of fact, one section of this strange kingdom—the Limbo of the Fathers—is permanently closed. After the Ascension of Jesus, there was no longer a reason to maintain the waiting room. Now, upon death, you are immediately delivered to paradise, purgation, or perdition. You cannot go to limbo even if all you want is a good night's sleep for all eternity.

Hell: A Real Scream, Without the Popcorn

Now for the really, really bad news. I hate to break it to you, but, according to the testimony of the saints, you, like billions of others, could end up in hell. Your chance of escaping eternity in a black pit with a pitchfork in your rear end, in the opinion of these experts, is about 1,000 to 1. To be saved from this fate, you must be free of original sin, you must be forgiven of mortal sin, and you must be in a state of sanctifying grace.

To be absolved of original sin, you must have received the sacrament of Baptism. That part is easy. If you are a Christian, you were probably baptized as an infant. If you were not baptized, simply submit yourself to any priest or minister. Some will sprinkle water on your head; others will dunk you in a tank. But, in either case, Baptism will wash away the sin of Adam.

St. Peter Speaks

There are seven deadly sins: pride, gluttony, envy, sloth, anger, lust, and covetousness.

For Heaven's Sake, Stay Sinless

To be free of mortal or serious sin is infinitely more difficult. To accomplish this, you must lead an exemplary life, including abiding by the following rules:

➤ You must not commit a mortal sin.
➤ You must never utter a blasphemy.
➤ You must never dishonor your parents.

➤ You must never sleep in on Sunday, when you should be in church.

➤ You must never steal anything big or anything from someone less fortunate than you.

➤ You must never utter a damaging untruth about another person.

➤ You must never engage in premarital or post-marital sex, let alone any sexual perversity.

➤ You must never break your solemn word, including your wedding vow.

➤ You must never commit a serious act of violence.

➤ You must never advocate abortion.

➤ You must never advance a godless cause, such as Marxism.

➤ You must never abandon the Catholic faith or rebuke Catholic doctrine.

➤ And, above all, you must never receive Holy Communion while in a state of mortal sin. To do so would be to commit an act of sacrilege, for which there might be no forgiveness.

St. Peter Speaks

Absolution is the remission of sin that the priest can grant a person who expresses sincere sorrow over his or her sins and promises not to commit such sins again. It comes from the Latin word *absolutio,* which means "acquittal."

Souls Must Be Scrubbed by Priests

If you have committed any of these sins, you must obtain complete forgiveness by going to Confession, obtaining *absolution,* and performing acts of penance. Performing acts of penance means that you must endure some measure of punishment for your offenses.

Finally, you must receive Jesus Christ into your system—that is, into your soul and body. This can be accomplished by receiving Holy Communion after completing the terms of your penance. By receiving the Eucharist, you receive sanctifying grace. Sanctifying grace is the grace that makes the soul acceptable for entrance into the Kingdom of Heaven.

Who Goes to Hell?

The list includes:

➤ All those who are consumed by worldly things, such as fame, glory, money, and sex

➤ All those who fail to turn to the things of God and the matters of the spirit

➤ All those who separate themselves from the Holy Catholic Church

Buddhist monks who live pure lives but deny the truth of Christianity are bound for hell. The same can be said of Hindu mystics. Pagans, pantheists, gnostics, and atheists are all bound for hell. This what the Catholic Church teaches. It maintains, in the words of St. Cyprian, that it is "the Ark of Salvation outside of which there is no salvation."

Now for the Good News: Some Non-Catholics Can Be Saved

Non-Catholics, however, are not necessarily sentenced to hell. If they are good and holy individuals, they might end up in purgatory. Such a good break can take place only if these individuals are born and raised in non-Catholic households. Those who willfully separate themselves from the Roman Catholic Church have little or no chance to escape the flames.

Don't scream! Don't yell! Don't throw this book in the fireplace! I am only presenting to you authentic Catholic doctrine.

Hell Is Even Worse Than You Can Imagine

Hell is meant to be a very scary place. St. Methodius, we are told, converted King Boris of Bulgaria to the Christian faith by drawing depictions of hell on the walls of the royal palace. Teaching of hell is meant to bring sinners to a state of attrition—sorrow for sin based on fear of punishment. Attrition is the first step toward contrition—sorrow for sin based on love of God.

In the gospels, Jesus says that sinners, after death, are sentenced to an everlasting punishment (Matthew 25:31–46). It is a place where they are bound and gagged, a place of utter darkness, a place where there is weeping and gnashing of teeth (Matthew 22:2–14). He further describes it as a place where "the worm does not die" and where "the fire is not quenched" (Mark 9:43–48).

In the Book of Revelation, St. John the Evangelist describes hell as a place where the damned are

Divine Revelation

Vatican II proclaimed that it is through the Catholic Church alone that the fullness of the means of salvation can be obtained. This is in keeping with the proclamation of the Fourth Lateran Council that no one can be saved outside the Universal Church.

Holy Cow!

Martin Luther, John Calvin, and the other leaders of the Protestant Reformation have been branded heretics by the Catholic Church, along with the first members of their congregations, but not the children who were born and raised in their churches.

tossed into a lake of burning sulfur, where they are "tormented day and night forever and ever."

St. Cyprian tells his readers that the condemned in hell will be burned forever but will never be consumed by the flames. "Weeping," he says, "will be useless and prayer ineffectual."

But while the body is perpetually burned, St. Augustine writes, the soul of the damned is eternally consumed by the "worm" of grief. This grief will consist of knowledge that he or she will be eternally separated from God and all that is good.

Some Saints Granted Personal Tours of the Devil's Domain

Several saints and mystics have been treated to a firsthand view of hell. The monk Tyndale in the twelfth century gave a graphic account of the place of perdition. In the center of hell, he said, the devil is bound to a burning gridiron by red-hot chains; his screams of pain and agony never end. His hands are free, and he periodically reaches out to seize one of the damned; his teeth crush them like grapes, and his fiery breath draws them down his burning throat. Assistant demons with hooks of iron plunge the screaming bodies of the damned alternately into fire or icy water. After this, the demons hang them up by their tongues, or saw them into pieces, or beat them flat on an anvil, or boil them in oil and strain them through a cloth. This sounds bad enough, but there's more. Sulfur is cast into the fire so that the stench is unbearable, and the fire gives no light, so the whole place is engulfed in horrible darkness.

Four hundred years later, St. Teresa of Avila found hell to be a place of unspeakable suffering, where the soul is continually torn from the body while the body is repeatedly dismembered and cast into flames.

In the twentieth century, Sister Lucia, who beheld the Virgin Mary at Fatima, was blessed with this bird's-eye view of the devil's domain:

> Plunged in the sea of fire were demons and souls in human form, like transparent burning embers, all blackened or burnished bronze, floating about in the conflagration, now raised into the air by the flames that issued from within themselves together with great clouds of smoke, now falling back

Holy Cow!

According to a recent *Time/CNN* poll, only 1 percent of Americans believe they are headed for hell.

Hagar the Hagiographer

St. Thomas Aquinas maintained that the "fire which will torment the bodies of the damned is corporeal," and he speculated that hell might be located in the bowels of the earth.

on every side like sparks in huge fires, without weight or equilibrium, amid shrieks and groans of pain and despair, which horrified us and made us tremble with fear.

Hell Might Have Different Levels

Some saints, such as St. Basil of Caesarea, maintain that there are different levels of hell, with varying degrees of pain and suffering. Dante upheld this view in his poem *The Divine Comedy* and said that hell is a place of mud, frost, filth, fire, ice, and venomous serpents. But, no matter what level you arrive at, the door will be locked and you will never escape. Your cries will be ignored, and your agony will be everlasting.

All the saints agree, however, on the following horrors of hell:

➤ Eternal separation from God

➤ Perpetual agony

➤ Everlasting darkness

➤ Exposure to the suffering of others, including their screams of pain, pleas for mercy, blasphemies, and rants against God

Divine Revelation

It is a heresy to believe in universal salvation, the teaching that all men will be saved.

Hell is the only place in this life and the next where the saints cannot help you. They cannot use their merits to obtain your release. They cannot plead your case before the heavenly tribunal. They cannot even pray for you, because such prayers would be in vain.

The Least You Need to Know

➤ Saying litanies of the saints can help reduce the amount of time a loved one must spend in purgatory.

➤ When sinners have paid penance for all of their sins in purgatory, they can move to Heaven.

➤ Limbo is the land of sleep for unbaptized babies.

➤ There are lots of ways to get into hell, but once you're there, there's no way to escape.

Part 2

A Primer to the Communion of Saints

Warning! If you turn the page, you will drop down a deep hole and land in a very strange world where sights can be sounds, where colors can be touched, and where taste can be seen. It is a world in which all your senses can be rearranged and in which you will behold such things as bodies materializing out of nowhere, beasts spouting Christian doctrine, and bedbugs becoming blessed stones singing songs. In this place, the extraordinary is common and the common is extraordinary. If you turn the page, you will fall into a wonderland, you will pass through the looking glass, and you will arrive at a new realm of reality. Some of you will be disturbed by the experience; some will be amused, and some will be inspired. You will laugh, you will sigh, and you will scream. Turn the page and the surreal becomes real, lives become legends, and fantasy becomes reality. You are about to enter the weird world of saints.

Whatever Happened to the Twelve Apostles?

Nobody ever claimed that the trip to sainthood was an easy one, and this certainly holds true for the 12 apostles of Jesus. Although the information on some of the apostles is sparse, records indicate that all but one of Jesus's closest followers were martyred for their beliefs. Beheadings, crucifixions, and flayings befell these holy men and other close associates of Jesus. Read on to find out how these early saints earned their place in Heaven and how you can contact them through prayer.

John the Baptist: Sainthood Is Not for Sissies

John the Baptist prophesied Jesus' coming, and John baptized Jesus in the Jordan River. John was the first of the Christian *ascetics,* living in the desert and subsisting on a diet of locusts and wild honey. He wore a cloak of camel hair with a leather belt around his waist, and he preached a fiery message of repentance. When the religious leaders of Jerusalem came to see him, John called them a "brood of vipers" and warned them of the coming wrath of God.

St. Peter Speaks

An **ascetic** is a person who turns from all worldly pleasures, including food, drink, sex, and society, to attain spiritual perfection.

Hagar the Hagiographer

Salome, the daughter of Herodias, performed an exotic and erotic dance for her stepfather, King Herod. As a reward, he gave her the head of John the Baptist on a silver platter.

St. John the Baptist condemned not only the religious leaders—the Sadducees and the Pharisees—but also King Herod, who, John said, committed an act of adultery by marrying his brother's wife, Herodias. For speaking against the royal couple, John was eventually cast into prison and beheaded (a fate that many saints have in common!).

When Jesus heard about the arrest of John, He said: "I tell you the truth: Among those born of women there has not risen anyone greater than John the Baptist: yet he who is least in the kingdom of heaven is greater than he." This enigmatic saying shows hagiographers that John the Baptist was the greatest saint of the Old Dispensation, that is, of all those who lived and died before Christ performed His act of atonement on the cross. He is greater than Abraham, David, Isaiah, or any other Old Testament figure, and he is greater than such New Testament figures as St. Ann and St. Elizabeth (his mother). But St. John the Baptist is a far lesser saint than the Virgin Mary, who is the holiest of all saints, and lesser than the Twelve Apostles.

St. John the Baptist remains the patron saint of Baptism, bird dealers, cutters, and people who suffer from epilepsy or convulsions.

Before the 12 apostles became saints, several people who are mentioned in the New Testament gained a place in glory. Can you match the following saints' names with their relationship to Jesus Christ? The following holy ones died before Jesus began His ministry:

Sts. Anne and Joachim	a. The prophets who recognized the infant Jesus as the Christ when He was presented in the temple for circumcision
The Holy Innocents	b. The parents of St. John the Baptist
Sts. Zechariah and Elizabeth	c. The parents of the Virgin Mary
Sts. Simeon and Anna	d. The three wise men who came from the East to adore the holy infant
Sts. Balthasar, Melchior, and Caspar	e. The 144,000 babies slaughtered by Herod the Great
St. Joseph	f. The father of Jesus

Answers: Sts. Anne and Joachim = c; The Holy Innocents = e; Sts. Zechariah and Elizabeth = b; Sts. Simeon and Anna = a; Sts. Balthasar, Melchior, and Caspar = d; St. Joseph = f

St. Peter Gets the Keys to the Kingdom

Among the 12 apostles, the greatest saint is St. Peter. The reason for this, according to Catholic thinkers, is simple. Jesus singled out Peter as the leader of the Church by saying:

> You are Peter, and on this rock I will build my church and the gates of hell shall not overcome it. I will give to you the keys of the kingdom of heaven; whatever you bind on earth will be bound in heaven, and whatever you loose on earth will be loosed in heaven. (Matthew 16:18–19)

By this so-called "Great Commission," Jesus gave Peter the keys to the Kingdom of Heaven and the power to forgive and bind sins. Bind sins! This means that St. Peter and his successors can bind you to your evil deeds forever, making you an *anathema* or an "accursed thing" in the eyes of God.

St. Peter's position of leadership is reasserted in other passages of Scripture. At the close of St. John's Gospel, Jesus again singles out Peter from the Twelve with this instruction: "Feed my sheep" (John 21:15-17). This passage, Catholics maintain, shows that St. Peter served as the Shepherd of the Christian flock.

Of equal importance to hagiographers is Luke 22:31-32 in which Jesus says to Peter: "I have prayed for you that your faith will never fail. You, in turn, must strengthen your brothers." This passage became the key text for the Church's affirmation of *papal infallibility*.

In the Book of Acts, St. Peter is represented as the unquestioned leader and chief spokesman for the apostles. Indeed, the other 11 apostles, including St. Matthias, who took the place of Judas Iscariot, remain figures of seemingly minor importance.

Holy Cow!

Protestants maintain that Jesus did not give the Great Commission only to Peter but to all 12 of the apostles.

St. Peter Speaks

The dogma of **papal infallibility** states that the pope is incapable of error when he makes an official pronouncement regarding faith and morals.

"Quo Vadis?" Wasn't That a Movie?

According to tradition, Peter established a church at Rome, where he was put to death during the reign of Nero. Peter was crucified upside down after he said that he was not worthy to be crucified in the manner of the Lord. The good saint was buried on Vatican hill, which, in time, became the site of St. Peter's Basilica.

Church historians say that Peter passed on his authority as head of the Church to his successors, who occupied his Holy See (from the Latin "sedes," meaning "seat") in the eternal city. These successors all served as the bishops of Rome and came to be called "holy fathers" or "popes."

Hagar the Hagiographer

In a second-century work called *Acts of Peter*, Peter is depicted as running from Rome at the outbreak of Nero's persecutions. Climbing Vatican hill, the disciple encounters Jesus heading in the opposite direction and asks: "Where are you going, Lord?" (In Latin, *"Quo vadis, domine?"*). Jesus replies: "I am going to Rome to be crucified." Hearing this, the chastised saint returns to Rome, where he is crucified upside down at his own request.

Holy Cow!

St. Peter was succeeded by St. Linus, who was promptly put to death by Roman officials. St. Linus was succeeded by St. Anacletus, who suffered a similar fate. The list of successors continues in an unbroken line to the present occupant of St. Peter's throne: the current Catholic pope.

A Prayer to St. Peter

St. Peter remains the patron saint of Rome, the Catholic Church, and watchmakers. You can invoke him for a blessing by reading aloud the following prayer (it's kind of long and will likely offend Protestants):

> O glorious St. Peter, who in return for thy strong and generous faith, thy profound and sincere humility, and thy burning love, was rewarded by Jesus Christ with singular privileges, and, in particular, with the leadership of the other Apostles and the primacy of the whole Church, and was made the foundation stone, do thou obtain for us the grace of a lively faith, that shall not fear to profess itself openly, even to the shedding of blood and the sacrifice of life itself, rather than surrender. Obtain for us, likewise, a sincere loyalty to our Holy Mother, the Church; grant that we may ever remain most closely and most sincerely united to the Roman Pontiff, who is the heir of thy faith and of thy authority, the one, true, visible head of the Catholic Church, that mystic ark outside of which there is no salvation. Grant, moreover, that we may follow, in all humility and meekness, her teaching and her advice, and may be obedient to all her precepts, in order to be able here on earth to enjoy a peace that is sure and undisturbed, and to attain one day in Heaven to everlasting happiness. Amen.

The Weird Gospels Produce Weird Legends

The lives of St. Peter and the 12 apostles form the first chapters of hagiography as recorded by later Church

Fathers, such as Origin, St. Clement, St. Ignatius, and St. Irenaeus. These pious accounts come from Christian folklore, and much of this folklore is contained in the questionable or "apocryphal" gospels that were in circulation in the second and third centuries.

Most Christians assume that from the beginning there were just the four gospels that comprise the New Testament: Matthew, Mark, Luke, and John. But there were dozens of gospels all claiming to profess the truth about Jesus Christ. In some of these gospels, Jesus visits distant lands, such as India and China, performs astonishing miracles (such as the child Jesus forming birds from clay and causing them to come to life), and utters outlandish sayings ("No man that is tempted shall enter the kingdom of heaven").

In the early churches were such texts as the Gospel of Truth, the Gospel of Thomas, the Gospel of Simon and Jude, the Gospel of Bartholomew, the Secret Gospel of St. John, the Gospel of St. Peter, … you get the idea. Not only were bogus gospels in circulation, but so were bogus epistles, such as the Acts of Paul, the Acts of Peter, the Acts of Andrew, and the Acts of Philip. The process of selecting the real gospels from the questionable gospels took a long time. The New Testament as we know it today did not come into existence until 367 A.D.

Divine Revelation

St. Peter's real name was Simon. Jesus changed his name to Peter (*petrus*), which means "rock." The faith of Peter is the rock upon which the Church is established.

Divine Revelation

Jesus called 12 apostles to represent the 12 tribes of Israel. The 12 tribes of Israel were descendants from the 12 sons of Jacob.

Holy Fairy Tales?

Turning to these strange gospels, along with the New Testament and early church letters, we can trace the early lives of the saints, including the 12 apostles, although it is impossible to separate the fact from the fiction. In these works, we encounter speaking lions, fire-breathing dragons, and even devout bedbugs. These sources for our knowledge of the apostles were later condemned as heretical by the Church and were judged "worthy of being committed to the flames." Yet, the ordinary Christians cherished these works, and they became the basis of the first cults of the saints.

St. Andrew: The X-Rated Life of the First Apostle

St. Andrew was the brother of St. Peter. Originally a disciple of St. John the Baptist, Andrew was the first apostle to be called by Jesus. In the gospels, he is presented as a worrier. He wanted to know where and how Jesus lived (John 1:38), how to feed the crowd of 5,000 when they had only five small barley loaves and two small fish (John 6:9), and how and when Jerusalem would be destroyed (Mark 13:4).

Following the feast of Pentecost when the 12 apostles received the gift of tongues, Andrew, according to pious tradition, spread the gospel to Greece where he exorcized demons, cured the desperately ill, and calmed a tempest. He also persuaded the wife of Aegeates, the Roman governor of Greece, to live in perfect chastity. The enraged governor threatened to torture Andrew unless his wife returned to the marriage bed. Andrew, however, told the good wife to remain steadfast. For this reason, the apostle was put to death on an X-shaped cross to which he was tied, not nailed. The saint lived two days in a state of suffering, still preaching to those who gathered around him about the importance of chastity in marriage. His remains were later transported from Greece to Constantinople.

In 1210, the crusaders recovered the head of Andrew from the Cathedral of St. Sophia and gave it as a present to Pope Pius II. In 1965, Pope Paul VI, in the spirit of ecumenism (Christian union), returned the relic to Constantinople. St. Andrew may not have been the head of the Church, but his head was venerated by the Church for hundreds of years.

Because he was a fisherman by profession, St. Andrew is the patron saint of fishermen, fishmongers, and sailors. If you are a fishmonger in need of a little "soul," invoke the saint by reading aloud this prayer:

> O glorious St. Andrew, you were the first to recognize the Lamb of God with your friend St. John. You remained with Jesus for that first day, for your entire life, and now throughout eternity. As you led your brother St. Peter to Christ and many others, draw us also unto Him. Amen.

St. Peter Speaks

The 12 apostles in alphabetical order are Andrew, Bartholomew (also called Nathaniel), James the Greater, James the Less, John the Divine, Jude (also known as Judas and Thaddeus), Matthias (the replacement for Judas Iscariot), Matthew (also known as Levi), Peter, Philip, Simon the Zealot, and Thomas (also known as Didymus).

Holy Cow!

The stories about St. Bartholomew come, in part, from a weird work called the Gospel of St. Bartholomew, which appeared in the second century. It was one of many questionable or apocryphal gospels and letters that were not included in the New Testament.

St. Bartholomew Gets Skinned in India

St. Bartholomew is also known in the New Testament as Nathaniel. We don't know much about him, except for the fact that Jesus called him "an Israelite, incapable of deceit." According to tradition, Bartholomew preached in India and Armenia. He allegedly was flayed alive by King Astyages and later was beheaded. His relics remain in the Church of St. Bartholomew, with the exception of his right arm. The arm ended up in England and was given by King Canute's wife to the Cathedral of Canterbury. Chaucer mentions it in *The Canterbury Tales*.

Because he was flayed, or skinned alive, St. Bartholomew remains the patron saint of butchers, furriers, dyers, leather workers, and shoemakers. For some reason, he is the saint to invoke if you suffer from a nervous disorder or twitching. If you want to invoke him, simply recite this prayer:

> O glorious St. Bartholomew, Jesus called you a person without guile, and you saw in this word a sign that He was the Son of God and the King of Israel. Obtain for us the grace to be ever guileless and innocent as doves. Amen.

Doubting Thomas Produces Potent Dust

St. Thomas is known as "Doubting Thomas" and Didymus, the "twin." In the gospels, he does seem to be a skeptic, but he is also one of the Lord's most loyal followers. When Jesus insists on returning to Judea to raise Lazarus, Thomas urges the others to make the trip, so that "we may die with Him" (John 11:7–16). At the Last Supper, Jesus tells the apostles that He is about to leave them and that they already know the place where He is going. Hearing this, Thomas cries out, "Lord, we don't know where you are going. How can we know the way?" Jesus responds by telling Thomas, "I am the way ...." Thomas, however, did not believe the reports of the Resurrection and said that he would believe only if he could see and touch the Lord's wounds. Jesus, of course, appeared to him and granted that request. Thomas then burst into the great cry that is climax of John's Gospel: "My Lord and my God!"

According to tradition, Thomas spread the gospel to Parthia, Persia, and India. In India, the apostle was ordered to build a palace because he was a carpenter by trade. When he was given 20 pieces of silver

Divine Revelation

It's a holy game of "The Name's the Same." The Blessed Virgin Mary had an older sister. Do you know her name? Her name was also Mary. Don't scratch your head. It's true. For proof, turn to John 19:25. This Mary, the sister of Mary, was the mother of three apostles. This second Mary stood at the cross along with the first Mary and a third Mary.

Holy Cow!

Seven of the apostles were closely related. Andrew and Peter were brothers, along with James the Greater and John the Divine. The group included three additional brothers: Simon the Zealot, Jude or Thaddeus, and James the Less.

to start the project, Thomas allegedly gave the money to the poor, incurring the wrath of the ruler. Subsequently, the doubting apostle was speared to death at a place called Colamine. Years later, the dust from outside his tomb was said to be potent enough to cure a boy of demonic possession.

There is a footnote to the life of St. Thomas. The story that he journeyed as far as south India is substantiated by historical fact. In the sixteenth century, Portuguese explorers landed on the Malabar Coast and found awaiting them a Christian community that traced its origins to the missionary work of St. Thomas. To this day, the descendents of this community call themselves "St. Thomas Christians."

St. Thomas is the saint to invoke against doubt. He is the patron saint of architects, builders, and construction workers. Want to get his attention? Say this prayer:

> O glorious St. Thomas, your grief for Jesus was such that it would not let you believe He had risen unless you actually saw Him and touched His wounds. But your love for Jesus was equally great, and it led you to give up your life for Him. Pray for us that we may grieve for our sins, which were the cause of Christ's sufferings. Help us to spend ourselves in His service and so earn the title of "blessed," which Jesus applied to those who would believe in Him without seeing Him. Amen.

It's No Magical Act: St. Simon Really Gets Sawed in Half

St. Simon, according to tradition, was the son of Cleophas, who was the brother of St. Joseph, the "father" of Jesus. His mother was Mary's older sister. This means that Simon was a first-first cousin of Jesus. Two of his brothers—St. Jude and St. James the Less—also numbered among the 12 apostles. Modern scholars now claim that Simon, Jude, and James were not cousins of Jesus, but his real-life brothers.

St. Peter Speaks

Zealots, at the time of Jesus, conducted guerilla warfare against their Roman oppressors with such homemade weapons as clubs and bows and arrows.

Because he is called a *zealot,* Simon is depicted as a rabble-rouser, intent upon sparking an open revolt against Roman rule. According to the early martyrologies, or stories of the martyrs, Simon was the bridegroom at the wedding feast at Cana. After seeing his "cousin" Jesus transform water into wine, Simon deserted his bride at the altar and, along with his brothers, became a chaste and holy disciple.

Tradition says that Simon eventually became the head of the Christian church in Jerusalem. After the burning of the Holy City in 68 A.D., Sts. Simon and Jude moved to Pella in Persia (modern Iraq). In 120 A.D., the brothers were arrested and sentenced to death. Simon was sawed in half, while Jude was hacked to death with a short sword or falchion.

St. Simon, you guessed it, is the patron of saw men and curriers. Do you need him for a favor? Recite this prayer:

> O glorious St. Simon, you were a cousin of Jesus and a devoted follower as well. You were called a zealot, indicating that you were willing to give your life for your religion and your freedom as a human person. Obtain for us the grace to be willing to give up our lives for Christ and to labor for the freedom and peace that only God can give. Help us to spend ourselves for God on earth and be received by Him in eternal bliss in Heaven. Amen.

St. Judas? You've Got to Be Kidding! Is There Really a St. Judas?

St. Jude is really not St. Jude. He is actually St. Judas or Thaddeus. His name has been changed to prevent him from being confused with the notorious apostle Judas Iscariot. Tradition says that he is the author of the short letter in the New Testament that bears his name. In the letter, St. Jude instructs the faithful to persevere in times of difficulty. For this reason, he is known as the patron saint of lost causes and remains one of the most popular figures in Heaven.

You can invoke St. Jude by reading aloud the following prayer:

> Most holy apostle St. Jude, faithful servant and friend of Jesus, the name of the traitor—who delivered the beloved Master into the hands of His enemies—has caused you to be forgotten by many, but the Church honors and invokes you universally as the patron of hopeless cases, of things almost despaired of. Pray for me, I am so helpless and alone. Make use, I implore you, of that particular privilege given to you, to bring visible and speedy help, where help is almost despaired of. I promise, O blessed St. Jude, to be ever mindful of this great favor, to always honor you as my special and powerful patron, and to gratefully encourage devotion to you. Amen.

Hagar the Hagiographer

Judas Iscariot should never be confused with St. Judas or St. Jude. The disciple who betrayed Jesus has been consigned to the lowest region of hell.

Divine Revelation

The Epistle of Jude is the shortest book in the New Testament. Consisting of 25 verses, it warns against false teachers who divide the church and lead believers astray.

It's So Ironic: St. James the Less Gets More Attention Than St. James the Greater

The younger brother of St. Simon and St. Jude is called St. James the Less, not because he is of less importance than St. James the Greater, but because he was shorter and younger. This St. James, according to tradition, is the author of the epistle bearing his name in the New Testament. In the epistle, he says that faith without good works is dead—a statement that infuriated Martin Luther and the Reformers.

Primitive accounts say that James the Less preached in Judea, Samaria, Syria, and Mesopotamia. When he returned to Jerusalem, James preached a fiery sermon from a tower of the Temple. The sermon so infuriated the ruling elders that they cast him from the high tower to the rocks below. James, however, survived the fall and continued to mumble pious words. The elders proceeded to stone him, as he blessed and forgave them. Finally, one of the elders smashed the skull of the chatty apostle with a club. In commemoration of the manner in which he forgave his murderers, St. James the Less has gained more prominence than St. James the Greater and is hailed as the patron saint of the dying.

Divine Revelation

According to Biblical scholars, Jesus had brothers and sisters. To prove this, they point to gospel passages, such as the following from Matthew: "Coming to His hometown, Jesus began teaching the people in their synagogue, and they were amazed. 'Where did this man get this wisdom and these miraculous powers?' they asked. 'Isn't this the carpenter's son? Isn't His mother Mary and aren't His brothers James, Joseph, Simon and Judas? Aren't all his sisters with us?'" (13:54–56). Catholics refuse to acknowledge this, claiming that to the end of her days, Mary remained a virgin. They say that the brothers and sisters were really the Lord's first cousins.

Want to contact St. James the Less? It's easy. Just recite this prayer:

O glorious St. James the Less, you were our Lord's cousin and, at the same time, His friend and follower. You wrote that every good and perfect gift comes to us from the Father of lights and that faith without works is useless. You preached the divinity of Jesus until your death as a martyr. Obtain for us from the Father of lights the great gift of a living faith in Jesus' divinity, which will inspire us to unstinting labor in the service of God and our fellow human beings and enable us to reach our heavenly destiny. Amen.

Sure, He's Dead, but He Might Do Some Good in Spain

St. James the Greater, in the estimation of Jesus, might really have been greater than St. James the Less. He was included in the Lord's inner circle. He was present at the raising of the daughter of Jairus (Mark 5:37) and the transfiguration (Mark 9:11), and he stood guard at the garden in Gethsemane while Jesus prayed (Matthew 16:37).

James the Greater is the only apostle whose death is recorded in the New Testament. According to Acts, the apostle was arrested for causing unrest among the Jews and was put to death by the sword (Acts 12:2).

Following his death, tradition says that body of the saint was "miraculously" *translated* (a nice way of saying "moved") from Jerusalem to Iria Flavia in northwest Spain. The residents of Iria Flavia were astonished to see the body materialize before them, and they placed the cadaver of James the Greater in a holy sepulcher. The sepulcher remained a famous attraction for pilgrims and tourists throughout the Middle Ages.

St. James the Greater remains the patron saint of chemists, apothecaries, druggists, and victims of arthritis and rheumatism. If you suffer an arthritic flare-up, call upon this saint with this prayer:

> O glorious St. James the Greater, because of your fervor and generosity Jesus chose you to witness His glory on the mount and his agony in the garden. Obtain for us strength and consolation in the unending struggles of this life. Help us to follow Christ constantly and generously, to be victors over all over difficulties, and to receive the crown of glory in Heaven. Amen.

St. John: The Lord's Favorite Disciple

St. James the Greater had a younger brother, St. John, who also became an apostle. As a matter of fact, his brother became not only a member of the inner circle with St. James and St. Peter but also the disciple most loved by Jesus. St. John became known as St. John the Divine, and he wrote not only the fourth gospel and three epistles but also the Book of Revelation.

Jesus called St. John and St. James "sons of thunder" because they wanted to call down fire from Heaven on the unbelieving Samaritans (Mark 3:17).

Hagar the Hagiographer

Why was St. John the disciple most loved by Jesus? This is what St. Augustine says: "Christ was pleased to choose a virgin for His mother, a virgin for His precursor (John the Baptist), and a virgin for His favorite disciple."

St. John was the only apostle who remained faithful to Jesus to the bitter end at Calvary. From the cross, Jesus looked down at his mother and the beloved disciple and said to Mary, "Dear woman, here is your son," and to John, "Here is your mother." From that moment on, the disciple took Mary into his house and cared for her until the time of her miraculous Assumption into Heaven.

According to tradition, John went on to establish churches throughout Asia Minor. Several pagans tried to put him to death. The high priest of the goddess Diana forced him to drink a poisonous concoction, but the drug had no effect upon him. Several years later, he was arrested by order of Emperor Domitian and was transported to Rome. At the Latin Gate, John was placed in a vat of boiling oil but emerged from the ordeal completely unscathed. The emperor then exiled the indestructible disciple to the island of Patmos, where he wrote the Book of Revelation.

Finally released from Patmos, John moved to Ephesus, where he was regularly transported (at the age of 98) to gatherings of the faithful. He constantly gave the gatherings the same advice: "My dear children, love one another" (1 John 4:7). When asked why he kept repeating the same thing to the same people, John replied: "Because it is the precept of the Lord, and if you comply with it, you do enough." St. Jerome wrote: "These words ought to be engraved in characters of gold and written in the heart of every Christian."

If you want to have your book published, or if you've swallowed some poison, say this prayer:

> O glorious St. John, you were so loved by Jesus that you merited to rest your head upon His breast and to be left in His place as a son of Mary. Obtain for us an ardent love for Jesus and Mary. Let me be united with them now on earth and forever after in Heaven. Amen.

Hagar the Hagiographer

St. John remains the patron saint of bookbinders, booksellers, publishers, and writers. This means that he is, by tradition and default, the patron saint of *this* book.

And Now for the Tale of St. John and His Bedbugs

We cannot leave the subject of St. John without relating the story of the sanctimonious bedbugs. On one of his trips, he was forced to spend the night in a bed that was teeming with bedbugs. After they crawled over the exhausted saint and bit him without mercy, John cried out: "I say unto you, O bugs, behave yourselves, one and all, and leave your abode for the night and remain quiet in one place, and keep your distance from me."

The next morning, John's traveling companions spotted thousands of obedient bedbugs patiently waiting outside the bedroom door. When John appeared revived and refreshed from a good night's sleep, he said to the bugs: "Since you have well behaved yourselves in hearkening to my rebuke, come unto your place." Hearing this, the good bugs scurried back to the bed and disappeared under the covers. This goes to show that saints are not only good examples, but great (and environmentally safe) exterminators.

According to tradition, John died in bed of old age. He was the only apostle who did not suffer martyrdom.

A Tax Collector for a Saint?

St. Matthew—the tax collector (formerly known as Levi)—is listed by hagiographers as a martyr, although no one knows whether he was burned, stoned, or beheaded. Matthew, of course, was not only great in math but also in verbal skills—he is alleged author of the first gospel. Of all the apostles, he would probably do best on scholastic aptitude tests (SATs).

St. Matthew is the patron saint not only of bookkeepers and accountants, but also of the Church's mission. This last honor was bestowed on him because he ends his gospel with the so-called Great Commission, in which Jesus says: "Therefore, go and make apostles of all nations, baptizing them in the name of the Father and of the Son and of the Holy Spirit, and teaching them to obey everything I have commanded you" (Matthew 28:19–20).

If you have a bookkeeping problem, you can invoke St. Matthew with this prayer:

> O glorious St. Matthew, in your Gospel you portray Jesus as the longed-for Messiah who fulfilled the prophets of the Old Covenant and as the new Lawgiver who founded a Church in the New Covenant. Obtain for us the grace to see Jesus living in His Church and to follow His teaching in our lives on earth so that we may live forever with Him in Heaven. Amen.

Holy Cow!

During the time of the apostles, travelers spent the night in places called "caravansaries." Such havens were always located around sources of water. The rooms were tiny and dingy, and travelers slept on cots that were usually infested with bedbugs.

Holy Cow!

Although he was the author of the first gospel and a very prominent apostle, St. Matthew's fate became blurred with the fate of St. Matthias, so it is virtually impossible to separate the tradition of one from the other.

Missing in Action: St. Matthias

Although no one is quite sure what happened to St. Matthias, his body ended up in Jerusalem, where it was discovered by St. Helena—the mother of Constantine, the first Christian emperor. This "replacement" member of the 12 apostles is not quite as popular as the others, and few devotions are directed to him. This might be a result of two factors: Most people confuse him with St. Matthew, and replacements (as with George Lazenby as James Bond) are never quite as popular as the original (Sean Connery in the same role).

Still, St. Matthias is hailed as the patron saint of alcoholics. You can call him to your case by reciting the following:

> O glorious St. Matthias, in God's design it fell upon you to take the place of the unfortunate Judas who betrayed his Master. You were selected by the twofold sign of the uprightness of your life and the call of the Holy Spirit. Obtain for us the grace to practice the same uprightness of life and be called by that same Spirit to wholehearted service of the Church. Then, after a life of zeal and good works, let us be ushered into your company in Heaven to sing forever the praises of Father, Son, and Holy Spirit. Amen.

Divine Revelation

Dragons are Biblical. In Revelation (12:1–5), St. John had a vision of an enormous red dragon with 7 heads, 10 horns, and 7 crowns on the heads. The dragon stood in front of a woman who was about to give birth so that he could devour the baby. The woman is identified by the Catholic Church as Mary. The dragon is the personification of the devil.

St. Philip Becomes the First Dragon Slayer

As for the last of the 12 apostles, St. Philip was the apostle who asked Jesus how much bread was needed to feed the multitude and who, looking at the 5,000 hungry followers, said: "Eight months' wages would not buy enough bread for each of them to have a single bite" (John 6:7). He was also the apostle who told Jesus that he wanted to see God the Father. To this request, Jesus replied: "Don't you know me, Philip, even though I have been among you such a long time? Anyone who has seen me has seen the Father" (John 14:9).

In 80 A.D., according to tradition, this rather inquisitive apostle suffered the same fate as St. Peter by being crucified upside down at Hierapolis in Phygia under the reign of Domitian.

Philip deserves special mention because he was the first saint to fight a dragon. The ferocious dragon guarded the Temple of Mars in Greece, and Philip managed to force the fire-breathing beast into submission with a cross.

The first dragon fighter remains the patron saint of bread makers and pastry chefs, not of dungeons and dragons. This, no doubt, is due to St. Philip's role in providing bread (but not cupcakes or French croissants) to the 5,000 hungry followers of Jesus.

If you are facing a dragon, call upon St. Philip by saying this prayer:

> O glorious St. Philip, at the Last Supper you said to Jesus, "Lord, show us the Father and it will be enough for us." Help us to make this our prayer also and to seek God in all things. Obtain for us the grace to know the Father and Jesus Christ whom He has sent—for in this does eternal life consist. Amen.

The Least You Need to Know

➤ John the Baptist set an example for subsequent saints by living a life of self-denial.

➤ St. Peter is called the "prince of the church" and "the greatest apostle" because he received the Great Commission from Jesus.

➤ Much of the information regarding the apostles come from strange gospels and epistles that were circulated in the early Church and were later condemned.

➤ Eleven of the twelve apostles (the exception being St. John the Divine) were put to death for their faith.

Chapter 5

Now Playing:
ST. PAUL

The man,
The Legend.

Guest Starring:
His
Apostles

Legends Versus Lives: St. Paul and His Disciples

In This Chapter

➤ St. Paul poses problems for Catholic saints

➤ St. Paul's life becomes legend

➤ Saints perform similar wonders

➤ Saints' lives are contained in martyrologies

What do St. Paul, Martin Luther, and a chronic case of constipation have in common? Well, one day Martin Luther, who suffered from constant constipation, sat on a toilet in a high tower and had a cathartic experience. He opened the scriptures and read a passage from Paul's letter to the Romans that said, "The just shall live by faith" (1:17). It was this passage that inspired Luther, a very devout Catholic monk, to begin formulating what eventually became the Protestant Reformation.

St. Paul—The Patron Saint of Protestants

Luther had been a very diligent monk who tried to win God's grace by good works. He spent days in prayer, he went without food and water, and he scrubbed the floors of the monastery. "I out-monked all the other monks," he said. But this one passage from Paul convinced Luther that he could not be justified by works because all works, even the most charitable and seemingly selfless, are insufficient and insignificant. As Isaiah said, they are like filthy rags. The Reformer believed that individuals can be justified only by their faith in Jesus.

Luther held that prayers and pleas to the saints produce no results. Pilgrimages to holy places fail to gain God's favor. The purchase of indulgences and the recitation of litanies, he maintained, are mere exercises in human futility. The only thing that matters is faith—pure and simple faith—in the saving work of Jesus Christ.

St. Paul Undermines St. Peter and the Heavenly Host

By reading St. Paul, Luther and the Reformers came to believe that the veneration of the saints in Heaven was heinous idolatry. The statues and images of the saints were stripped from churches. The relics were removed from altarpieces. The images of the holy ones were cast into bonfires. These things were done to rid Christianity of pagan or "papal" idolatry.

Holy Cow!

Did a bowel movement really cause the Protestant Reformation? That is the contention made by psychologist Eric Erikson in his book *Young Man Luther*.

Divine Revelation

St. Paul was originally Saul of Tarsus, who was originally a persecutor of the Christians. He encountered the risen Christ on the road to Damascus and was struck blind. Three days later, when "something like scales fell from his eyes," he was baptized and began a new life as the apostle Paul.

The Reformers discovered that St. Paul in his epistles undermined the doctrine of saints as divine intercessors by claiming that Jesus Christ alone remains the one Mediator between God and man (1 Timothy 2:5). Because Christ alone is the Mediator, the saints have no power, no authority, and no claim or right to God's attention. The saints, the Reformers said, have no merits in a divine treasure chest—merits that were earned by their exemplary lives and good works. The saints, even the most pious martyrs, are totally without merit in the eyes of God. They, like everybody else in the Kingdom of Heaven, are justified only by faith.

The dispute between St. Peter and St. Paul arose over the question of the Gentiles. Both apostles ate and drank with the Gentiles. Both accepted the Gentiles as brothers. Both maintained that Gentiles do not have to submit to the Hebrew rite of circumcision in order to be accepted in the community of saints. Everything was fine and dandy until some leaders of the Jerusalem Church showed up in Antioch, where the two Apostles were living. In the company of these leaders, St. Peter shied away from all contact with the Gentiles. He wouldn't join them at table. He wouldn't break bread with them. He wouldn't associate with them. St. Peter's hypocrisy was so galling that St. Paul screamed at him in front of everybody. He said: "You are a Jew, yet you live like a Gentile and not like a Jew. How is it, then, that you force Gentiles to follow Jewish customs?" (Gal. 2:14). Firmly reprimanded by St. Paul. St. Peter got off his high horse and, once again, became one of the *goys*.

Many Protestants love this passage. It undermines the concept of Peter's supremacy and the notion of papal infallibility. It serves to endear them to St. Paul, and, in their own way, to venerate him in much the same way that Catholics venerate St. Peter.

Another factor endeared St. Paul to Protestants. He did not submit to the authority of St. Peter. Occasionally, Paul was downright insubordinate to the great Prince of the Church. "When St. Peter came to Antioch," Paul wrote in his letter to the Galatians, "I opposed him to his face, because he was clearly in the wrong" (Galations 2:11). Paul defied the authority of Peter, just as Luther and the Reformers opposed the authority of the pope.

Holy Cow!

The German philosopher Friedrich Nietzsche said that St. Paul was the "inventor" of Christianity.

Hey, Paul's Not a Mensch

But, although he may be loved by Lutherans, Methodists, Presbyterians, Baptists, and Episcopalians, St. Paul is the saint most detested by the Jews. After all, he was a Jew who turned against Judaism. Because God had sacrificed His own son to free people from sin, Paul believed, it was clear that the laws of Moses were not adequate to reconcile people to God. The law was holy and good, he said, but it could not break the enslaving power of sin, not even for the most pious Jew.

Believing that the followers of Christ were free from the law, Paul accepted the Gentiles into the fellowship without reservation and even took uncircumcised converts into the Holy Temple at Jerusalem. Pious Jews were outraged. What could be more of an effrontery to the God of Abraham, Moses, and David?

Divine Revelation

In his epistles, St. Paul reflects on the "folly" of Christ who became victorious by his defeat on the cross. He writes: "God chose what is foolish in the world to shame the wise; God chose what is weak in the world to shame the strong; God chose what is low and despised in the world, even things that are not, to bring to nothing things that are."

St. Paul May Be Smart, but He's Not Really Cute

Catholics throughout the ages have not really warmed up to St. Paul in the same manner that they have to rough-and-gruff St. Peter and kind and gentle St. Jude. Small wonder. St. Paul isn't really warm and cuddly. Nor is he particularly attractive. In the apocryphal Acts of Paul and Thecla, he is described as follows: "A man small of stature, with a bald head and crooked legs, in a good state of body, with eyebrows meeting and a nose somewhat hooked." This is the one and only vivid description we have of any of the apostles.

This small, bald guy with a hooked nose turned out to be the greatest Christian missionary. He traveled more than 10,000 miles over his lifetime and experienced incredible adventures. In his second letter to the Corinthians, Paul maintains that he was flogged by irate Jews on many occasions, that he was cast into prison; that he was beaten with rods three times, and that he was stoned and left for dead. He says that he went for long periods of time without food and drink; that he endured several shipwrecks, once spending a night and a day in open sea; and that he was besieged by bandits and cut-throats as he journeyed throughout the Roman Empire.

Holy Cow!

Luther and the other Reformers used St. Paul to undermine the concept of the saints as intercessors by pointing to 1 Timothy 2:5–6, where the apostle writes: "There is one God and one Mediator between God and men, the man Christ Jesus, who gave Himself as a ransom for all men—the testimony given in its proper time."

The Story of Paul and the Lion Who Became a Pussycat

Paul's exploits were embellished by pious legends that were recorded in such apocryphal sources as the Acts of Paul. One story involves a baptized lion. In Ephesus, the stalwart saint was forced to face a hungry lion "of huge size and unmatched strength" in an arena. But, as soon as the lion was loosed, it crawled over to Paul like a good little kitten and lay at his feet. (The spectators, it seems, were unaware that the apostle had encountered the same lion in the wilderness some time before and had preached to it. The beast had professed belief in Jesus and had submitted to Baptism.) At this point, a tremendous hailstorm rained from Heaven, killing many people and animals. In the wake of the storm, the baptized lion and Paul returned to the wild.

Hagar the Hagiographer

Albert Schweitzer, the great Protestant missionary and author of *The Quest for the Historical Jesus*, says that St. Paul is the patron saint of Protestant thought.

According to ancient martyrologies, Paul was beheaded on the outskirts of Rome on the same day and in the same year that Peter met his Maker. For this reason, they share the same feast day. Their bodies were buried five miles apart. But, on the feast day, popes celebrate solemn High Mass at St. Peter's and do not take the short trip to St. Paul Outside the Walls. Few hagiographers can blame them. St. Paul has created too much trouble in the Kingdom of Heaven.

Divine Revelation

St. Paul is a sexist, just like St. Peter. In his first letter to the Corinthians, St. Paul writes, "Man did not come from woman, but woman from man; neither was man created for woman, but woman for man" (1 Corinthians 11:8). In the eyes of feminists, St. Peter is no better. In his first letter, he says, "Wives be submissive to your husbands, so that, if any of the nonbelievers do not believe the word, they may be won over without words by the behavior of their wives, when they see the purity and reverence of your lives. Your beauty should not come from outward adornment, such as braided hair and the wearing of gold jewelry and fine clothes. Instead, it should be that of your inner self, the unfading beauty of a gentle and quiet spirit, which is of great worth in God's sight" (1 Peter 3:1–4).

In the art of the Church, St. Paul is presented not as the great lion of God (as he remains in Protestant thought), but as a rather benign and bald figure walking down a country road with his furry friend, the baptized lion. He remains the patron saint of evangelists, snake handlers, and laypeople. If needed, St. Paul may be summoned by this prayer (which is not offensive to Protestants):

> O glorious St. Paul, after persecuting the Church, you became by God's grace its most zealous apostle. To carry the knowledge of Jesus, our divine Savior, to the uttermost parts of the earth, you joyfully endured prison, scourgings, stonings, and shipwreck, as well as all manners of persecutions, culminating in the shedding of the last drop of your blood for our Lord Jesus Christ. Obtain for us the grace to labor strenuously to bring the faith to others and to accept any trials and tribulations that may come our way. Amen.

Holy Cow!

Before the Reformation, legends meant the lives of the saints. The holy legends were read to the monks and nuns at every meal.

Forget the Lives, Give Us the Legends!

The story of the lion is significant because it points to a fundamental fact of hagiography: The lives of the saints are not based on Biblical witness but on the testimony of tradition. In the early Church, the priest was obliged to present the people with a lecture (a *lectio* in Latin). The lecture was usually read rather than recited, so it became known as a *legenda* or "legend" (meaning "that which must be read"). The people did not like dry lectures on theology, such as interpretations of passages from St. Paul's epistles. They preferred stories about the lives of the saints that imparted easy-to-grasp moral lessons. For this reason, the lives of the saints, until the time of the Reformation, were called "the legends of the saints."

Before the Reformation, *legend* did not have a negative connotation. It did not signify a story that was untrue. The "legends" included facts that were historically genuine facts that could be substantiated either by visible cures, by tangible miracles, or by the testimony of other saints. Sure, some of the legends were pious fabrications with little basis in fact, but many were not.

Two rules were established for the acceptance of legends:

➤ The extraordinary is commonplace in the life of a saint.

➤ The signs and wonders, such as cures, apparitions, visions, *stigmata*, pleasant odors, and incorruption, that are attributed to a saint must not be unworthy of his or her moral and spiritual character.

St. Peter Speaks

A **stigmatic** is a person who bears the supernatural wounds of the crucified body of Jesus Christ.

Naturally, today much more stringent regulations are in place for sainthood. But until the sixteenth century, pious folk stories, to a large degree, were accepted as true. They were true because they came from tradition.

You Have to Admit It: The Saints Are Kind of Boring

Reading the lives of the saints can be an exercise in monotony. One life does not seem different from another life. This is because the legends are not different from one another. Most relate the same information:

➤ Saints can control elements: water, rain, wind, hail, fire, and sunlight. They can cause earthquakes. They can force volcanoes to erupt. They can create a tempest in a teacup.

➤ Saints can enlarge or diminish objects. They can dissolve a mountain into a speck of dust or transform a drop of water into a flowing stream.

➤ Saints can transcend gravity. They can levitate and, at times, fly through the air.

➤ Saints take part in battles, especially against such evil things as dragons.

➤ Saints are served by animals from wild beasts to bedbugs.

➤ Saints communicate with the heavenly host.

➤ The heavenly host proclaim the identity of saints to others by making bells ring or stones sing.

➤ The saints behold visions of Heaven, purgatory, and hell.

The Disciples of St. Paul

St. Paul's disciples are also hailed and venerated as saints. Paul called St. Timothy "my beloved son in faith" and sent him two stirring epistles in which he directs his disciple to correct teachers of false doctrine and to appoint bishops and teachers. Paul also advised Timothy to drink a little wine for his stomach problems (1 Timothy 5:23).

According to tradition, Timothy became the first bishop of Ephesus. He was stoned and clubbed to death after denouncing the pagan festival of *Katagonia,* a celebration held in honor of the Greek god Dionysus, who died and rose from the dead. His relics were later (to use a hagiographer's favorite word) *translated* or "moved" to Constantinople in 356. Cures at St. Timothy's shrine in the eastern capital are mentioned by St. Jerome and St. John Chrysostom.

St. Paul's "beloved son in faith" has left a strange legacy. Despite his closeness to Paul, Timothy is really not held in high esteem by Protestant fundamentalists. Perhaps they piously realize that Timothy probably took the apostle's advice and imbibed an alcoholic beverage. Catholics, however, love to pray to this good saint every time they suffer from gastrointestinal discomfort or flatulence.

Moreover, St. Timothy is more than likely highly distressed in Heaven by the fact that Dionysus— the pagan god who inadvertently caused his death—was mistakenly acclaimed a saint in the fourth century.

Got tummy problems? Invoke St. Timothy by this prayer:

> O glorious St. Timothy, well known for your gentleness, you were a most faithful disciple of St. Paul and, like him, traveled much to bring the good news to all people. The letters that Paul wrote to you reveal your zeal and

Hagar the Hagiographer

The relics of St. Timothy were discovered in Jerusalem during the reign of Constantine. For some strange reason, they were located near the remains of St. Andrew and St. Luke.

Divine Revelation

In his first letter to St. Timothy, St. Paul says, "The love of money is the root of all kinds of evil. Some people, eager for money, have wandered from the faith and pierced themselves with many griefs" (1 Timothy 6:10).

inspire us with confidence. You, too, were cast into prison, and you, too, gave your life for Christ. So with confidence, we dare to ask, please obtain relief for my stomach distress, if it be God's will. Amen.

Hagar the Hagiographer

Because St. Titus is the saint to be invoked against freethinkers, he probably should be invoked against Martin Luther, who (according to Albert Schweitzer) is the patron saint of free thought.

Divine Revelation

When people swooned over his good looks in Greece, they called St. Barnabas Zeus (because he was so awesome) and St. Paul Hermes (because he was short and talkative), St. Barnabas and St. Paul told the crowd: "We too are only men like you. We are bringing you good news, telling you to turn from these worthless things to the living God, who made heaven and earth and sea and everything in them" (Acts 14:15).

St. Titus: Don't Lose Your Head, or, Keep Your Mind Closed to New Ideas

St. Titus was also one of Paul's favorite disciples and his personal secretary. Paul called him "my true child after a common faith" (Titus 1:4). Titus was also the recipient of an epistle from the apostle that was included in the New Testament. In the letter, Paul instructed his "true child after a common faith," who had been left in Crete, to address the problem of the Cretans who were liars, evil brutes, and lazy gluttons. To make matters worse, Paul wrote, they were easily corrupted by false doctrines.

According to tradition, Titus took this advice and became the first bishop of the Christian congregation in Crete. He remained with the disagreeable Cretans until 110 A.D., when he finally died of old age.

But death wasn't the earthly end of Titus. His head was brought to Venice after the Saracen invasion in 823 and, to this day, is venerated in St. Mark's Cathedral.

St. Titus is invoked against all freethinkers and has been invoked against any skeptical readers of this saintly work.

Something else is special about St. Titus. He was a Gentile and never submitted to the rite of circumcision. This means that he was (hallelujah!) the first *goy* in Heaven.

St. Barnabas: A Hunk of a Saint to Swoon Over

St. Barnabas, another of St. Paul's companions, plays a prominent part in the early chapters of Acts. He accompanied Paul on the apostle's first overseas mission, first to Cyprus (where they converted a Roman proconsul), and then to the mainland of Asia Minor.

We know from Acts that St. Barnabas must have been a real hunk. Women in one town in Greece swooned over him and believed that he must be a god. Only with difficulty could St. Barnabas prevent the women from offering him gifts and favors.

St. Barnabas accompanied St. Paul back to Jerusalem to meet with the council of the disciples and to discuss the question of circumcision for converts. After this, the two men parted, and St. Barnabas slipped from the pages of history.

This saint has been the victim of a great deal of confusion. He is listed in the martyrologies and mentioned in the Catholic Mass as an apostle, even though he was not one of the 13 (including St. Paul). To make matters worse, the *Acts of Barnabas*, an apocryphal epistle which Christians believed told of the miracles and deeds of St. Barnabas, really records the acts of Bar-Nahba, a believing Muslim.

A prayer in praise of St. Barnabas is as follows:

> "God, our Father, you filled St. Barnabas with faith and the Holy Spirit and sent him to convert the nations. Help us to proclaim the Gospel by word and deed. We ask this through our Lord Jesus Christ, who lives and reigns with You and the Holy Spirit, one God forever and ever. Amen."

Hagar the Hagiographer

The Jewish parents of St. Barnabas called him Joseph. When he became a Christian, he sold all his goods and took the name "Barnabas," which means "son of consolation." In Acts, St. Luke describes him as "a good man, full of Holy Spirit and of faith" (6:24).

A Gospel Writer Finally Gets Translated—But Not into Another Language

St. Mark, who accompanied St. Paul on a missionary trip to Cyprus, is recognized as the author of the second gospel. According to tradition, he became the bishop of Alexandria and was martyred by burning during the reign of Trajan (98–117 A.D.). His charred remains were translated to Venice and remain under the high altar of St. Mark's—appropriately enough, next to the holy head of St. Paul's other buddy, St. Timothy.

St. Mark is depicted in medieval art as a lion, which brings us back to the baptized lion who, because he was saved, must have lost his pride.

The evangelist is celebrated as the patron saint of attorneys, victims of insect bites, and those who suffer from scrofulous diseases.

Learn a Lesson from St. Philemon

To understand more about the establishment of legends, let's take a look at two of St. Paul's other friends: St. Philemon and St. Onesimus. We know from Paul's short note to Philemon that he was a Christian, probably living in Colossae, and that Apphia, who is also greeted in the note, may have been his wife. We know that Paul sent this letter from his prison cell in Rome and that St. Timothy was with him. The note informs Philemon that Paul is returning to his care a runaway slave called Onesimus. We know that Onesimus was a troublesome slave who was of little use to his former master. But Paul informs Philemon that Onesimus has become a Christian and a good and devout disciple who has helped Paul in times of trouble. Therefore, Paul says that he should be received no longer as a slave but as a dear brother who can serve Philemon in his Christian endeavors.

That's all we know from the letter. But the legend or life of St. Philemon tells us that he was a bishop of Colossae who took Onesimus into a house and lived with him as a brother before confirming the former slave as bishop of Bera. The legend also tells us that Philemon was stoned to death with his wife, Apphia, for witnessing to the faith. Onesimus, the slave, became a stellar example of equal opportunity. He went on to become bishop of Alexandria, where he suffered martyrdom and gained a crown in Heaven.

Divine Revelation

The Letter to Philemon is St. Paul's shortest epistle. Like the Epistle of St. Jude, it consists of a mere 25 verses.

How do we know these things? How can we be sure that these stories were not made up by some crazy monk in a medieval monastery? Hagiographers say that we can accept such legends as having a basis in historical fact because the names of St. Philemon, St. Apphia, and St. Onesimus are mentioned in ancient martyrologies, such as the Apostolic Constitution. Statements about their latter lives are also contained in the writings of St. Irenaeus and St. Ignatius.

Of course, such evidence that comes from hearsay and secondhand sources would be dismissed in a court of law and ruled unacceptable for a research paper. Still, there is some evidence, even though the evidence is unreliable.

A Saint Without a Legend Is Like a Dog Without a Tail

This brings us to the last of the esteemed Protestant saints: St. Stephen. Protestants like St. Stephen and are willing to have their churches named after him because this guy is a real, flesh-and-blood, honest-to-goodness Biblical character. His story is recorded in the Book of Acts, along with the details of his death. There is no need to rely on *martyrologies* or apocryphal letters or statements of other saints to substantiate the facts about him. They are clearly and unequivocally contained in the New Testament.

St. Luke, the author of the third gospel and the book of Acts, tells us that Stephen was one of the seven men chosen to settle disputes between Hellenistic (Greek-speaking) and Hebraic (Aramaic-speaking) Jews over the distribution of food. Stephen was consecrated for this work because the apostles laid their hands upon him. This means that he was a duly ordained minister, a fact that endears him even more to present-day Protestants.

Like all real saints, Stephen performed great wonders and manifested many miraculous signs among the people. He also rubbed a lot of the traditional Jews, who failed to recognize Jesus as the Messiah, the wrong way. They instigated a slander campaign, saying that Stephen spoke about the destruction of the temple.

Eventually, the newly ordained minister was arrested and dragged before the ruling elders in Jerusalem, who questioned Stephen about the charges. The good saint stood up and began to deliver a speech. At first, his words were well received and the elders saw that "his face was like the face of an angel" (Acts 6:15).

Stephen went on to provide a summary of the origins of the law and of God's covenant with the Jews. The elders were lulled into complacency and, more than likely, were set to release him. But then Stephen's speech turned truly and utterly radical. In building the temple, Stephen said, Solomon had not served God. "The Most High," he remarked, "does not live in houses made by men" (Acts 7:48). The speech got worse. Stephen proceeded to attack the judges directly:

> You stiff-necked people with uncircumcised hearts and ears. You are just like your fathers: You always resist the Holy Spirit! Was there ever a prophet your fathers did not persecute? They even killed those who predicted the coming of the Righteous One. And now you have betrayed and murdered him—you who have received the law that was put into effect through angels but have not obeyed it. (Acts 7:51–53)

When the elders heard these remarks—especially the disparaging words about their fathers, they were furious so much so that they "gnashed their teeth at him" (Acts 7:54).

St. Peter Speaks

Martyrologies are the early accounts of the Christian martyrs that were kept by early Christian churches to commemorate the anniversaries of their deaths.

Divine Revelation

St. Stephen's interpretation of the teachings of Jesus was explosive because it profoundly challenged the Law of Moses and set the course for the separation of Christianity from Judaism.

But Stephen continued. He looked up to Heaven and said: "I see Heaven open and the Son of Man standing at the right hand of God" (Acts 7:56).

Hearing this, the judges covered their ears and screamed at the top of their lungs. Then they grabbed him and dragged him to a place of execution outside the city walls and proceeded to stone him. Before they proceeded to lift heavy boulders to crush Stephen's skull, they removed their robes and placed them at the feet of a young man named Saul, who, of course, became Paul, the great Christian apostle and the subject of this chapter.

St. Peter Speaks

St. Stephen is remembered as the first **proto-martyr** of the Church. He is called a proto-martyr because he set the prototype for subsequent Christian martyrs.

Hagar the Hagiographer

St. Augustine (also a favorite of Protestants) wrote, "If Stephen had not prayed, the Church would not have gained Paul."

St. Stephen Was Dead a Long Time Before He Finally Got a Life!

The entire account of St. Stephen is contained in two chapters of Acts. But his feast day is not celebrated on the day of his martyrdom and entrance into the Kingdom of Heaven. His feast day is the day in which his relics were translated from Jerusalem to Rome.

You see, even after his death, Stephen managed to get a life or a legend. The legend concerns a devout priest named Lucian who, in 415 A.D., was led by an angel to St. Stephen's burial place in Jerusalem. Lucian found not only Stephen's casket—but also the caskets of St. Nicodemus and St Abibas. When the priest opened St. Stephen's coffin, a sweet fragrance filled the air and miracles were recorded throughout the Holy City.

When St. Stephen's relics (along with the stones that had been used to kill him) arrived in Rome, there was a great celebration, accompanied by reports of miraculous cures. He became venerated not only for his spiritual example but also for his earthly remains. In 444, the saint became so popular that the Empress Eudocea built a stately church over the spot where he had been buried. Four hundred years after his death, the martyr got a life.

Naturally enough, St. Stephen remains the patron saint of bricklayers, stonemasons, and (for good reason) victims of headaches. The way the holy saints died is the way they are best remembered.

The Least You Need to Know

➤ St. Paul undermines the Catholic doctrine of the communion of saints.

➤ Like the other saints, St. Paul became the subject of popular piety.

➤ Many legends surround St. Paul's disciples.

➤ St. Stephen became the first Christian martyr and serves as the prototype of Christian martyrdom.

Chapter 6

The Holy Martyrs: How to Obtain Real Death Benefits

In This Chapter

➤ Christians are called "Haters of Humanity"

➤ Saints provide role models

➤ St. Perpetua becomes a superstar

➤ Bad times produce more persecutions

➤ More persecutions produce more Christians

You can't really blame Nero. Rome, the eternal city, had burned to the ground, and some people thought he was responsible: They accused him of causing the conflagration so that he could rebuild the city according to his own grandiose plans. Others said that he even played the lyre and sang while Rome burned. Everyone was in an uproar. They had lost their homes and possessions. Everything was in ashes. Somebody had to pay. When they blamed Nero, he quite naturally blamed others. "It wasn't me," he said. "It was the Christians. They are haters of humanity."

How the Christians Became So Hated

And so a great pogrom, or mass execution, began. The Christians were rounded up from every section of the city and cast into prison. The Romans, who lost their loved ones, their homes, their businesses, and their possessions, cried out for their blood, and Nero had to placate them.

The Christians in Rome came from all levels of society. The majority, however, were low-paid Greek-speaking immigrants. Slaves were attracted to the new religion, as were women (some from well-to-do families).

Great games were staged in which Christians were put to death for the amusement of the people. Accounts of these early persecutions appear to be accurate because they come from Roman sources. Tacitus, for example, provides the following account of the first Christian Holocaust:

Mockery of every kind was added to their deaths. Covered with the skins of beasts, they were torn by dogs and perished, or were nailed to crosses, or were doomed to flames. These served to illuminate the night when daylight failed.

Nero Was Bad, but Domitian Was Worse

This was bad, but the worse was yet to come. In 95 A.D., Emperor Domitian made a concerted effort to rid humanity of "the deadly superstition of Christ." Thousands were put to death throughout the Roman Empire, including many of the Lord's original disciples. The pogrom under Domitian was particularly severe because the emperor demanded to be worshipped by all of his subjects.

Starting with Julius Caesar, a number of Roman rulers were deified after their death. But Domitian scandalized the Empire by demanding that his contemporaries worship him while he was still alive. Christians, of course, could worship no person as divine, except Jesus, who was God made man.

St. Ignatius Imparts Hope and Inspiration

After Domitian bit the dust (proving, once and for all, that he was not divine), the persecutions began again under the reign of Trajan. Throughout the empire, Christians were rounded up and put to death. One such Christian was St. Ignatius of Antioch, who was martyred in 105.

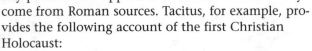

Holy Cow!

Nero was an unabashed hedonist who loved orgies and debauchery. He had his 19-year-old wife murdered so that he could marry his mistress, and then he killed his mistress. He also wrote poetry, designed palaces, played the lyre, and thought of himself as a talented singer. Before he killed himself, he sighed: "Alas, what an artist is dying in me."

Divine Revelation

The letters of St. Ignatius are among the most valuable possessions of the Church because they shed light on Christian belief and practice less than 75 years after the Ascension of Christ into Heaven.

We know a great deal about Ignatius because he was the writer of seven very spirited letters held in honor by the early Christians.

Ignatius had been the bishop of Antioch for more than 40 years when he was arrested for his refusal to worship the Roman deities. At the age of 70, he was bound in chains and transported to Rome. On this fateful journey, the old bishop wrote these words to his followers: "Come fire, come cross; grapplings with wild beasts, cuttings and manglings, wrenching of bones, hacking of limbs, crushing of the whole body; let cruel torments of the devil come upon me; if only I attain unto Jesus Christ."

When his followers attempted to come to his aid, Ignatius urged them to do nothing to rescue him. Bound in chains that he called "spiritual pearls" and vexed by 10 soldiers whom he called his "leopards," the old saint traveled across much of Asia Minor on foot before setting sail for Rome.

The End of Ignatius Is Not Ignoble

When he arrived in Rome, Ignatius was sentenced to be fed to wild beasts for the amusement of the public. The old saint received the sentence with joy and thanksgiving. When scores of grieving Christians sought him out in his jail cell, Ignatius told them that martyrdom would result in instant union with God.

According to legend, Ignatius was gobbled up by two particularly ferocious lions in the Flavian amphitheater—the place we now call the Coliseum.

Hagar the Hagiographer

Tradition says that St. Ignatius was a persecutor of Christians before he became a convert and a disciple of St. John the Evangelist. He is depicted in Christian art as being present when St. John went on to meet his Maker.

St. Cecilia, or, All for a Song

Another victim of this early persecution was St. Cecilia. She was a Roman girl of noble birth who became a Christian as a young child without her patrician parents' awareness. They remained unaware even when she began to act a little weird. She fasted from food and drink for long periods of time, and she wore a horribly uncomfortable hair shirt for penance under her regular clothes. Eventually, Cecilia's father arranged, despite her protests, for her to be married to a young pagan named Valerian.

On their wedding night, Cecilia told Valerian that she could not submit to the conjugal act until he submitted to Christian baptism. Filled with lust for

Hagar the Hagiographer

St. Cecilia is the patron saint of music. The official prayer to her goes like this: "St. Cecilia, pray for inspiration for all Christian musicians, especially those in charge of our sacred liturgies. Amen."

his new bride, Valerian agreed. When her dutiful husband set off to find a priest, Cecilia spent the time in prayer. Hours later, after being baptized, Valerian entered the bedroom to find a giant angel with flaming wings singing a beautiful hymn to his virgin wife.

Holy Cow!

In 756, Aistulf, the barbarian invader, sought to steal the body of St. Cecilia from her shrine in Rome. Hearing of this horrible plan, Christians removed her body to a hiding place. The problem was, they later forgot where they had hidden it. Finally, Pope Paschal I had a dream that enabled him to locate the missing body.

Holy Cow!

When Christians were tried in Roman court, such as the court of Pliny the Younger on the Black Sea, they were compelled to kneel before a raised dais, where the magistrate sat with two assessors. Those who failed to kneel were immediately sentenced to death.

After this experience, Valerian became a good and sincere Christian who spent all his time and money helping to spread the gospel. In time, Valerian and his brothers (who also converted to the new religion) were arrested for refusing to make sacrifices to the pagan gods. They were such sincere spokesmen that they made their executioner a Christian before he could raise his axe to chop off their heads. The executioner, then, agreed to die with them.

The next day, Roman soldiers were ordered by the emperor to kill Cecilia, whose eloquence had converted hundreds of pagans to Christianity. The soldiers attempted to burn her in her bathroom, but the attempt failed. After she emerged from the flames, the soldiers tried to cut off her head, but they only succeeded in leaving her mortally wounded. She prayed that she would be allowed to stay alive until her house became consecrated as a church. When the consecration took place, three days later, Cecilia went on to meet her Maker.

Pliny Relates Plenty on Christians

We know even more about the persecutions under Trajan because of records kept by Pliny the Younger, a Roman governor of the combined provinces of Bithynia-Pontus. His records state that Christians who were hauled into his court were given an opportunity to recant their faith. Those who cursed Christ and made an offering to the pagan gods were set free. But those who remained obstinate in their beliefs were put to death.

Curious about Christians, Pliny the Younger investigated the strange religion and discovered, as he records in his letters, that the accursed Christians met before dawn to "chant verses" in praise of "Christ as a God." The food they shared, he noted, was "ordinary and harmless," and they did not appear to be dangerous.

Emperor Trajan responded to Pliny's letters by saying that all those convicted of being Christians must be put to death for the sake of humanity.

Zounds: St. Zoe Opposes Zeus

More were martyred during the reign of Hadrian (117-138). The so-called Acts of the Martyrs, the first hagiography, dates from this period, which tells the inspiring tale of St. Zoe.

Zoe and her husband Hesperus were slaves who had been freed by their good Christian master Catalus. They had two sons and settled down to a nice comfortable life in Constantinople. They educated their sons as Christians but became rather lax in their practice of their religion.

When the persecutions broke out in 135, Zoe and her family were arrested. Because Zoe and Hesperus were less than devout, they were permitted to go free. But their two sons were tortured without mercy for refusing to worship the pagan gods. The wife and husband were moved to repentance and recommitted their lives to Christ. They asked to join their sons in the torture chamber, where they were subjected to every conceivable kind of humiliation. Finally, the entire family was put to death in a massive furnace.

St. Zoe is the patroness of family unity. If you are experiencing disruption in your family, try the following prayer: "May the intercession of St. Zoe bring about unity of faith in families, based not on doing the minimum required, but on heroic love of God and neighbor. Amen."

Yet Another Round of Persecutions

In 155, some 40 years after the death of St. Ignatius, a new wave of persecutions suddenly broke out in Smyrna (modern-day Izmir in Turkey). Hundreds of Christians were put to death, including St. Polycarp, the bishop of the province.

Some Carp About St. Polycarp

St. Polycarp was so revered that he never removed his own shoes. That menial task was always performed by disciples who were eager to serve him.

The account of this Christian saint comes from a letter he wrote to the Philippians, as well as a second-century document called "The Acts of Polycarp."

Holy Cow!

Hadrian was the most brilliant of all the Roman emperors. He publicly burned all tax records so that the people would be freed from government oppression, established public welfare, reorganized Roman law, rebuilt towns and cities, and made Rome, the most beautiful city in the world. Unfortunately, he also persecuted Christians.

Brought before the Roman proconsul, Polycarp refused to curse Christ and to make an offering to the gods. "Eighty-six years I have served Jesus and He never did me any wrong," said the saint. "How can I blaspheme the King who saved me?"

The provincial city's lions were too well-fed from a steady supply of Christians to devour the crusty old Polycarp. And so, the brave and unbowing bishop was ordered to be burned at the stake.

His Bones Are Worth a Fortune

When the executors attempted to nail the saint to the stake, Polycarp said, "He who grants me to endure the fire will enable me also to remain on the pyre unmoved." When the pile of wood was set to blaze, the flames formed a circle around the saint and failed to consume him. Polycarp died only when one of the executioners reached into the pyre to stab him in the heart.

Hagar the Hagiographer

When St. Polycarp was put to death, along with 12 of his disciples, a fragrant smell emanated from his blood "as if it were the wafted odor of frankincense or some other spice."

Hagar the Hagiographer

Got a terrible earache? No problem! Just invoke the name of St. Polycarp, who specializes in aural problems.

The devotion to the old bishop was so great that soldiers were warned not to allow Christians to take his remains, "else they will abandon the Crucified, and begin worshipping this one."

Despite this warning, some disciples of Polycarp were able to carry off a few of his bones. These remains were considered by the Church in Smyrna to be "more valuable than gold." This is the first reference made to the relics of a martyr.

One of the most cherished prayers in Christendom is the following prayer, which Polycarp said before he died on February 23, 155:

> Lord, Almighty God, Father of your beloved and blessed Son Jesus Christ, through whom we have come to the knowledge of Yourself, God of angels, of powers, of all creation, of all the race of saints who live in your sight. I bless You for judging me worthy of this day, this hour, so that in the company of the martyrs I may share the cup of Christ, Your Anointed One, and so rise again to eternal life in soul and body, immortal through the power of the Holy Spirit. May I be received among the martyrs in Your presence today as a rich and pleasing sacrifice. God of truth, stranger to falsehood, You have prepared this and revealed it to me and now You have fulfilled the promise. I praise You for all things. I bless You, I glorify you, through

the eternal priest of Heaven, Jesus Christ, Your Beloved Son. Through Him be glory to You, together with Him and the Holy Spirit, now and forever. Amen.

Hey, Marcus Aurelius, Why Don't You Practice What You Preach!

Marcus Aurelius, the Caesar who served as a Stoic philosopher, launched a fresh wave of persecutions that lasted from 161 to 180. These persecutions were conducted in the wake of several natural disasters, including earthquakes and floods, that occurred throughout the Roman Empire.

The most brutal of these events took place at Lyons in the summer of 177. Hundreds of Christians were rounded up as enemies of the state and subjected to terrible punishments. The trials and tribulations of these martyrs were carefully recorded in yet another martyrology. The 90-year-old bishop of Lyons, St. Pothinus, was beaten so severely that he died two days later. Many of the victims were confined to dark, dank, and airless dungeons, where they died from the inhuman conditions or strangulation by their jailers. Others, who called themselves "athletes of the faith," were flogged repeatedly or roasted on red-hot iron chairs before being cast to wild beasts.

Holy Cow!

Marcus Aurelius is the emperor who came closest to Plato's ideal of a philosopher-king. A generous ruler, he increased the number of people who were eligible for free corn from the state and forgave unpaid taxes. In his *Meditations,* he proclaimed his love for the human race. Few think of him as the hater of Christians that he was.

St. Blandina: No Bull, She's Gored to Glory

One of the most famous martyrs of Lyons is St. Blandina. The young woman was tortured until her persecutors were too tired to continue flogging and flailing her. Blandina was then dragged into the amphitheater and nailed to a kind of cross as prey for the lions and tigers. When none of the beasts dared to bite her, the young woman was returned to her cell for more torture and torment. Throughout her ordeal, Blandina continued to

Hagar the Hagiographer

The account of the martyrdom of St. Blandina is preserved in a letter from the surviving members of the Church in Lyons to the Church in Asia Minor.

encourage her fellow prisoners about their place in the Kingdom of Heaven. Finally, she was tied in a net and tossed to a wild bull. By that time, even the pagan spectators were moved by her incredible courage.

Are you the victim of torture or torment? Does your boss pick on you? Are you the victim of ridicule? Have you been falsely accused of something? If you answer "yes" to any of these questions, St. Blandina is the saint for you. She intercedes for all victims of torture (physical and well as mental) and all people who have been falsely accused.

Just Toss Us a Bone, for Heaven's Sake

Following the persecutions, Christians begged for the bodies of the holy martyrs, but the Roman soldiers left the bodies to rot for several weeks in the hot sun. Then the bodies were burned and the ashes were cast into the Rhine river, for fear that they would rise again to exact revenge.

At this time, Tertullian, the father of Latin theology, wrote, "The blood of the martyrs is the seed of the church." The deaths of these early Christians not only attracted new converts, but they inspired new Christian soldiers who wanted to give their lives in the service of Christ.

Five Reasons Christians Were Really Irksome to Pagans

By now you must be wondering why the Christians were so offensive to the Romans, even mild-mannered Romans like Marcus Aurelius. It seems almost incomprehensible. The Christians were creating no trouble. They believed in submitting to Roman authorities and upholding the law. They didn't get drunk and destroy property. They didn't misbehave in the public baths and spas. They didn't attend orgies and wouldn't steal a dime. So why all this fuss about them? Why all the arrests? Why the persecutions? Why the mass executions? The reasons, according to Church historians, are as follows:

Divine Revelation

The Flavian Amphitheater in Rome was a regular site for gladiatorial contests, wild beast shows, circuses, and Christian executions. Its name since the Middle Ages has been the Coliseum.

➤ Christians refused to participate in pagan worship. For this reason, they seemed downright unpatriotic because the gods were the protectors of the Roman Empire.

➤ Christians appeared to be cannibals. They spoke about partaking the body and blood of their Savior. Maybe, at their secret meetings in the catacombs, they were eating young children.

➤ Christians appeared to practice incest. At their services, they gave their brothers and sisters the kiss of peace.

➤ Christians promoted marital difficulties. They often advised women to refrain from having sex with their spouses because they believed that chastity—even within marriage—was a virtue.

➤ Christians had no use for the world and worldly pleasures. They considered themselves citizens of some eternal Kingdom, not the eternal city of Rome. For this reason, they were misanthropes: haters of all mankind.

The persecutions continued under Commodus, the unsavory son of Marcus Aurelius, and the soldier-emperor Severus, as the mighty empire suffered economic decline, barbarian invasions, and widespread rebellions.

The Ever Popular St. Perpetua Gets X-Posed

In present day Tunis stands an arena where the famous Christian martyrs Perpetua and her maid Felicitas, along with several of their companions, met their glorious end. A celebrated work entitled *The Passion of Perpetua and Felicitas,* published immediately after their deaths, records the sufferings of the 22-year old Carthaginian woman and her devoted maid. According to the account, the pious Perpetua entered the arena singing a psalm, while "abashing with the high spirit in her eyes the gaze of all spectators." A savage bull, unleashed on Perpetua, knocked her to the ground. But she immediately arose undaunted and began to fix her disheveled hair, knowing "it was not proper for a martyr to loosen her hair, lest she seem to mourn at the moment of her glory."

Holy Cow!

The reign of Commodus (180–192) was marked by economic decline, palace conspiracies, barbarian threats, and wholesale executions. To amuse himself, he often dressed in gladiatorial armor and killed unarmed opponents in the arena. On New Year's Eve in 192, his wrestling partner performed a public service by strangling him to death to the applause of onlookers.

Holy Cow!

Before she was put to death, St. Perpetua was stripped naked. The Roman spectators commented on the beauty of her breasts. St. Felicitas, Perpetua's old maid, was also stripped, but no one had a kind word to say about her sagging boobs.

Now prim and proper, Perpetua joined her maid in the middle of the arena and stood perfectly still. The crowd screamed that the women should be spared, but Perpetua and Felicitas displayed no emotion. The mood turned ugly as the crowd began to call out for their blood. The two women exchanged the kiss of peace and then were hacked to pieces by gladiators.

This account became wildly popular in the first Christian centuries. From Carthage to Alexandria, it was read at the start of every church service. Finally, St. Augustine was forced to warn the faithful not to accord *The Passion of Perpetua and Felicitas* the same status as the gospels.

St. Peter Speaks

When Christianity became the official religion of the Roman Empire, the Bishop of Rome assumed the title of **pontifex maximus.** That's why the pope is called a pontiff.

Holy Cow!

"The gladiatorial games are prepared," wrote a third-century Church Father, "that blood may gladden the lust of cruel eyes." Though some enlightened pagans opposed the games, most favored them, and the Roman people just couldn't get enough of them. Church Fathers wrote fiery tracts to discourage Christians from attending the gory spectacles.

Great Party Causes Terrible Hangover

The worst persecutions originated in 248, the year of Rome's 1,000-year anniversary. The eternal city was aglow with thousands of torches. Crowds packed the Campus Martius, the site of pagan pageants. The Palatine and Capitoline hills were teeming with people, who were laughing, dancing, and drinking the free-flowing wine. Government workers tossed coins and bread into the crowd. It was a great toga party.

On the riverbank overlooking the Tiber, the emperor, in his role as *pontifex maximus,* or high priest of the Roman religion, sacrificed lambs and goats to the Fates, who controlled the destinies of people and governments. Massive white bulls and heifers were paraded along the river and sacrificed to Jupiter, the god of Rome, and his sister and wife, the goddess Juno. A chorus of boys and girls, chosen from the aristocracy, sang ancient hymns to Apollo and Diana.

Things Go from Bad to Worse

It was the party of parties, a celebration of patriotism. All good Romans took part in the festivities. They cheered and waved and had a grand old time. But guess what? The Christians refused to take part in the celebration. And the Romans, the good Romans, were offended. The Christians benefited from the *pax Romana*—the peace of Rome—from Roman prosperity and from Roman welfare. They were seen as ungrateful. But, even worse, they were disrespectful to the gods. They made no offerings, they sang no hymns, and they offered no prayers. This spelled trouble. Dishonored gods were dangerous gods. And, if the gods really got mad, the Roman people would be subject to years of plague and drought and hardship.

After the celebration, the fears of the Romans came to fruition. Barbarians crossed the Danube, the empire experienced a grain shortage, plague popped up in portions of the city, and civil war erupted in various provinces.

And You Thought Nero Was Nasty

On January 3, 250, Emperor Decius officiated over the annual sacrifice to Jupiter and to the other gods of Rome. He ordered all residents of every province in the empire to follow his example. Commissions were set up in every town and village to administer imperial edict. Everyone who offered a sacrifice to the gods was presented with a certificate or "libellus" to show that he or she had obeyed the emperor's command.

The government wasted no time in arresting those who defied the order. St. Fabian, the Bishop of Rome, was arrested, put on trial before Decius himself, and executed on January 20, 250. The bishops of Antioch and Jerusalem were arrested and died in custody.

If You Sacrifice, We'll Never Speak to You Again

"Where are your papers?" the Roman officials asked, after knocking at the door. Those who could not produce written proof that they had sacrificed to the gods were rounded up and cast into prison. It was a time of widespread fear and terror. Neighbors told on neighbors. Many Christians, fearing torture, offered sacrifice to the gods and received certificates. Others refused and were put to death.

In Alexandria, St. Dionysius provided an account of Christians who were forced to sacrifice:

> When called by name, they approached the impure and unholy sacrifices. But pale and trembling, as if they were not to sacrifice, but themselves to be victims and the sacrifices of the idols, they were jeered by many of the surrounding multitude, and were obviously equally afraid to die and to offer the sacrifice.

Divine Revelation

St. Fabian was chosen pope because a dove flew into the church and landed on his head during the papal election. He was the most unlikely candidate to become a bishop in the assembly because he was a layman.

Hagar the Hagiographer

St. Dionysius miraculously escaped martyrdom during the great persecution under Decius. He was tried before a Roman magistrate in Egypt and was deported to Kufra, where he converted thousands of Libyans. He later returned to Alexandria, where he resumed his duties as bishop.

The Martyrs Who Were Not Murdered

Things got even worse for Christians in Alexandria when a horrible outbreak of the plague ravaged the Egyptian city. So virulent was the plague that every house contained dying victims. The bodies of the dead were cast into the street, where they rotted in heaps under the merciless sun.

Hagar the Hagiographer

I know what you're thinking! Hey, Hagar, why is this chapter so long? There are over 10,000 officially recognized saints in the Kingdom of Heaven, and the overwhelming majority of them—over 7,000—were early Christian martyrs. I could go on, but space is limited.

Christians, who had been forced to hide and conduct their meetings in secret places, emerged from their shelters to attend to the dead and dying. At tremendous risk to themselves, they nursed the sick, washed the bodies of the dead, and prepared mass graves. Many of these good Christians became infected and died after caring for others. They later were acclaimed as true martyrs of charity and were added to the calendar of the saints.

How many Christians were put to death? No one can say with certainty. But it is true that thousands were martyred before Decius was killed in battle in June, 251. Six years later, thousands more came to a glorious end when Emperor Valerian ordered that "all persons under Roman law must conform to the Roman ceremonials" and, under the punishment of death, outlawed gatherings of Christians. Among the victims was Pope Sixtus II, the Bishop of Rome, who was beheaded in his Episcopal chair, along with four of his deacons.

For a Saint, It's Okay to Lose Your Head

Another victim of Valerian's persecution was St. Cyprian, who wrote *On the Unity of the Church,* a work that said that all Christian unity must be centered on the Bishop of Rome, who is the rightful successor of St. Peter. The African saint also said that he who does not have the Church as a Mother does not have God as a Father. St. Cyprian was martyred in Carthage. It took several strokes of the axe to chop off his head. To the very end, the saint lived up to his reputation for being difficult.

Before St. Augustine wrote *The City of God,* St. Cyprian was considered the most profound of the early Christian writers, because Tertullian and Origen, really great and even more profound Christian writers, had been condemned as heretics.

It's a Bird! It's a Plane! No, It's St. Restituta!

Another glorious martyr who was put to death under the reign of Decius was St. Restituta. This holy woman was a Roman of noble birth who had been converted to the faith by her chambermaids.

When persecutions erupted in Sora, Italy, the Lord appeared to Restituta and asked her to go there. When she consented, an angel appeared before her with flapping wings and flew her to the city. Many persons, including Roman soldiers, were converted to the faith because of the many miracles she performed in the marketplace.

Upon being informed of Restituta's flight into Sora, the authorities arrested her, bound her in chains, and cast her into a dark dungeon. Periodically, they removed her from the dungeon to prod her with red-hot pokers and to whip her until she fell unconscious. The good Restituta steadfastly refused to recount her faith.

For over a week, the young woman lived without food or water, naked and in chains. One day, when the jailers looked into her dungeon, they discovered a flock of angels removing her chains. Beholding this sight, they fell to their knees and became God-fearing Christians. The next day, Restituta was beheaded, before she could perform any more miracles or convert any more guards.

St. Peter Speaks

St. Restituta is a favorite saint of women in prison. Such women are encouraged to mouth the following devotional: "May the prayers of St. Restituta come to the assistance of all those in prison for their faith and those to whom they may witness during their confinement."

And You Thought Diocletian Was Decent

For the next 40 years, Christians experienced another period of relative tranquility. Then the worst of all persecutions took place under an emperor named Diocletian.

Diocletian was a bit of a fruitcake. He wore a diadem set with pearls, and he ordered all visitors to not only bow before him but to prostrate themselves on the floor in his presence. He also fancied that he was the one and only true son of Jupiter.

St. Peter Speaks

By the turn of the fourth millennium (300 A.D.), there were more than five million Christians in the Roman Empire.

On February 23, 303, the emperor issued an order that all Christian churches and all Christian writings throughout the empire should be destroyed. Two months later came another decree that condemned all Christian clergy to prison. The prisons immediately became packed. This necessitated the third and final decree that all Christians who refused to worship Jupiter and the gods of Rome were to be put to death. Entire towns and villages were destroyed. In Phrygia, all of its inhabitants were burned to death for refusing to deny their faith and to sacrifice to the pagan idols.

The Pope Who Became a Pagan to Avoid Torture

The bloodshed was even greater than during the persecutions under Decius. The rolls of the martyrs increased by hundreds, even thousands, of names in every part of the empire, except Gaul and Britain. Eusebius, the first great church historian, tells us that people were stripped naked in torture chambers; men and women were flogged until flesh hung from their bones; bones were scraped with shells, while the victims remained alive; fingers were pierced with sharp reeds that were pushed under nails; eyes were gouged out and cast into pails; molten lead was poured down the throats of screaming women and children; skulls were smashed with clubs; severed heads were stacked in piles at places of public execution; and crosses surrounded countrysides.

The deaths were so horrific that several Christian leaders—including Marcellinus, the Bishop of Rome—recanted the faith and offered sacrifice to the pagan gods.

The Bloodshed Backfires

But the persecutions backfired. Thousands of spectators at arenas were moved by the courage of the Christians and the steadfast faith they manifested in the face of death. The accounts of the heroism of the martyrs spread from Christian community to Christian community. Romans from all walks of life were attracted to the new faith like never before.

Eventually, the Christians were cheered when they appeared before the masses, and the gladiators were jeered.

St. Anastasia: Proof That It Pays Off to Have Friends in High Places

One of the favorite saints from this period of persecution is St. Anastasia. This saint came from a noble Roman family and married a pagan, even though she was a Christian herself. During the reign of terror under Diocletian, she hid many fellow Christians in her palatial house. At first, the Romans didn't bother her—they thought that because Anastasia was married to a good pagan boy, she must be a fine and

Holy Cow!

It's true! Marcellinus was a pope who, when confronted with torture, denied the Christian faith and made offerings to the gods of Rome. Small wonder he never attained sainthood.

St. Peter Speaks

Every saint in the Kindom of Heaven has a feast day. Originally, this was their *dia natalis,* or the day they died as martyrs and were reborn as saints in Heaven.

upstanding pagan herself. But, when notified that she was harboring enemies to the realm, they arrested her, cast her into prison, and attempted to starve her to death.

During this ordeal, Anastasia began to pray to St. Theodota, a holy woman who had been cast to the lions with three of her sons the previous year. St. Theodota responded to Anastasia and nightly appeared in the prison cell to feed her. Fearful of her influence with the heavenly host, her guards freed her.

Once freed, Anastasia set sail to come to the aid of Christians in far-off provinces. A storm arose and the crew abandoned the ship, while the pious woman and her Christian companions prayerfully stayed aboard. Suddenly, St. Theodota appeared at the helm and piloted the ship to land.

After converting pagans throughout the Empire, Anastasia was taken to Palmaria, where she was burned alive.

Lucy in the Sky with Diamonds

St. Lucy was a beautiful young woman of Greek lineage who lived in Sicily. When she became a Christian, her pagan boyfriend became outraged. He reported her to the authorities and she was dragged before a magistrate. Because she prided herself on her virginity, the magistrate ordered that she be cast not into prison, but into a brothel.

Hagar the Hagiographer

St. Anastasia remains the patron saint of those lost at sea. Christians who feel abandoned by everybody are encouraged to invoke her assistance.

Holy Cow!

Prostitution was legal in ancient Rome, but, by law, brothels were kept outside the city walls and could only open at night. Fees were adjusted to bring promiscuity within the limits of every pocketbook.

When the soldiers tried to carry out the order, they found that Lucy had become immovable. Try as they may, they could not budge her. Frustrated, they covered her with oil to slip her into a crate. But Lucy had become as solid as granite. The guards next attempted to set her on fire. But—even though she was doused with oil—Lucy proved to be nonflammable. Finally, the guards were forced to hack her to pieces with swords and axes.

St. Lucy is invoked as the patroness of the blind and the visually impaired, since her name comes from the Latin word *lux*, meaning light. Here is one prayer by which you can obtain her intercession: "Relying on Your goodness, O God, we humbly ask You, through the intercession of St. Lucy, Virgin and Martyr, to give perfect vision to our eyes, that they may serve for Your greater honor and glory. St. Lucy, hear our prayers and obtain our petitions. Amen."

Hey, Guys, Don't Mess Around with St. Agnes

No discussion of the saints of the Great Persecution would be complete without a word or two about St. Agnes. Agnes was a beautiful and affluent girl of 12 who caught the eye of lusty pagan teenagers. One of these lads approached her and made an indecent proposal. Agnes shunned his attention and advances by telling him that she had pledged her heart and her life to Jesus Christ.

Upon making this statement, Agnes was arrested and cast into prison. When the Roman officials attempted to make her pay homage to the pagan gods, the young woman simply made the sign of the cross. This act of piety made the Roman officials furious. And so, they decided that this good virgin should be sent to a brothel so that anybody with a denarius or two could purchase her favors.

Agnes was transported to a seedy Roman brothel. The first customer to come up with the right coin for a naughty act with Agnes was the teenager who had turned her in to the authorities. When he took off the young girl's clothes, the lad was frustrated because her long hair shielded the private parts of her body. In a fury, the boy tossed Agnes to a cot and attempted to force his way upon her. As soon as he touched her holy body, the randy boy was struck blind. He fell to his knees and begged for mercy. Agnes forgave him, and his sight was restored.

Hagar the Hagiographer

St. Agnes is the saint who can best protect women from rape and other forms of sexual violence. She can be invoked by reciting the following prayer: "St. Agnes, intercede for us that we may be protected from rape and other forms of violence. Intercede for all those who do not know the Lord and seek pleasure instead in sexual sin. Through Christ our Lord, Amen."

Hearing of the miracle, the authorities sentenced Agnes to be burned at the stake as a Christian witch. When her executioners attempted to light the fire, they were immediately ignited like human torches and burned to ashes before the stunned spectators. Eventually, a soldier managed to put her to death by stabbing her in the heart.

Diocletian Cracks Up and Grows Cabbage

In the midst of this turmoil, Diocletian suffered what historians believe to be a nervous breakdown. He issued one more harsh edict against the Christians and resigned as Caesar. He spent his remaining years in a humble palace on the Adriatic (in present-day Split, Yugoslavia), where he became a cabbage farmer.

The persecutions came to an end in 312, when Constantine, beheld a vision of the cross in the heavens before going into battle against his imperial rival, Max-entius. The vision came with a slogan: *In hoc signo vinces* ("By this sign, you will conquer"). Constantine had crosses painted on the shields of his soldiers and routed his rival at the Mulvian bridge.

Upon becoming Caesar, Constantine became a Christian and issued the Edict of Milan, which granted toleration to Christians throughout the Empire. The age of the Christian heroes had come to an end.

Holy Cow!

Constantine, the first Christian emperor who presided over the Council of Nicea (the first ecumenical council of the Church), committed too many sins (including murder) to become a saint. His mother, however, is the much-loved St. Helena.

The Least You Need to Know

➤ Nero blamed Christians for the burning of Rome, and the first persecutions began.

➤ Christians were believed to be atheists, cannibals, lovers of incest, and disrupters of peace and serenity.

➤ The greatest period of persecution occurred during the reigns of Decius (circa 250 A.D.) and Domitian (circa 300 A.D.).

➤ The persecutions served only to produce millions of new Christians.

➤ The golden age of martyrdom came to an end when Constantine beheld a vision and became a believer.

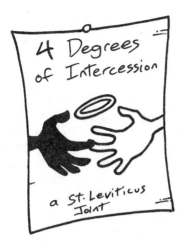

Chapter 7

The Intercession of the Saints (Plus: How Many Saints' Lives Are Really Legends!)

In This Chapter

➤ The difference between worship and veneration

➤ The four degrees of intercession

➤ The meaning of feast days

➤ Feast days produce legends

➤ Legends produce lives

"It's not idolatry," many Catholic theologians say. "We do not pray to the saints as gods. We merely pray to the saints that they will intercede for us before God. After all, the saints are *alive.* We hold this as a matter of faith, and they stand before the celestial throne, not as mannequins, but as persons. If this is true, why can't we ask them—just like we ask our family and friends—to do us a favor? Why can't they obtain a blessing for us? Why can't they plead our case and present our petitions before Almighty God?"

The Power of the Saints

Do Catholics pray to the saints? It all comes down to a matter of semantics—that is, a matter of religious word play. Technically, Catholics say that they really do not pray to the saints. They simply "invoke" or "call upon" the saints to pray for them. It all comes down to a distinction between "worship" and "veneration." Worship or adoration, according to Catholic theology, must be offered only to God as He is manifest in three distinct persons. But veneration or reverential respect must be accorded to the angels and saints.

The distinction represents a very fine line—that often has become blurred. After all, non-Catholics maintain, prayer is prayer!

The belief in the power of the saints arose during the first three Christian centuries, the time of the great persecutions. Evidence that these early Christians believed that saints could intercede with God on their behalf can be found in the early martyrology of the Church of Alexandria, which relates the following story of Potamiaena interceding on behalf of her prison guard in a way that many people might not find so pleasant.

St. Peter Speaks

Catholic theologians make a distinction between worship (*latria*) and veneration (*dulia*). Only God can receive latria, but saints are due good measures of dulia.

St. Peter Speaks

Intercession, in the study of the saints, refers to ability of saints to plead with God on behalf of sincere believers. It is the primary function of a saint. They are lobbyists in the Kingdom of Heaven.

Hey, St. Potamiaena, Forget the Favor!

In 202, members of a catechetical, or religious training school for converts, were put to death in Alexandria. Among these martyrs was a beautiful girl named Potamiaena. Before she was put to death, Potamiaena managed to befriend her prison guard, a Roman centurion named Basileides, and convert him to Christianity. The next day, a weeping Basileides was forced to lead his newfound friend to a place of execution. Potamiaena told him to stop crying because she had wonderful news for him. She had managed to intercede with Christ for him so that he, too, would receive the favor of experiencing martyrdom. Basileides received this news with joy, while Potamiaena was lowered into a cauldron of boiling pitch. The next day, as if by a miracle, Basileides was led into a courtyard and was promptly beheaded.

This story, located in the early martyrology of the Church of Alexandria, relates the fact that these early Christians believed in the concept of *intercession*.

Intercession: Not Just for the Living

Not only can the saints intercede for the living, but, as other early legends show, they also can intercede for the dead. We are told that St. Perpetua, while in prison, prayed for the eternal fate of her young brother, Dinocrates, who had died when he was 7. She first saw him in a place of pain and suffering, where he cried out for a drink of water. Perpetua awoke in a state of despair and fell on her knees to pray for Dinocrates. She prayed for several days and nights. Finally, she had a vision of her young brother being welcomed by the Lord into the Kingdom of Heaven.

Listen, Quinctianus, I'd Rather Die Than Have You Touch Me

So, the living can intercede for the living and the dead. Now it gets even more complicated. The dead, according to these early "lives," can intercede for the living.

For proof of this, let's turn to the tale of St. Agatha, who was put to death in 250. Young, beautiful, and rich, Agatha could have had it made as a Roman maiden in the province of Sicily. Instead, she decided to live as a holy virgin, dedicated to God. When Emperor Decius announced his edicts against Christians, the Sicilian magistrate Quinctianus tried to blackmail the beautiful virgin. He said that he would not have her arrested because of her faith, if she would agree to have sex with him. Naturally, Agatha was appalled by this suggestion and said that she would rather die.

And Now for the Seediest Brothel in Sicily

Quinctianus, however, had another punishment in mind. He handed Agatha over to the madam of the seediest brothel in Sicily. Agatha did what any good Christian would do. She refused to accept any customers. The madam, in turn, sent her back to the evil magistrate.

Outraged, Quinctianus had the virgin beaten, cast into a stinking pit, and tortured. He then tried again to make the saint consent to sex. As steadfast as ever, Agatha flatly refused.

The Private Parts That Reappeared

At this point, the magistrate commanded that the pious maiden be stripped naked. Once the guards removed Agatha's clothing, Quinctianus admired

Holy Cow!

It's funny how things happen in the community of saints. Dinocrates was suffering in purgatory. At the request of St. Perpetua, the young boy was lifted from the flames and was granted a place in Heaven. Because he is in Heaven, Dinocrates is a saint.

Divine Revelation

St. Agatha was right not to give in. The New Testament says that no one who engages in fornication or acts of sexual impurity will enter the Kingdom of Heaven (1 Corinthians 6:9).

the beauty of her body and then ordered his guards to cut off her breasts. Agatha protested by saying, "Cruel man, have you forgotten your mother and the breast that nourished you, that you dare to mutilate me this way?" Quinctianus repeated the order, and Agatha was rendered breastless.

Cast back in her cell, Agatha prayed to St. Peter. When she awoke in the morning, the saint discovered that her breasts had regrown and that now they had become even more beautiful than before. When the magistrate beheld her stunning new figure, he ordered her release, fearing that the young virgin was a demon or a witch.

Holy Cow!

St. Agatha was not the only saint with beautiful breasts. For proof, turn to the previous chapter and read the account of St. Perpetua. She had every Roman in the arena goggling at her.

Hagar the Hagiographer

Tradition says that St. Agatha said this prayer when she found herself in the hands of her enemies: "Jesus Christ, Lord of all, Thou seest my heart; Thou knowest my desires. Do Thou alone possess all that I am. I am Thy sheep: make me worthy to overcome the devil."

Mt. Etna's Still Not Erupting

Several years later, Agatha was arrested again by the same magistrate for spreading the faith to all who would listen. This time, the evil Quinctianus ordered that she be rolled on red-hot coals until she expired. His order was carried out. Agatha was near death when an earthquake erupted. In the destruction, the magistrate's guards were killed and Quinctianus fled for his life. Agatha thanked God for an end to her pain and suffering and was transported into glory.

Her story is important in this study of saints. It shows that the dead can help the living. St. Peter answered Agatha's prayer and performed a miracle on her behalf. But there is more to learn from her story. Legend has it that carrying the veil of St. Agatha, which was taken from her tomb in Catania, has averted volcanic eruptions from Mt. Etna. What's more, St. Agatha's intercession, on behalf of the people of Malta, who venerate her as their patron saint, reportedly saved Malta from Turkish invasion in 1551. Not only did the dead St. Peter come to the aid of the living St. Agatha, who cherished him as her patron, but the dead St. Agatha came to the aid of the living people of Malta, who turned to her as their patron.

Small wonder that St. Agatha is one of the most popular saints. She is the patroness of breast cancer, breast disease, nurses, single laywomen, and wet nurses. She is invoked for protection against fire, earthquakes, and eruptions of Mt. Etna. If you want to contact her, just present the following petition:

Dear virgin and martyr, whom the church recalls in her liturgy, you heroically resisted the temptations of a degenerate ruler. Subjected to long and horrible tortures, you remained faithful to your heavenly spouse. St. Peter, we are told, gave you some solace and so you are invoked by nurses. Encourage them to see Christ in the sick and to render true service to them. Amen.

It's True: Dead Saints Do Favors for Dead People

Now it gets even weirder. So far, we have learned the following:

➤ Living saints can intercede for living people.

➤ Living saints can intercede for dead people.

➤ Dead saints can intercede for living saints and living people.

The fourth and final thing you must know about intercession is this startling fact:

➤ Dead saints can intercede for dead people!

Don't scream! Don't yell! According to hagiography, it's true. St. Gertrude the Great of Helfta devoted her life to meditation of the Sacred Heart of Jesus. In many of her visions, she was transported to the afterlife, where she saw souls screaming in agony. Gertrude prayed for these souls until the time of her death.

As the legend tells it, upon ascending into Heaven, Gertrude was singled out for her concern over the suffering souls and was named the patron saint of purgatory. This is a position of considerable prominence in the afterlife. Every time a prayer is offered to St. Gertrude, 1,000 souls are released from purgatory. This means that we could empty this place of perdition in a matter of months by constantly saying this simple prayer:

> Eternal Father, I offer Thee the most precious blood of thy divine son, Jesus, in union with the Masses said throughout the world today, for all the holy souls in purgatory, and for

Hagar the Hagiographer

St. Gertrude was a great Christian mystic who beheld many visions, which she wrote about in her journal in great detail. For centuries, novices in convents throughout the world were required to read her journal and perform the spiritual exercises (including self-flagellation) prescribed in its pages.

Divine Revelation

God is called *omnipotent* because He is all powerful, *omniscient* because He is all knowing, and *omnipresent* because He is at all places at the same time. The saints do not have these powers and abilities. This is why they are not gods or demigods.

sinners everywhere, for sinners in the universal church, those in my own home, and within my own family. Amen.

It Began with an Anniversary Party

When you think about it, the veneration of the saints began in an understandable way. During the periods of terrible persecutions, the names of the martyrs and the dates of their martyrdom were written in record books kept by the Christian congregation. Every year, the faithful gathered to celebrate the anniversary of the martyr's death. At the anniversary, they recalled the martyr's heroic acts so that the saint would be an inspiration to others. The record books in which they recorded the deaths of the martyrs were called martyrologies, and their readings of the lives of these heroes were called legends.

Hagar the Hagiographer

On the day of the anniversary of a martyr's death, the congregation to which the martyr belonged would gather together in celebration of his or her achievement. The celebrations would consist of a church service, a reading about the saint, and a communal meal or feast. This is why the day on which a saint is honored is called his or her feast day.

In time, the real lives of the individuals behind the names were forgotten and became embellished by pious folklore. This is evident in the sagas of some of the greatest saints, including St. Eulalia.

She Should Have Stayed on the Farm

St. Eulalia is the most famous virgin martyr of Spain. All that we really know about her is that she was a young woman who was put to death in Merida in 304. But a legend arose around her that makes it impossible to separate the fact from the fiction.

According to the legend, Eulalia was only 12 when word came that all those who refused to offer sacrifices to the pagan gods would be put to death. Eulalia's mother, knowing the piety and devotion of her daughter, decided to take the young girl into hiding in the country. But Eulalia fled from the hiding place at night and presented herself before a Roman judge in Merida to witness to him about her faith.

Holy Cow!

It was not uncommon for girls of 12 and 13 to be married in ancient Rome; the ideal age for walking down the aisle was 14. A girl who was 19 and unmarried was considered an "old maid."

Just Shut Up and Pass the Salt!

The judge attempted to talk the young girl into making an offering to the gods, telling her that the offering would take only a minute and consist only of presenting a little salt and incense before a statue. He was even kind enough to hand her a pinch of salt and a measure of incense. Upon receiving this offering, Eulalia threw it to the ground and stepped on it. When the judge cried out in alarm, she spat at him.

The judge was incensed. After all, he was only trying to be nice. So, he ordered that the bold 12-year-old be sent to the torture chamber. After placing her in shackles, the torturers proceeded to tear the flesh from her abdominal regions with sharp meat hooks. Eulalia welcomed every tear within her flesh as a trophy from Christ.

Next, the executioners lighted torches and placed the flames against her breasts. Instead of screaming in agony, the young saint uttered words of thanksgiving. Eventually they set fire to her hair so that she became encircled by smoke and fire.

The Saint Gives Romans the Bird

When Eulalia uttered a prayer with her dying breath, a white dove suddenly popped out of her mouth and winged up to Heaven. The sight of the bird so startled the executioners that they ran screaming from the torture chamber, never to return.

This same strange legend was attributed to another St. Eulalia, St. Eulalia of Barcelona. To complicate matters, it was further attributed to saints named Aulaire, Aulazie, and Olalla. So was there really a St. Eulalia of Barcelona? Maybe, maybe not.

Nevertheless, St. Eulalia of Merida became a superstar among the saints. By 360, many hymns were written to her, and Prudentius, a Spanish bishop, spoke of the hundreds of pilgrims who came to the shrine of Merida to venerate her bones. He said that the good saint, now next to the throne of God in Heaven, "beholds them, and being made propitious by hymns, protects her clients."

The Spanish saint remains the best person in Heaven to protect "clients" from miscarriage and from rain. She can also be invoked to produce rain and hailstorms. In addition, she can cause runaway children to return home. A prayer to this saint goes like this: "St. Eulalia, ask God to give us strength to overcome our fear of looking ridiculous by speaking the truth to those who stand against Christ and His Church. Amen."

Divine Revelation

The dove in Christianity is the symbol of the Holy Spirit. When Jesus was baptized by St. John the Baptist in the River Jordan, the Spirit of God descended as a dove from Heaven and remained upon Him.

Hagar the Hagiographer

St. Eulalia is depicted in Christian art with a cross, a stake, and a dove. Despite the fact that she may have never lived, St. Eulalia was a favorite saint of St. Augustine.

Sebastian: Seems Like a Good Name for a Soldier

The intrusion of folklore into the lives of the saints is also evidenced in the story of another famous saint, St. Sebastian. All that we truly know about this saint is that his name appears in a Roman martyrology and that the body of a Christian named Sebastian was buried in the catacombs of Rome.

A legend arose about this man and his bones. The faithful came to believe that Sebastian was a captain in the Praetorian Guard, who lived in Diocletian's imperial palace and became the emperor's most trusted soldier and private protector. When Christians were arrested and sentenced to death, Sebastian visited them in prison, bringing them supplies and comfort. Gradually, the soldier got to know the prisoners and was converted to the new faith.

Sebastian spread the gospel to his friends and fellow officers, Marcus and Marcellian, who also became Christians. Marcus and Marcellian next introduced Sebastian to their parents, Nicostratus and Zoe. Nicostratus suffered from a crippling case of gout, and Zoe was a deaf mute as a result of an accident. Sebastian made the sign of the cross over the couple, and husband and wife were immediately healed of their infirmities.

Holy Cow!

Some saints, sorry to say, never existed, even though they are the subjects of widespread devotions. The Roman Catholic Church acknowledges this fact and also admits that it is impossible to sort fact from fancy in the accounts of the heroes and martyrs.

Hagar the Hagiographer

St. Sebastian was not the first Roman soldier to become a saint. That honor belongs to St. Longinus, who was present at the Lord's Crucifixion.

Talk About Ingratitude! After All I've Done for You ...

Sebastian went on to perform many more miracles and to convert hundreds of pagans to Christianity, including the governor of a Roman province. Eventually, word of Sebastian's Christian faith reached Diocletian. The emperor summoned Sebastian to appear before him. Foaming at the mouth with rage, the emperor accused him of shameful ingratitude and criminal conspiracy. Sebastian objected to these charges, saying, "I pray daily for thy safety and the prosperity of the state."

Diocletian ordered that Sebastian be tied to a tree and shot to death by arrows. This was the Roman form of a firing squad. The saint was shot with dozens of arrows and left for dead in an open field.

St. Irene to the Rescue

Hours later, a Christian widow named Irene went to remove Sebastian's body from the tree, only to discover to her amazement that the saintly soldier was still alive. The good Irene took Sebastian to her house and nursed him back to health.

Upon his recovery, Sebastian reappeared before the emperor, who thought he was seeing a ghost. The saint told the cowering Diocletian, "You will have no peace until you cease from shedding innocent blood."

The Story of St. Sebastian Really Stinks

After he regained his senses, the Emperor sentenced Sebastian to be cudgeled to death and ordered that his body be thrown into a sewer. His orders were obeyed. A group of soldiers clubbed the saint to death and dumped his body down a manhole.

A lovely young Christian named Lucina removed the saint's body from the sewer and properly buried him in her rose garden along the Appian Way.

In 367, Pope Damascus built the basilica of San Sebastian over his tomb, and it became one of most famous of Christian shrines.

Saints Don't Have Sex, but They Can Reproduce

None of the details about St. Sebastian has a basis in fact, not even the assertion that he was a soldier. Still, the pious legend served to create several other saints, including St. Marcus, St. Marcellian, St. Nicostratus, St. Zoe, St. Irene, and St. Lucina, all of whom are equally groundless in history. Additional stories about St. Sebastian gave rise to legends about even more pious figures, including St. Tiburtius, St. Susanna, and St. Caius. This shows that saints are spiritually prolific. They produce other saints at an amazing rate and in an amazing way. In this way, we can consider them like heavenly gerbils.

Holy Cow!

Ancient Rome was really quite modern. The Romans developed highly sophisticated aqueducts so that water flowed into the city. The city contained 700 wells, 700 fountains, and 130 reservoirs, along with a public sewer system.

Divine Revelation

Legend gives rise to more legend. Sts. Marcus and Marcellian, according to pious folklore, were not only brothers, but twin brothers. After their buddy St. Sebastian was clubbed to death, they were arrested and tossed into prison. By the time their day of execution came, they had converted not only their fellow prisoners but also their captors.

The legend of St. Sebastian does not end with the creation of his shrine, nor his production of other saints. His legend gives rise to other legends. In the fourteenth century, the Black Death spread throughout Christendom, killing one third of the population. One priest said that being exposed to the plague was like being exposed to "nature's archers." Archers! The image of St. Sebastian, tied to a tree, immediately came to mind of good Christians. People turned to him by the thousands for salvation, and he received renewed popularity.

Hagar the Hagiographer

St. Sebastian was not the first saint to be cast in a Roman sewer. According to legends, the first saints to suffer this indignity were Sts. Irenaeus and Abundus. But the great thing about saints is, no matter what you do to them, they always smell sweet.

Holy Cow!

The pagan practice of sleeping in a temple so that a god could speak to you in a dream was transferred to the sanctuary of Sts. Cosmas and Damian in Sicily, where many Christians spent the night so that the saints could speak to them in their sleep.

Oh, Please!

Even to this day, despite the fact that his story has no basis in fact, St. Sebastian's legend continues to give rise to new legend. Because he is often depicted as a naked youth, with a muscular body and an angelic face, who is pierced with arrows, St. Sebastian has become the favorite saint of the gay and lesbian community.

St. Sebastian is celebrated as the patron saint of archers, athletes, ironmongers, soldiers, lace workers, and plague victims.

All They Want Is a Little Recognition

The saints had become recognized as powerful intercessors, and the people realized that it was good to have friends they could call on in high places. Eventually, the feast days of the saints became celebrated with long processions and solemn religious services.

By the fourth century, after Constantine beheld his vision, bishops encouraged believers to call upon the holy martyrs during times of need. St. John Chrysostom (344–407) gave this instruction: "When you perceive that God is chastening you, turn not to God's enemies, but to His friends, the martyrs, the saints, and those who are pleasing to Him and have great power." Similarly, St. Cyril of Jerusalem said: "We honor and commemorate those who have died before us: patriarchs, prophets, apostles, and martyrs, in order that, by their prayers and intercessions, God may receive our petitions."

All of this occurred not without a problem. Pagan converts, who had a natural bent toward polytheism, began to worship the saints and martyrs as demigods. To make matters worse, many pagan gods were given Christian names and crept into the community of saints. The pagan gods Castor and Pollux became Sts. Cosmas and Damian, and the goddess Victoria became St. Victoire. Noting this phenomenon, Claudius of Turin (a ninth-century archbishop) bitterly complained that many converts to the faith of Christ "have not abandoned their idols, but only changed their names."

The Least You Need to Know

➤ Saints are venerated, not worshipped.

➤ Saints can intercede for living and dead people.

➤ Feast days are days on which a congregation celebrated the martyrdom of one of its members.

➤ Many of the saints of the Church probably never existed.

Chapter 8

Hey! These Apologists Won't Say They're Sorry!

In This Chapter

➤ How Christians defended the faith

➤ What constitutes a Christian apology

➤ Tertullian, the "Father of Theology"

➤ Origen defines world order

➤ St. Catherine becomes a radical feminist

The pagan war against Christianity was waged not only by the sword (and countless methods of torture) but also with words. Roman writers took out their poison pens to depict Christianity as a ridiculous religion that could appeal to only the dregs of society: slaves, menial workers, idiots, crazy old widows, and gullible young housewives.

Works appeared depicting Jesus of Nazareth as a really crazy prophet who called himself "King of the Jews." One work, *The Acts of Pilate,* described the Roman governor as a just and kind man who was forced to nail Jesus, a simple nutcase, to a cross because of the bloodthirsty demands of the Jewish people. Later, according to this account, the 12 apostles, embarrassed that their leader had died like a common criminal, stole the body of Jesus from a tomb and spread stories about His Resurrection.

Holy Cow!

In his satire, Lucian writes, "Christians despise all things non-discriminately, and consider them common property. So if any con man comes among them, he can walk away with their goods and possessions."

Hagar the Hagiographer

Pagans were shocked that Christian "brothers and sisters" exchanged kisses on the mouth and believed that they were practicing incest. For this reason, St. Atenagoras, a second-century apologist, said that a liturgical kiss must be discreet and "carefully guarded." He cautioned that a defiled kiss "excludes us from eternal life."

The Pagans Take Aim at Christians—This Time with Their Pens

For the first Christian century, churchmen could disprove these claims with the testimony of the first followers of Jesus, many of whom were still alive. After all, the resurrected Jesus appeared not only to several women and the 12 apostles, but also, as St. Paul records, to more than 500 of His disciples.

Hey, Lucian, Don't Call Me a Jackass!

A Roman named Lucian wrote a satire in which Christians are portrayed as so stupid that they elect a cynic named Peregrinus Proteus as a "prophet, a cult leader, and a community chief." Proteus ends up writing preposterous commentaries on the Bible that Christians acclaim as profound.

The attack on Christians spilled over into the visual arts. In murals discovered in an ancient imperial palace on the Palatine Hill, Christians are depicted as worshipping a crucified man with the head of a jackass.

Flash! Second-Century News! Christians Called Unnatural!

The first real serious threat—a threat that couldn't be dispelled by a simple testimony—came from a Roman philosopher named Celsus. This guy, who has all but disappeared from the pages of history, created just as many intellectual problems as such relatively modern movers and shakers as Darwin, Marx, Nietzsche, and Freud.

Celsus said that Christianity is philosophically silly because it separates man from the rest of creation. "They say that God made all things for man," the pagan writes, "but this is not true. Do not plants grow for animals as well as humans?" Man, in the vast scheme of things is no better than a fly or a bug. Celsus claims that God's care is for all creatures, not just one creature.

You Really Think Jesus Is a Bad Example?

Speaking of God, Celsus declared that monotheism is completely unnatural. Polytheism reflects the real created order: There is a special god for every planet, every country, every city, and every household. All the gods are embodied in the emperor, whom all men are obliged to serve. A good emperor, like a good god, displays the Roman virtues of loyalty, manliness, courage, and fortitude. According to Celsus, Jesus did not display these virtues. Christ wept tears before facing Pilate and displayed weakness on the cross. As a divine figure, the pagan proclaims, Jesus set a bad example.

Turning to the subject of the Resurrection, Celsus wrote, "If Jesus really wished to display His divine power, He should have appeared to the actual men who had reviled Him rather than a group of weak-kneed disciples."

God Does Love Frogs and Worms

As for the Christians themselves, Celsus describes them as an arrogant group of nonentities, "frogs holding a symposium around a swamp or worms a convention in a pool of mud, saying that God loves them."

Now the writings of Celsus were downright nasty, and they raised the dander of many Christians. To combat this stream of bad press from the pagans, a few educated Christians became press agents of the movement, stating that Christ is the hope for mankind and that Christians are model citizens.

The writings of Celsus were burned after Christianity became the official religion of the Roman Empire. But long passages of his work are quoted by Christian writers, such as Tertullian, Origen, and Macarius Magnes.

Let's Get This Straight—These Guys Won't Apologize

These press agents were called *apologists* not because they tried to apologize for their beliefs, but because they sought to defend the faith. As a matter of fact, these writers were not sorry about anything except the state of the world and pagan morality.

Holy Cow!

Celsus was a Roman who took the time and trouble to read the books of the Christians. He shows us the early Church as it appeared to outsiders: a movement still Jewish in outlook, divided among different factions; an ideology that rejected reason among human virtues; and an organization that looked forward to the end of the world in a blaze of glory.

St. Peter Speaks

An **apology,** in works of classical antiquity, is an essay in defense of a philosophical or moral position. It comes from the Greek work *apologia,* meaning "defense."

The first great Christian apologist was a gentle scholar from Samaria by the name of Justin Martyr, who taught Christian religion in his rooms above a bathhouse in Rome.

Divine Revelation

Logos is the Greek word for "reason" and for "word." The Gospel of John begins by saying, "In the beginning was the Word ("Logos"), and the Word was with God, and the Word was God. He was with God in the beginning. Through Him all things were made; without Him, nothing was made that has been made" (1:1–3). This passage shows that St. John had been trained in Greek philosophy.

Divine Revelation

St. Justin said that Christians are not the enemies of humanity, but the hope of mankind. "To put it simply," he wrote in his *First Apology*, "what the soul is in the body, the Christians are in the world."

St. Justin Says That Christians Are Not Complete Idiots

In his First Apology, St. Justin tried to show that Christian monotheism is natural because it upholds the principle of unity in the universe. All things in the universe are not chaotic, but harmonious. Everything that occurs in nature occurs with a discernible regularity. This shows that the universe is controlled not by a multitude of gods, but by one God.

This might seem of little consequence to us, but it was an amazing claim in the second century. Justin was showing that Christian faith is not opposed to the dictates of reason. He was saying, in fact, that Christian faith is reasonable and that anybody who is truly reasonable—truly philosophic—will come to accept the new faith.

It's All Greek to Us, Too!

The Gospel of John, St. Justin wrote, states that the world was created by the word of God. The Greek word for word is *logos*. Plato, in his works, spoke of the creative power of the divine Logos. Therefore, Plato, without knowing it, was a Christian.

Jesus displayed human emotions, St. Justin continued, because He was a real man. He was not a god pretending to be a man. He was like us in all things, except sin. Jesus wept. He sweated blood and tears. He cried out on the cross because He was truly man. And He performed miracles, He controlled the elements, and He rose from the dead—all because He was truly God.

Please, St. Justin, Don't Lose Your Head in This Argument!

But the greatest proof of the truth of the Christian religion is evident in the lives of its converts who were transformed from whores and thieves into good and obedient citizens. Justin wrote, "With us you will find many unlettered people, tradesmen and old women, who are uneducated, unsophisticated, and inarticulate, but they show the reality of our religion by their acts and blameless lives."

The pagans did not take very kindly to Justin's arguments. A Roman philosopher named Crescens succeeded in having Justin arrested for spreading sedition. Dragged before a magistrate in 165 as a plague broke out in the city, Justin was asked, under threat of death, to recant his faith. The apologist refused and said, "We ask nothing better than to suffer for the sake of our Lord Jesus Christ and so be saved." After making this statement, he was hauled into a courtyard and beheaded.

Hagar the Hagiographer

St. Justin Martyr is the patron saint of philosophers, philosophy, and apologists. It's ironic that the first Christian philosopher was put to death under the reign of pagan philosopher Marcus Aurelius.

Fronto Gets St. Irenaeus Irked

More pagan attacks on Christianity continued to appear. M. Cornelius Fronto, the tutor of Marcus Aurelius, said that Christianity should not be looked upon as an outshoot of Judaism. It should be viewed as a new and depraved religion in which participants performed unspeakable acts. Fronto said that he had attended one Christian banquet. After a lavish meal, he wrote, the Christians engaged in dark, lustful embraces, and then separated by brother and sister to engage in open acts of incest.

Enter St. Irenaeus, who said that Christianity was a not a new and depraved religion but an evolved form of Judaism. His key word, as an apologist, was *harmony*. There is complete harmony between the Old and New Testaments, he wrote, between the sin of Adam and the cross of Jesus, between the words of the prophets and the teachings of the apostles, and between the God of creation and the God of salvation. There is also harmony among all Christian churches because they all look to the Church of Sts. Peter and Paul as the guardian of right belief. Pagans may be exposed to the teachings of off-the-wall Christians, who don't know right doctrine from wrong doctrine, he said, and for true Christian faith, they must look to Rome. In this way, he wrote, the pagan world will come to know the harmony between Greek thought and Christian theology. Far from engaging in carnality and incest, Christians live for the soul rather than the body, like true philosophers.

Hagar the Hagiographer

According to tradition, St. Irenaeus was converted to the faith by St. Polycarp (remember him from Chapter 6, "The Holy Martyrs: How to Obtain Real Death Benefits"?) and might have followed the old saint to Rome. He became Bishop of Lyons in 177 and played an important part in determining the date of Easter.

Holy Cow!

The early Church included many heretics. The Docetists said that Jesus did not have a real body. The Gnostics said that the God of the Old Testament was not a real god (but merely a demigod). The Manicheans said that there were two real Gods—the God of the Old Testament and the God of the New Testament and Satan. The Arians said that Jesus was not the eternal Son of God, but a "creature" because He had been created in time. The church faced not only enemies without, but also enemies within. St. Irenaeus spent most of his life refuting the bizarre statements of heretics.

Can't You Leave Him Alone When He's Dead?

The words of St. Irenaeus were wasted on the Romans, but they strengthened the stature of the Roman church among Christians. In 202, the apologist was put to death in Asia Minor.

St. Irenaeus is venerated as one of the holiest Christian saints because of his statements about the supremacy of the Church of St. Peter (that is, the Catholic Church) above all other Christian congregations. Irenaeus' body was buried under the Church of St. John in France, which became known as the shrine of St. Irenaeus. Calvinists sacked this sacred shrine in 1562 (Protestants never liked this saint), and his relics were cast away with the rubble.

Holy Cow!

Although he is not a saint, Tertullian was the first theologian to formulate the doctrine of the Trinity. The basis of this doctrine is found in primitive baptismal formulas, which stipulated that converts be baptized "in the name of the Father, the Son, and the Holy Spirit."

This Guy Has a Wacky Sense of Humor!

One of the greatest Christian apologists was Tertullian, who is hailed as the "father of Latin theology." Once, when asked how he, an educated pagan, could believe in the superstition of Christians, Tertullian said, "I believe because it is absurd. Jesus was buried and rose again from the dead. It is certain because it is so incredible." He thought that his reward in Heaven would be seeing his enemies burn in hell: "How I shall marvel, laugh, rejoice and dance with glee at the sight of seeing the despisers of Christ groaning in the depths of darkness!"

Tertullian was a terrific defender of the faith. When Roman magistrates arrested Christians in Carthage on charges of disloyalty, Tertullian defended them with an eloquent letter. He assured the Roman court that Christians "are always praying for all emperors, for a safe dynasty, brave armies, a faithful Senate, and a quiet world under Roman rule."

Tertullian wrote another tract in which he attempted to show how the great thinkers from Socrates to Seneca were (when all is said and done) Christian prophets. Future Christian saints, including St. Cyprian, imitated his work and called him "the master apologist."

The Saint Who Was Locked Out of Heaven

But guess what? The father of "Latin theology" never made it into the communion of saints. At the end of his life, he decided that the world was coming to an end and joined a group of doomsday prophets called the Montanists. He also came to think that there was no way of reconciling pagan thought to Christianity. "What has Athens to do with Jerusalem?" he wrote. "What has the Academy to do with the Church? Away with all attempts to produce a philosophical Christianity."

What's more, he became more disagreeable. He condemned all Christians who became soldiers, all parents who did not veil their daughters, and all priests and bishops who restored sinners to communion. Finally, he called the pope a dirty old man and a shepherd of adulterers. This was the last straw. The greatest of Christian apologists became condemned as a heretic. What a pity!

Divine Revelation

The Montanists, the sect that Tertullian joined, believed that they were filled with the Holy Spirit. They uttered prophecies and spoke in tongues. They experienced religious ecstasies and often fell in trance. All in all, they were like modern Pentecostals. They were also very strict. They advocated celibacy, endured long fasts, and looked forward to the Lord's Second Coming.

Christianity Gets Caught Up in Technicalities

Clement of Alexandria, however, gained admission to the glorious fellowship. St. Clement was born in Athens and traveled widely in his youth, seeking wisdom from renowned teachers of many schools before converting to Christianity. As an apologist, he sought to make the faith acceptable to his fellow intellectuals. He said that a study of philosophy prepares one for the truth of Christianity. "Greek philosophy," he wrote, "provides for the soul the preliminary cleansing and training required for the reception of the faith, on which foundation the truth builds up the edifice of knowledge."

In the wake of Clement, Christian theologians started using strange philosophic terms to explain Christianity. Eventually they used such words as *homoiousious* and *homoousious, hermeneutics,* and *homiletics,* and *transubstantiation* and *consubsantiation.* Reading Christian theology was kind of like reading Greek. This trend has continued into modern times, so when you attend theological school, you are bombarded with such words as *soteriology, ontology, ecclesiology,* and, of course, *Christology.* In other words, St. Clement gave churchmen the means of at least sounding like college professors.

Hagar the Hagiographer

Why did St. Clement stress the intellectual aspects of Christianity by quoting Plato and other Greek philosophers in almost every page of his works? Clearly, he was writing in response to critics who said that Christianity was based upon superstition and blind belief. The pagan Celsus had written, "Some of these stupid Christians do not want to provide any reason for what they believe. They keep saying such dumb things as, 'Don't ask questions, just believe,' or, 'Your faith will save you.'"

Holy Cow!

Eusebius, the first official historian of Holy Mother Church, says that Origen cut off his privates "both to fulfill the Savior's saying, and also that he might prevent all suspicion of shameful slander on the part of unbelievers. For, as young as he was, he used to lecture on divine things to women as well as men."

Now This Is Really Extreme!

St. Clement's successor in Alexandria was a most peculiar man called Origen. When Origen was 17 years old, in 202, his father was arrested as a Christian and was sentenced to death. The lad wanted to join him in prison and martyrdom, but his mother prevented him from appearing before the authorities by hiding his clothes. The father was beheaded, and Origen decided to undergo his own type of martyrdom. He fasted much, slept little and always on the bare ground, subjected himself to cold and nakedness, and, as a final gesture, castrated himself.

Yes, you read the last sentence correctly. This great Church Father castrated himself. This sounds completely insane, but Origen thought he was only complying with the teachings of scripture. In Matthew 19:11–12, Jesus says:

Not everyone can accept this word, but only those to whom it has been given. For some are eunuchs because they are born that way; others were made that way by men; and others have renounced marriage for the kingdom of heaven. The one who can accept this should accept it.

Origen accepted it because he really wanted to get to Heaven.

Eunuchs Can Be (Believe It or Not) Very Productive

Origen devoted his life to explaining Christianity in philosophic terms. God, he said, is the First Principle of all things, and Christ is the Logos or Reason that organizes the world. The world, he believed, is heading for perfection. After the final conflagration, there will be another world with another long history, and then another and another. Man, too, is headed for perfection. After death, the soul will pass through many places for purification until it enters the heavenly kingdom.

St. Demetrius, the Bishop of Alexandria, and other Church officials read his 6,000 books (that's right, 6,000) and were amazed at his erudition. But they also realized that his writings were kind of crazy, and they condemned him as a heretic. They especially disliked his vision of universal salvation.

The Man Who Moved Mountains

One of Origen's disciples and a staunch defender of the faith with the pen was St. Gregory Thaumaturgus, a.k.a., Gregory the Wonderworker. He was a Biblical scholar who answered nagging questions concerning the gospels, like what were the pigs that became possessed by the demons from Legion doing in Palestine, a place where pigs were detested and held to be unclean? And, how can scripture say that Jesus and His disciples were threatened by a storm on the Sea of Tiberius, when that sea is little more than a mud puddle? And why do the four evangelists disagree on so many

St. Peter Speaks

St. Gregory the Wonderworker is one of the most famous of Christian saints. He is the first recorded person to whom the Virgin Mary appeared. He is the right saint to call upon in times of earthquake and flood.

Divine Revelation

It's true. Saints can move mountains. In the Gospel of Matthew, Jesus says: "I tell you the truth, if you have faith and do not doubt, not only can you do what was done to this fig tree, but also you can say to this mountain, 'Go, throw yourself in the sea,' and it will be done. If you believe, you will receive whatever you ask for in prayer" (21:21-22).

101

details of the life of Jesus, including His genealogy? St. Gregory became the first New Testament scholar by providing detailed responses to such queries.

Hagar the Hagiographer

Several epistles defending the truth of the Christian religion against the pagan philosophers were written by St. Venantius, the patron saint of leaping. He suffered a most unusual martyrdom. The saint survived not only the usual tortures of scourging, burning, beating, and being fed to wild beasts, but also being tossed from a high cliff. As soon as he struck the ground, he bounced back up to praise the Lord. He kept doing this until the pagans cut off his head

St. Peter Speaks

According to one legend, St. Catherine was an Egyptian queen, known for her great beauty, who became "mystically married" to the Christ Child. He allegedly gave her a ring that she never removed from her finger.

He also became known as a "second Moses" because of his ability to work wonders. This guy could put Harry Houdini and David Copperfield to shame. When the river Lycus threatened to flood, he turned back the raging waters. When two brothers fought over the rights to their father's lake, St. Gregory solved the problem by making the lake dry up with the turn of his cloak.

Once, when returning from the wilderness, St. Gregory decided to spend the night in a pagan temple. Upon entering the temple, the good saint naturally made the sign of the cross to purify the air.

The next day, the temple priest tried to call forth his usual oracles, but the demons said they could not return to the temple because St. Gregory had cleansed it. The angry priest demanded that the saint rectify the situation. Happy to comply, the saint handed the priest a paper on which he had written this command: "Gregory to Satan: you have my permission to come back now." The high priest, upon reading this, discovered that all the demons had returned.

Surprised that all the pagan gods would obey Gregory's instructions, the temple priest asked the Wonderworker to explain the faith to him. Shocked by the doctrine of the Incarnation and the concept of spirit passing into matter, the priest asked for a sign that this doctrine was true.

The old saint commanded the priest to look at a mountain and then, by the wave of his arms, managed to transport the mountain from one place to another. Needless to say, this was enough to convert the priest to leave home, family, and his fiends in the temple to be trained as Gregory's disciple.

Will Jesus Marry the Queen of Egypt?

Among the philosophical defenders of the faith during the time of the great persecutions is St. Catherine of Alexandria, who was one of the first women to behold a vision of the Virgin Mary.

Catherine was born of a noble family and devoted herself from childhood to study. She read the works of the great Greek philosophers. She read the works of the Roman stoics and cynics. Finally, she read the works of St. Clement and became a Christian.

Hagar the Hagiographer

The feast day of St. Catherine of Alexandria falls on November 25, immediately before the beginning of Advent. Throughout the Middle Ages, the church outlawed marriages during the seasons of Advent and Lent. November 25, therefore, became a sort of deadline for women to get engaged. For this reason, unmarried women said the following prayer to St. Catherine:

A husband, Saint Catherine, A good one, St. Catherine, A handsome one, St. Catherine, A rich one, St. Catherine, And soon, St. Catherine!

St. Catherine Frustrates the Emperor

When persecutions broke out again in Alexandria, Catherine could not hold her tongue. She boldly went before the Roman emperor and scolded him for his cruelty. She also raised questions about the pagan religion that the dumbfounded Maxentius, despite his schooling in philosophy, could not answer. In frustration, the emperor summoned 50 of the most renowned philosophers throughout the empire to answer her nagging questions and to silence the saint once and for all.

These sages appeared in the imperial palace to confront the combative Catherine. But, after a few hours of debate, they admitted to Maxentius that they could not answer her questions nor refute her claims. Outraged at the failure of these sages to controvert one Christian woman, he sentenced all 50 to be cast into a blazing furnace and for their ashes to be dumped in a dung heap.

Hagar the Hagiographer

In 1760, Alban Butler published his great work *Lives of the Saints*, which provides the stories of thousands of saints. It remains the classic text on hagiography. Butler wrote the book as an apologist to increase devotion to the saints during the period of enlightenment.

And Now She Gets Even with His Wife

Realizing that Catherine was a woman of profound wisdom and understanding, Maxentius attempted to persuade her to become his consort and adviser. When the saint refused, the emperor had her cast into prison with common criminals and riffraff.

Being naturally persuasive, Catherine managed to convert all her fellow prisoners to the new faith. What's more, she converted the prison guards. Finally, she even managed to convert Faustina, the emperor's wife, when she came to see the remarkable woman.

Holy Cow!

One of the voices urging St. Joan of Arc to pick up the sword and fight for the honor of France was that of St. Catherine.

As a result of all this converting, Catherine was fastened to a spiked wheel that was to be turned over a press until her bones were crushed and her blood was spent. But, as soon as they turned the wheel, it rolled from the axle and crushed the executioners along with a small group of spectators.

The emperor then ordered to have the troublesome saint beheaded. Legend has it that as soon as her head rolled off her body, angels carried her body to Mt. Sinai and placed it in a beautiful sarcophagus, where it still remains.

The First Female Church Father? Are You Serious?

Because of her skills as a philosopher, St. Catherine is hailed as the "first female Church Father." Is this a terrific oxymoron? She is also celebrated as the patron saint of wheelwrights, students, and college professors. You may obtain her services simply by saying this prayer:

St. Catherine of Alexandria, great apologist of the faith, intercede for all students, professors, and evangelists that they may find the words not only to defeat the enemies of truth, but also to become instruments of conversions. Amen.

Great Idea! Passing Out Tracts to the Pagans!

St. Cyprian, the bishop of Carthage, tried to answer these charges in a religious tract called "That the Idols Are Not Gods." The zealous saint and his fellow churchmen spread throughout the city much like modern zealots distribute tracts to revelers in New Orleans during Mardi Gras, to business people at airports, and to senior citizens at shopping malls.

In his tract, St. Cyprian said that the gods of Rome have no power to do anything. For centuries, they have been honored and worshipped by the people of Carthage and yet they allowed the plague to appear and to spread throughout the pagan city. Petitions to these gods are silly, since the gods are merely dumb idols. Persecutions are equally of no use, since pagan gods are incapable of being appeased, pleased, or displeased. How, he asked, can you appease a carved piece of wood or a thing of marble?

If You Think About It, A Plague Isn't Really Funny!

If they are real, the saint continued, then they must be demons, leading the populace astray by falsehoods and evil deeds. After all, aren't the pagan gods known to be tricksters, who love to play practical jokes on mere mortals? What better prank than a plague? If the gods are not merely false gods, they are cruel and deceitful demons that must be exorcised in the name of Christ.

It was a classic apology. It presented the Christian case in the correct form of a disputation. What's more, it tried to show that Plato, like all real philosophers, denied the concept of polytheism and upheld belief in one Supreme Being. By setting forth this apology. St. Cyprian may have won the argument, but he also lost his head.

St. Peter Speaks

When his death sentence was announced, St. Cyprian cried out: "Thanks be to God!" He was beheaded after giving his executioner twenty-five gold pieces and saying, "Hurry up, and get on with it."

Lactantius Has Last Laugh

The final intellectual attack on Christianity by the Romans came from a prolific pagan named Porphyry who attempted to show that the stories about Jesus were flights of fantasy. He also said that Christians are so stupid and pig-headed that they cannot be reconverted to paganism by the forces of logic and reason. Such efforts, he said, are like trying to write a letter on the surface of water, where liquid closes over every stroke.

This batch of bad pagan press caused Lactantius to write a long tract entitled "On the Deaths of the Persecutors." In this work, he outlined a history of God's wrath against the tormentors of Christians. Beginning with Nero, who died at his own hand, Lactantius maintained that all who persecuted Jesus and His followers had died a horrible death.

Hagar the Hagiographer

Lactantius wrote a poem called "The Phoenix" in which he compares the Egyptian myth of the Eastern bird that lives as long as a thousand years, dies in flames, and rises from its own ashes to the life, death, and resurrection of Jesus. He was the first person to relate a pagan myth in a positive way to Christian truth.

Hagar the Hagiographer

According to his legend, Cyprian was a practitioner of sorcery and the black arts before he became a Christian. A young pagan named Aglaides approached Cyprian and asked him to place a spell on a beautiful girl named Justina, so that he could seduce her. Cyprian tried with all of his skills as a wizard to gain control over Justina. But Justina was a Christian virgin, who was protected by the Virgin Mary. Finally, he called upon the devil to help him in weaving the right spell. The devil could not weaken Justina's resolve, but still demanded the payment of Cyprian's soul for his efforts. Cyprian mimicked Justina by making the sign of the cross. The devil shrieked in horror and disappeared. Cyprian sought forgiveness for his sins as a sorcerer, submitted to Baptism, and became a priest.

Detailing the deaths of the persecutors, Lactantius also wrote about the lives and deeds of the holy martyrs. In this way, he became the first Church historian and the very first hagiographer.

When Can We Stop Apologizing?

The apologists did not stop apologizing after Christianity became an accepted religion in 312 with the conversion of Constantine. Throughout the centuries, new intellectual attacks arose that required new defenders of the faith:

➤ When Rome fell, Christians were blamed for the downfall, and saints such as St. Augustine had to write fresh texts in defense of Christianity.

➤ When Islam appeared, theologians such as St. Anselm of Canterbury had to prove that Christians were not guilty of worshipping three gods, as the Moslems proclaimed from a thousand minarets.

➤ When Aristotle was rediscovered and posed an intellectual uproar in the twelfth and thirteenth centuries, saints such as St. Albertus Magnus and St. Thomas Aquinas arose to show that the great Greek philosopher was really a Christian in disguise.

➤ When the Protestant reformation erupted, apologists such as St. Charles Borromeo and St. Francis de Sales appeared to defend the Church against charges of idolatry and doctrine (such as the veneration of Mary and the saints).

➤ In the age of enlightenment, apologists such as Blessed John Henry Cardinal Newman were called upon to declare that faith is not contrary to demands of reason and scientific discovery.

➤ In modern times, apologists such as Jacques Maritain, Gabriel Marcel, and C. S. Lewis defended the faith against the forces of nihilism, existentialism, and secular humanism.

This just goes to show that it's never too late to offer an apology. In fact, the right apology can give an excuse for you to escape the fires of purgatory and enter the community of saints. But remember, never say you're sorry in defending the faith. If you sincerely apologize, your apology will be worthless in the opinion of the community of saints.

The Least You Need to Know

➤ Roman writers attacked Christianity as a religion based on lies and mass deception.

➤ The first serious attack on the Christian religion came from a pagan writer named Celsus.

➤ St. Justin showed that Christianity is in harmony with Greek philosophy.

➤ The first female "Father of the Church" was St. Catherine of Alexandria.

➤ Apologies are not expressions of sorrow but statements of defense.

Part 3

The Middle Ages: When Sainthood Was in Flower

When Jesus was born, Heaven was practically empty, except for God and His angels. Within 1,000 years, the celestial kingdom actually became crowded with more than 25,000 canonized saints before the heavenly throne. There was a saint for every occasion (Baptism, Confirmation, Matrimony, and happy death), for every affliction known to mankind (insanity, epilepsy, cancer, kidney disease, bowel obstructions, hemorrhoids, and insomnia), for every profession (butchers, bakers, candlestick makers, and even floozies), for every nationality (Irish, English, French, Spanish, Italian, Russian, Polish, Hungarian, and Outer Mongolian), for every living creature (ducks, geese, dogs, cats, and even rats), and for almost everything imaginable (including the proper saints to call upon against fire, floods, snakebites, insects, moles, mice, wolves, and vampires).

Come back to a time when bones were precious, when dragons were real, and when miracles were commonplace occurrences. Turn the page and enter an age of holiness and enchantment.

Chapter 9

White Martyrdom: Confessors Open the Back Door to Heaven

In This Chapter

➤ The concept of a "confessor"

➤ The first monks

➤ The organization of monasteries

➤ The desert fathers

➤ The Rule of St. Benedict

Think about it! It's the year 324, and you, as a good Christian, want to be a martyr so that you will go straight to Heaven, but the time of the great persecutions is over. No Christians are being put to the sword, tied to stakes, or tossed to lions. Almost everybody is now a Christian: The soldiers are Christians, the magistrates are Christians, and even the emperor is a Christian. As a matter of fact, the emperor now presides over Church councils and determines Church doctrine.

Now That It's Legal, It's No Fun

The Bishop of Rome, who just 10 years earlier had to hide in the catacombs, is now called the Supreme Pontiff and lives in the Lateran Palacea, a lavish gift from the emperor. He lives like a king, walks around in royal robes, wears a silly hat, and gives orders that must be obeyed. If you disobey the "Holy Father" (as the Bishop of Rome is now called), the emperor will have you arrested or cast into exile.

What's more, the Holy Father, a.k.a. the Supreme Pontiff, surrounds himself with a select group of other priests called a "college," much like the pagan high priest did. These priests are called *cardinals* because they support the pope in his jurisdiction of the church. The cardinals also wear funny hats.

It's getting kind of crazy. When you go to church, you no longer sneak away to a secluded place in the hills or on the upper floor of someone's house; instead, you go to a great basilica on Vatican Hill, built from the stone and marble of pagan temples that used to stand there. Just 10 short years ago, a basilica was a pagan building whose central area, the apse, was filled with the statues of emperors who were worshipped as gods, but now the apse is filled with statues of saints, and candles are burning before the statues!

St. Peter Speaks

Cardinal comes from the Latin *cardo* meaning "hinge" or "support." In the fourth century, cardinals were priests who were incardinated to serve the Bishop of Rome.

At Least Pagans Had Some Fun ...

Now when you go to church, you don't sit before a deacon or presbyter who talks to your fellow believers just like an ordinary guy. You don't sit around a common table in memory of the Last Supper to break bread and share a glass of wine. Oh, no! All that has changed! Now you sit before a high altar where priests and bishops, wearing the stoles and vestments of the pagan priesthood, recite a fixed liturgy with great solemnity. The priests and bishops also sprinkle the people with holy water and incense, just like the pagans used to do.

Holy Cow!

The original Basilica of St. Peter was built by Constantine over the burial place of St. Peter. Early basilicas contained courtyards for pagans who wanted to come and listen to the Gospel readings at church services.

It's all so disheartening! The statues of Isis and Horus have not been destroyed as false idols; instead, they've been renamed. Now Isis is Mary, and Horus is Jesus. The birthday of the god Sol was now the birthday of our Lord. And the resurrection of the pagan god Attis during the spring solstice is now Easter.

Good News: You Can Become a Christian Hero

To top it all off, because Christianity is an accepted religion, Christians are no longer killed for their beliefs, meaning that people are no longer being martyred and entering the Kingdom of Heaven as saints. You want to become a real Christian hero—just like St. Sebastian or St. Agatha—but how can you? There must be another way to gain a crown in Heaven.

Well, cheer up, there is another way: You can become a "confessor." By becoming a confessor, you can suffer a slow martyrdom of the flesh by leading a life of perfect chastity. This is not as easy as it seems. To live a life of perfect chastity, you must remove yourself from all worldly enticements and worldly pleasures. You must avoid not only the occasion of sin, but also the very possibility of sin.

It's Time to Take Off Your Clothes and Head for the Desert

You're probably wondering, "How can I do that?" Well, if you remain in the city or even in the country, you might meet someone you are attracted to. If this happens, you might have an impure thought about sexual congress. In fact, in your mind, you might even consent to such an act. If this happens, you have committed mortal sin, and, therefore, you will be locked outside the pearly gates.

There is only one thing you can do. You must go off by yourself into the wilderness. Only in this way can you strengthen your spirit and mortify your flesh. You must follow the example of St. Antony.

St. Peter Speaks

In 321, Constantine made Sunday a legal holiday and put into effect the first "blue laws." He issued an edict that read: "All judges, city-people and crafts-men shall rest on the venerable day of the Sun." Along with celebrating Sunday as "the Lord's day," many Christians also observed the Jewish Sabbath (Saturday), until the church forbade it in 360.

Divine Revelation

St. Paul says that the state of chastity is the perfect state for true believers: "I would like you to be free from concern. An unmarried man is concerned about the Lord's affairs—how he can please the Lord. But a married man is concerned about the affairs of the world—how he can please his wife—and his interests are divided. An unmarried woman or virgin is concerned about the Lord's affairs: her aim is to be devoted to the Lord in both body and spirit. But a married woman is concerned about the affairs of this world—how she can please her husband. I am saying this for your own good, not to restrict you, but that you may live in a right way in undivided devotion to the Lord" (1 Corinthians 7:32–35).

If You Want to Be a Saint, Get Rid of the Farm

St. Antony was the son of a well-to-do Egyptian Christian family. When he was about 20, his life was radically changed when he walked into a church and heard a reading from the Gospel of Matthew. The reading told of a rich young man who asked Jesus how to obtain eternal life. Jesus told him, "If you want to be perfect, go sell your possessions and give to the poor, and you will have treasure in Heaven. Then come and follow me!" (19:21).

Hagar the Hagiographer

Much of our knowledge about St. Antony comes from a biography by St. Athanasius, an early hagiographer. The biography, which appeared in 357, was hugely popular.

Divine Revelation

The way to perfection lies in self-denial and turning from the things of this world. In the Gospel of Matthew, Jesus says: "If anyone would come after me, he must deny himself and take up his cross and follow me. For whoever wants to save his life will lose it, but whoever loses his life for me will find it" (16:24–25).

Wanting to be perfect, Antony divided the 200 acres of his fertile family estate among the citizens of his town. Then he sold his possessions and gave the money to the poor, keeping a small amount for his young sister.

The next day, he returned to church and heard this message from Matthew's gospel that seemed to be directed to his ears only: "Therefore, I tell you, do not worry about your life, what you will eat and drink; or, about your body, what you will wear" (6:25). The message was clear: Antony had to turn from the material world.

Please, St. Antony: Do Us a Favor and Wash Your Feet

The saint set off to live a life of complete self-denial in the Egyptian desert. St. Athanasius wrote in his famous biography of this saint:

> Antony was daily a martyr to his own conscience and to wiles of his flesh. His discipline became more severe as he continued his life of fasting and abstinence. He wore a garment of hair next to his skin that he never removed for the rest of his life. St. Antony never bathed his body to free himself from filth. He refused to even wash his feet or to put them in water.

In a short period of time, the young ascetic was set upon by the devil. At first, the devil appeared to him as a voluptuous young woman, but he chased her away with a stick. Then the tempter came in the form of a dragon. Antony chased him away with a cross. Finally, the evil one came in the form of a young boy.

When the boy appeared before him, Antony asked him to identify himself. The boy said, "I am called the spirit of fornication." Hearing this, St. Antony said, "The Lord is my helper and I will destroy His enemies." Hearing this, the boy fled into the darkness.

This Tomb Would Have Been Really Terrific Without Satan

After battling more demons in various disguises, Antony decided to lock himself in an abandoned tomb. He ate only one meal a day—bread and water—that a pious Christian left outside the entranceway. Night and day, he fought demons that attacked him with supernatural strength.

During his fifteenth year in the tomb, Antony experienced particularly ferocious assaults from Satan, who kept appearing in hideous and horrifying forms. Alas, the saint was driven to scream out in horror. As soon as this happened, a shaft of light broke through the darkness and drove the devil away. Seeing the light, Antony asked: "Where were you, my Lord and my Master? Why weren't you with me from the beginning of my conflict to alleviate my pain?" A voice answered, "Antony, I was here the whole time. I stood by and saw your combat. And because you manfully withstood the enemy, I will make your name famous throughout the world."

Hagar the Hagiographer

Consider this advice from St. Antony: "The devil dreads fasting, prayer, humility, and good works. He is not able even to stop my mouth which speaks against him. The illusions of the devil soon vanish, especially if you arm yourself with the sign of the cross. The devils tremble at the sign of the cross of our Lord, by which He triumphed over and disarmed them."

How to Be a Martyr Without Being Murdered

The Lord was as good as His word. In a matter of weeks, disciples appeared at his tomb, seeking instruction on how to live as holy ascetics. Antony gave them advice, until more appeared with the same request.

Seeking solitude, St. Antony again went off to the desert and took up residence in a cave on top of Mt. Pispur. Almost immediately, others, seeking a life of self-denial, moved into other caves in the area. Soon the mountain was thickly populated with Christians seeking the straight and narrow way to Heaven.

It got kind of out of hand. By the time Antony had lived in this cave for 20 years, more than 50,000 disciples took up residence in the desert. Many were not prepared for this "white martyrdom," so St. Antony set down rules that they had to follow. The rules were simple:

Holy Cow!

The life of a desert monk was grueling. Food and water were scarce, and caves were the only places of shelter. Temperatures in the Egyptian desert near Thebes could boil past 110° F, and fierce windstorms were frequent.

➤ Ascetics had to live alone, without any communication with others, let alone the outside world.

➤ They could eat only one meal a day, and that meal must consist of bread, water, and a few nuts. They could not eat anything else—not even a piece of fruit.

➤ They had to spend all day and all night in prayer and contemplation.

➤ They had to perform acts of mortification, such as hitting themselves with sticks or piercing their flesh with thorns.

➤ They had to engage in constant warfare against the principalities and powers of this wicked world.

Those who turned from the world to live in desert places were called "monks," from the Latin word *monachi,* meaning "solitaries." Along with Antony, a host of other holy monks became highly celebrated in Christian circles.

If You Thought Antony Was Weird, Wait Until You Meet Paul the Hermit

Another holy monk was St. Paul the Hermit, who lived for 90 years without speaking to anyone. The holy hermit was discovered in a cave in Upper Egypt by St. Antony, who had been commanded by God to set out in search of Paul. When the saints at last met, Antony was more than 90 and Paul was more than 113. Wondering how he had lived so long in such a frail condition, Antony discovered that he was fed by a raven that delivered a half of a loaf of bread to him every day without fail. The good raven increased the ration to a full loaf the day after Antony's arrival.

Hagar the Hagiographer

Of all the goods in the world, the thing St. Antony most admired was St. Paul's tunic, which the holy hermit had woven from palm leaves.

Knowing that he was near death, Paul said to his visitor, "Thou hast been sent by God to shelter this poor body in the ground." The holy hermit then asked Antony to bring him a cloak that had been a gift from St. Athanasius. Antony obeyed and set off to fetch the garment. On his return journey, he saw the soul of Paul ascending to Heaven, accompanied by angels, the 12 apostles, and the prophets of the Old Testament. At the mouth of the cave, Antony found Paul's body, which he wrapped in the cloak. But he was too weak to dig a grave. After he said some prayers, two lions appeared and dug a hole for the hermit so that he could be properly buried.

After leaving Paul, Antony found a new desert spot to call home—a place near the Red Sea that he called Inner Mountain. There he planted a little garden and resolved to spend the remainder of his life as a "daily martyr to his conscience, ever fighting the battles of faith." Again, hundreds sought him out to learn how to live as monks. When Antony died, his disciples decided to bury him secretly and never revealed the spot.

A Real Saint Is Merciful to Mosquitoes

Other great desert fathers emerged, such as St. Hilarion. This holy man lived in a swamp outside Gaza and never stopped any of the zillions of mosquitoes who infested the place from attacking his body. He cut his hair once a year, at Easter, and he lived on a diet of a few figs and vegetables that he grew in his tiny garden.

His reputation for holiness (and the ability to perform miracles) spread far and wide, so hundreds of other monks came to live in the bog. This greatly upset Hilarion, who said, "The world is surrounding me and I am receiving my reward in this life. If I wish to be found deserving of divine mercy, I must hide myself to pray and suffer."

I Want to Be Alone!

The good saint tried to head for the hills alone, but the great multitude of monks who looked to Hilarion as a role model refused to let him go on his merry way to white martyrdom. Finally, Hilarion was forced to go on a hunger strike until his disciples released him from his virtual prison.

No one wanted to be alone more than Hilarion. He moved to the Egyptian wilderness, where disciples sought him out. Then he stole away to the Libyan desert, where his flock found him again. Next he

Hagar the Hagiographer

St. Antony is the patron of basketweavers and brush makers because he advised his disciples to busy themselves by weaving mats and making baskets. He is also the patron of gravediggers because he helped the lions bury St. Paul the Hermit. If you want to invoke him (especially if you have eczema), say the following prayer: "O glorious St. Antony, you who could perform wondrous miracles, touch my skin that it may be smooth and my soul that it may be pure. Amen."

Hagar the Hagiographer

The wisdom of the desert fathers became legendary, and their advice on the ascetic life was recorded in a book entitled *Sayings of the Desert Fathers.* One example comes from St. Arsenius: "Be solitary, be silent, and be at peace."

Holy Cow!

Tens of thousands of Christians set off to desert regions to follow the examples of the desert saints. By 340, St. Athanasius noted, "The desert has been transformed into a city by monks." By the end of the fourth century, one traveler reported that the number of desert dwellers was equivalent to the population of Jerusalem and Alexandria.

St. Peter Speaks

An **ascetic** is a person who denies himself all earthly pleasures. It comes from the Greek word *asketes,* meaning a monk or a hermit.

sailed to Sicily, hoping that no one would find him as he made baskets and begged for bread. But guess what? Someone just happened to yell out: "Hey, aren't you that holy man Hilarion?"

And Now for the True Story of 101 Dalmatians

In despair, the harassed Hilarion decided to head out for a place where he could not speak the language and where his old friends from the desert were unlikely to show up. So he went to Dalmatia. But because he was a saint, people understood him when he spoke. For this reason, Hilarion became surrounded by 101 Dalmatians.

In desperation, he fled from Dalmatia to Cyprus, where he died at the rather young age (for an *ascetic,* anyway) of 80.

I've Heard of Insomnia, but This Is Ridiculous!

Another desert father and disciple of St. Antony was St. Pachomius, a Roman soldier who became famous as one of the holiest and most formidable of monks. He went 50 years without lying down. This has to be the all-time record for sleeplessness. Pachomius believed that sleep was a worldly pleasure that must be avoided because it kept a person from complete devotion to God.

This saint also had the gift of tongues. Pachomius could talk to anybody in any language, although, as is fitting for a monk, he spoke only when necessary.

Be a Good Monk: Memorize the Bible

Naturally, the fame of this great insomniac spread far and wide, and monks from all corners of Christendom came to camp near his cave. Finding the monks noisome and unruly, Pachomius, always the good soldier, forced them to live a regimented life, not in separate caves as solitaries, but in separate cells as members of the same community. This community was to be closed from the outside world by walls. Everyone who entered this habitat of monks or "monastery" was obliged to live by the following regulations:

➤ They had to wear habits made of rough wool with a cowl that prevented them seeing each other at meals.

➤ They had to come together for one communal meal consisting of bread, water, a few figs, and raw vegetables, and they were expected to fast for the remainder of the day and night.

➤ They could not speak to one another for any reason.

➤ They had to come together once a day for prayer.

➤ They had to receive Holy Communion on the first and last day of every week.

➤ They had to learn the Bible—both Old and New Testaments—by heart.

Soon monasteries popped up in desert areas throughout Christendom. By the time he died, Pachomius, who was called "abba" or "father" by the monks in his care, had established nine such religious communities on the banks of the Nile.

Don't Mess with St. Marcarius

Another desert father, St. Marcarius, told how he came to seek God in the wilderness. When he was a young *anchorite,* or religious hermit, this chaste saint was accused of seducing a young girl. The townspeople sought him out and nearly beat him to death. But when the girl went into labor, the infant refused to leave her womb for days, despite her best efforts. "I know why I can't deliver," she finally said. "It is because I accused that holy man and accused him unjustly." When she said this, the baby was delivered from her womb in perfect health. The townspeople went to search for the wrongfully accused Marcarius to make amends, but he had fled to the barren serenity of the desert.

After several years of fasting and prayer, Marcarius gained the ability to perform miracles. Once a merchant died after taking a large sum of money in trust, and his widow was unable to find it. The widow and her children were about to be sold into slavery to satisfy the debt when Marcarius was called. The saint went to the merchant's grave and called out, "Where did you put the money?" A voice answered: "I hid the money in the house, at the foot of the bed." Those who beheld this event

Holy Cow!

According to his legend, St. Pachomius traveled across the Nile on the back of a crocodile when he wanted to visit his sister. This story is probably fictitious because the saint thought it was sinful to look at, let alone talk to, a member of the opposite sex.

St. Peter Speaks

An **anchorite** is a person who retires to a solitary place for a life of religious seclusion. It comes from the Greek *ana-choretes,* meaning a recluse.

were terrified, but Marcarius explained, "It is not for my sake that this happened, for I am nothing, but it is because of the widow and the orphans that God has performed this miracle, God wants the soul to be without sin and grants it all that it asks."

How to Become a Spiritual Athlete

Like other desert fathers, Marcarius was a great spiritual athlete. He was so ascetic that he wore sandbags on his shoulders in the desert, and his diet consisted of raw beans, except during Lent, when he ate only an occasional cabbage leaf. He was very kind to animals—no less so than St. Francis of Assisi. He once cured a young hyena of blindness. In gratitude, the hyena's mother brought him a sheepskin. Racked with guilt over swatting a fly, Marcarius retreated naked into the desert for six months, allowing insects to feed upon his flesh.

Hagar the Hagiographer

When the monks approached St. Pachomius to pray for his close friend and disciple St. Theodorius, St. Pachomius said, "Though abstinence and prayer be of great merit, yet sickness, suffered with pain, is much greater."

Because he was a confectioner by trade, St. Marcarius is hailed as the patron saint of pastry chefs. This is a strange distinction for a guy who gobbled only raw beans and a few cabbage leaves. Still, before you bake a cake or a pie, invoke his name and your dessert will become truly delicious.

Hagar the Hagiographer

St. Martin of Tours, another holy desert father, was the first Christian other than a martyr to become a saint. He initiated a new form of exorcism whereby the afflicted expelled demons from their system by vomiting and defecation. He died on November 11, 400. November 11 was the day in which pagans tasted new wine in honor of the goddess Vinalia. For this reason, St. Martin is the patron saint of drunkards and innkeepers. Got a drinking problem? Try this prayer: "O glorious St. Martin, by your chaste and holy life, you cured lepers, restored the dead to life, banished demons, and converted thousands to the faith. Grant that we may be ever vigilant, ever faithful, and ever sober in our Christian walk. Amen."

Even Maggots Need a Break Now and Then

But the hands-down greatest Christian athlete of all time was St. Simeon. He entered a Syrian monastery at the age of 13 and immediately began practicing amazing feats of athletic asceticism. He wound chains around his body until his flesh was raw and then remained immobile for days. He tied a rope of twisted palm leaves so tightly that it ate into his skin and it became infested with maggots. When the maggots fell from his skin, he carefully placed them back on his open sores so that they would not suffer from separation. Simeon's excesses became so extreme that he was expelled from the monastery as a fanatic.

Undaunted, Simeon descended into a deep well, where he stayed for weeks without food. Finally, he was rescued by other solitaries in the area.

But Where Do You Go to the Bathroom?

That's when he got a really great idea. He decided to live on top of a pillar that he erected near Antioch in Greece. He stayed there for four years, as crowds began to gather around him every day to beg for his blessings and prayers. Simeon moved from that pillar to another pillar that was even higher—30 feet tall. Even that pillar was too low, so he erected one final pillar that was more than 60 feet high. St. Simeon stayed on top of this pillar for the remaining 35 years of his life.

During Lent, Simeon ate nothing; he ate only once a week for the rest of the year. He preached to large crowds every day. People came from far and wide to see him—he even attracted the attention of the Roman Emperor Marcian and his wife, Eudoxia.

He became known as Simeon Stylites (*stylos* is the Greek word for "pillar"). After his death, a succession of pillar saints appeared to take his place, including St. Simeon Stylites the Younger, who sat on a pillar for 45 years.

St. Simeon Stylites, the most famous of the desert anchorites, remains the patron of shepherds. Want to talk to him? Say this prayer: "O holy St. Simeon

Hagar the Hagiographer

Although St. Simeon Stylites was clearly insane, he should not be confused with St. Simeon Salus, the patron saint of madness. Simeon Salus was a monk who went to such limits to humiliate himself, including covering his body with dung, that he was called "salos" or "mad." He should be invoked by anyone who is on the verge of a nervous breakdown.

Holy Cow!

Supplies were delivered to St. Simeon by a basket. On special occasions, visitors could visit him by climbing a ladder. The base of his pillar still stands in the ruins of a Syrian church.

Stylites, you kept the devil and his demons at bay throughout your long and holy life. Protect my flock from all the beasts that would prey upon them. Amen."

Hagar the Hagiographer

Because of his organizational skills, St. Basil the Great is celebrated as the patron saint of hospital administrators. Need to call on him? Say this prayer: "O glorious St. Basil, may my work as a hospital administrator reflect the goodness and mercy of my Lord and Savior. Amen."

But Freaks Are Fun!

The monastic movement was becoming a Christian freak show. And so, some sensible "abbas," or abbots, set out to reform it. One such reformer was Basil the Great, the great saint of the Greek Orthodox faith who stopped monks from sitting on pillars and being show-offs by having them engage in manual labor for the benefit of the monastic community and in intellectual pursuits (including, of course, the complete memorization of scripture).

St. Basil is worthy of note because he comes from the most distinguished family of saints in the history of Christianity. His grandmother (St. Macrina), both of his parents (Sts. Basil the Elder and Emmelia), two of his brothers (Sts. Gregory of Nyssa and Peter of Sebaste), and his sister (St. Macrina the Younger) have been officially canonized. Even though all of these were good and holy people, the names of so many members of the same family in the litanies or lists of the saints still seems to reek of holy nepotism.

Need a Cold Shower? Jump in a Bramble Bush!

The great reformer of the monastic movement was St. Benedict. As a student in Rome (circa 490), St. Benedict feared spiritual contamination from his godless companions. For this reason, after performing his first miracle (repairing by prayer a broken dish), he retreated to an underground cave at Subico, where he lived for three years, dressed in animal skins and fed (you guessed it) by a raven. During this time, he was besieged daily by the devil. One day, the tempter came to him in the form of a black bird that flew into the saint's face, reminding him of a gorgeous girl he had seen in Rome. To rid himself of any impure thoughts, St. Benedict ripped off his clothing and immediately jumped into a bramble bush. He was never troubled by sexual desire again.

Let's Have No More Monkey Business in Monte Cassino

Gradually, news about St. Benedict spread, and the saint was joined at his cave by so many disciples that he established a new religious order. At Monte Cassino, 85 miles outside Rome, he built a monastery and established a Rule that—once and for all— would end the monkey business among monks. This is how the Rule worked: Once a monk was admitted to St. Benedict's monastery, he was forbidden to speak, he had to refrain from tears and laughter, and he had to walk with his eyes constantly to the ground. What's more, the monks could not own anything: "not a book, writing tablet, or an instrument for writing—not a single thing."

The daily schedule wasn't much fun, either. The monks had to work three hours in the morning in the garden, at the flour mill, or in the bakery. After work, they had to spend two hours studying sacred scripture or the lives of the saints. In the afternoon, they were granted two hours in their cells for prayer and meditation, followed by a return to hard labor until sunset. St. Benedict's motto was "to work is to pray."

Monks were not fed until noon—and, during the season of Lent, not until dusk. From mid-September to Easter, they received only one meal a day; in the summer months, they received two because the work was harder. At all times, this schedule of work and sleep had to be regaled by something called "the Divine Offices."

It's Bad Enough: Let's Forget About Nocturns and None

The "Divine Offices" were periods of communal prayer, in which the monks together recited psalms, read from the scriptures, and listened to sermons and admonitions. Every day in the monastery was the same, all governed by these "canonical hours":

➤ **Nocturns:** At 2 A.M., the bell rang and the monks rose from their flea-infested cots and went to the chapel to sing some psalms and say some prayers.

➤ **Lauds:** At 5 A.M., the bell rang and the monks had to gather to recite the morning prayers.

➤ **Prime:** At 6 A.M., the bell rang and the monks had to gather again to celebrate Mass at the start of day.

➤ **Terce:** At 9 A.M., the bell rang and the monks had to leave their chores to gather in prayer and devotions.

Holy Cow!

St. Benedict's great monastery at Monte Cassino was razed to the ground by Lombards, restored, then sacked by Saracens, rebuilt, and finally destroyed a final time by the Allies in World War II, who mistakenly believed it to be Nazi headquarters.

Holy Cow!

St. Benedict based his canonical hours on the sacredness of the number 7. Psalm 119, he noted, says that the Lord should be praised seven times a day, along with once in the middle of the day and once in the middle of the night.

➤ **Sext:** At noon, or the sixth hour of daylight, the bell rang and the monks again had to leave their chores to meditate on the sufferings of the Lord.

➤ **None:** At 3 P.M., the bell rang and the monks had to leave their cells (where they should have been praying, fasting, or performing a bit of self-flagellation) to join in communal prayer and thanksgiving.

➤ **Vespers:** At 6 P.M., or sundown, the bell rang, not for dinner, but for another session of prayer, readings, and devotions.

➤ **Compline:** At 9 P.M., the bell rang and the monks had to cease working for the day to praise God for their lives as penitents.

During the next 600 years, the Benedictines set up hundreds of monasteries that brought intellectual, social, and agricultural enrichment to vast regions of Europe. They also brought hundreds of new saints to Heaven. In fact, Heaven was becoming so crowded with confessors that St. Peter, in 1234, had to restrict the number of new entries into the Kingdom of Heaven.

The Least You Need to Know

➤ After the age of the martyrs, Christians sought new ways to sainthood.

➤ White martyrdom meant putting to death earthly desires.

➤ The desert fathers became Christian superheroes.

➤ St. Benedict regulated all aspects of monastic life.

Chapter 10

The Brides of Christ: Good Grief! There's a Harem in Heaven

Good news! It can still happen. A woman in this day and age can become a Bride of Jesus Christ. As a matter of fact, at this writing, the Lord has more than 113,000 living brides and millions of dead brides (dead in the sense that they no longer inhabit planet Earth).

Want a Perfect Husband? You, Too, Can Become a Bride of Christ

To become a Bride of Christ, a woman must enter a convent and take solemn vows before a priest or bishop. There is a widespread misunderstanding about vows. Priests don't take vows. Religious sisters don't take vows. Only those who live in a cloistered environment, such as a monastery or a convent, take vows.

The Honeymoon Is Heaven

Before taking her vows, a candidate for the nunnery kneels before the priest, who asks, "Are you resolved to preserve to the end of your days in the holy state of virginity and in the service of God and His Church?" If this sounds attractive, the candidate answers, "I am." The priest then asks, "Are you resolved to accept solemn consecration as a bride of our Lord Jesus Christ, the Son of God?" If she has gone this far, the candidate usually answers, "I am." The priest then proclaims, "Thanks be to God."

After offering a prayer of consecration, the priest reads this passage from the Song of Solomon: "Rise, my love, my fair one, and come away!" In response, the initiate, holding a candle, kneels before the priest to receive her veil and ring. The priest says, "Dearest daughter, receive your veil and ring that are the insignia of your fidelity to your Bridegroom, and never forget that you are bound to the service of Christ, and to His Body, the Church." The newly consecrated nun responds by saying, "Amen."

Upon the completion of this ceremony, the new Bride of Christ embarks on a three-day retreat, known as her honeymoon. Then she sits down with her fellow nuns for the wedding feast.

Divine Revelation

The idea of Christ taking a virgin as His bride comes from Old Testament imagery about God's marriage to Israel. Isaiah writes, "As a young man marries a maiden, so will your sons marry you; as a bridegroom rejoices over his bride, so will your God rejoice over you" (62:5).

Hagar the Hagiographer

One of the first consecrated virgins, apart from the Blessed Virgin Mary and the members of her family, was St. Petronilla, the daughter of St. Peter. According to the Roman martyrology, this virgin refused to wed Flaccus, a Roman nobleman, but arrangements for the wedding were made despite her wishes. Three days before the scheduled ceremony, Petronilla began fasting and praying that she would be spared from the plight of losing her virginity and her chance at sainthood. When the wedding guests arrived, they found the young woman dead at the foot of her bed. St. Petronilla is the patroness of France (along with St. Joan of Arc).

Nunsense—No Nun Is a Bad Nun

This is the surest and the easiest way for a woman to become a saint. If you stay in the world and get married, your chances of getting canonized are less than 1 in a billion. Your chances are lowered to 1 in 10 million by becoming a *nun*.

Bride of Christ?

I know, I know, many of you are shaking your heads and saying, "This sounds nuts. Where did this idea come from?" Strangely enough, it comes from scripture. In his first letter to the Corinthians, St. Paul encouraged young women to refrain from marriage to achieve the "angelic state" of single-minded devotion to Christ (1 Corinthians 7:8–9). Such women were granted a place of honor in the early church. By 200 A.D., virgins and widows assumed vows of chastity before the congregation in a solemn ceremony.

St. Peter Speaks

Nun comes from the Coptic (Egyptian) word for "good" or "beautiful." It was applied to one of the first convents for women that was established in Egypt by St. Pachomius.

It Beats Sending Them to College

In some Christian communities in ancient Rome, parents made vows before the altar in the names of their newly born daughters, committing them to lives of perpetual chastity. This might have been the Christian equivalent to the pagan practice of infanticide—that is, the putting to death of female babies. Tertullian condemned this practice in his treatise "On the Veiling of Virgins," pointing out that these vows were often later ignored and that in Christian churches were many pregnant virgins.

The leaders of the early church spoke of these consecrated virgins as the "Brides of Christ." Tertullian wrote to the virgins of Carthage, "You have married Christ, to Him you gave your flesh and to Him you pledged your maturity." To break this vow, St. Cyprian said, was to commit adultery. Such acts of adultery to Christ in the fourth and fifth centuries were punishable by death.

This Stuff Is for the Birds

Many of these consecrated virgins became great saints, including St. Dorothy. A beautiful Christian maiden of Cappadocia, Dorothy was desired by the

Hagar the Hagiographer

St. Augustine spoke about the problem of a widow who had made a vow of perpetual virginity in the name of her infant daughter, only to discover, to her horror, that her daughter later refused to honor this commitment. Faced with the terrible spiritual consequences of breaking a solemn vow, the good mother shunned all offers of marriage and lived as a chaste widow for the rest of her life.

Hagar the Hagiographer

St. Dorothy is the patroness of brides, florists, and gardeners. Getting married? You might need the help of St. Dorothy. If so, say this prayer: "O glorious St. Dorothy, grant that our marriage may be holy, pleasing, and chaste, so that it may be blessed. Amen."

Roman governor Fabricus but refused his offer of marriage. Fabricus sent his two pagan sisters to plead his case, but the good saint converted them to the faith. Fabricus was outraged. Dorothy was jailed (where she was fed by angels), cast into a pot of boiling oil (which she turned to sweet-smelling balm), and stretched on an iron bed over flames (which merely tickled her beautiful body). Finally, in frustration, Fabricus had her beheaded in a public courtyard.

A witness to this execution named Theophilius sarcastically asked Dorothy to send him flowers from her "heavenly garden." After her death, a child appeared before Theophilius with a bouquet of beautiful flowers and a basket of apples. After tasting one of the apples, Theophilius was converted, executed, cut into small pieces, and fed to the birds.

Talk About Child Abuse!

Another holy virgin who became an inspiration for young Christian women was St. Barbara. This saint was the beautiful daughter of a real nutcase named Diocorus. She was so ravishingly beautiful that he locked her in a high tower so that young men might never lust after her. In the tower, she dedicated her life to the Lord and pledged her life (and her virginity) to Him. While Diocorus was away on business, he ordered that an elaborate bathroom be built in his daughter's tower. After Barbara took a bath in the tub (which was really a small swimming pool), the water acquired magical healing power that could rid people of any affliction. People stood underneath the tower so that the good virgin could sprinkle them with her holy water.

Holy Cow!

The difficult straits off the California coast were called Santa Barbara by Spanish mariners, who called upon the saint to guide them from her tower in Heaven.

Seeing the crowd, Diocorus decided to remove the walkway from the tower and to enclose his daughter's living quarters with windows. Construction workers showed up and installed two windows. Upon hearing Barbara's tearful pleas, they added a third in honor of the Holy Trinity. At the sight of the third window, Diocorus knew that his daughter was turning the tower into a shrine. He drew his sword to slay his child, but Barbara jumped out of the new window and ran off to the wilderness.

St. Barbara Becomes Explosive

Barbara lived in the desert for many years as a holy hermit, until an evil shepherd discovered her whereabouts and ran to inform Diocorus. Upon being captured by her abusive father, Barbara cursed the evil shepherd, turning his sheep into locusts and him into stone.

Barbara was dragged before the civil authorities and was ordered to renounce her faith. Naturally, she refused. For this reason, she was stripped and flogged, was hung between two trees, was struck on the head with a mallet, and had her breast hacked off. Finding her impossible to kill, Diocorus decided to take matters into his own hands and dragged his daughter to the top of a mountain. He forced Barbara to her knees and raised his sword above her neck to cut off her head. A mighty thunderclap was heard, and "fire from Heaven" struck Diocorus and reduced him to a mound of ashes. To this day, all who handle explosives remain under St. Barbara's care.

Hagar the Hagiographer

Young women are encouraged to invoke St. Barbara by saying this prayer: "St. Barbara, intercede for all girls and women of your name, and all Christians, that they may be so full of the Holy Spirit that they would rather die than renounce their religion. Amen."

Two-Timing the Lord?

Gradually, Christian women who had been deflowered for some nefarious reason or forced into marriage could still be accepted as Brides of Christ, provided that they spent the rest of their lives in perfect chastity. Witness the case of St. Melania the Younger. At a tender age, she pledged her virginity to Jesus, but when she turned 14, her father forced her to marry a wealthy Roman named Valerius Pinianus. This wasn't a good idea because she was already engaged to the Son of God.

After two of her children were born stillborn, Valerius realized that he had made a terrible mistake in taking Melania's maidenhead. The couple prayed and received a vision that they should live as brother and sister in perfect chastity. Valerius sold his property and gave the money to the poor and to free 8,000 slaves. Many of the freed slaves joined Melania to live in her *convent* for consecrated virgins.

St. Peter Speaks

A **convent** is a community of persons who are devoted to the same religious life. It comes from the Latin *conventus*, meaning "assembly."

Now Prostitutes Are Marrying Jesus? What Next?

The heavenly harem came to attract not only married women, but also reformed women of the street. One such sinner was St. Mary of Egypt, who became a very important real person in the early Church. When Mary was a young woman (circa

Hagar the Hagiographer

St. Mary of Egypt is the patroness of penitent women and reformed prostitutes. If you are experiencing sexual temptation, invoke her with this prayer: "St. Mary of Egypt, teach us not to give in to despair no matter how heavy our sins may be. Intercede for all prostitutes, men who seek the services of prostitutes, and all others who engage in sexual sin. Ask the Lord to send us special grace to find peace and hope, especially in times of temptation. Amen."

Hagar the Hagiographer

St. Pachomius and his sister organized a monastic convent for women at Tabennisi in Egypt. The 400 women who lived there divided their time between manual labor and prayer (private and common). They raised their own food, cleaned and decorated the chapel, and made clothes for the monks who lived across the river.

320 A.D.), she ran off to Alexandria, where she lived as a prostitute for 17 years. Upon becoming a Christian, she became aware of the magnitude of her sins and, following the example of St. Antony, went to live in the desert wilderness of Jordan. For the next 47 years, she lived alone, subsisting on a diet of dates and wild plants. She also never wore clothes. She was dressed only in her long thick hair that flowed over her body.

One day, a monk named Zosimus came upon Mary and asked her (no, not to part her hair) to relate to him her story. At her request, Zosimus returned to her desert hideout the following year and found her on the other side of the Jordan River. When Zosimus called her, Mary walked across the water to meet him. One year later, the faithful monk returned again, only to find her dead body and this message that she had written in the sand: "Father Zosimus, bury the body of lowly Mary. Render earth to earth and pray for me. I died the night of our Lord's Passion, after receiving the divine and mystic banquet." When Zosimus began to dig her grave, a lion appeared to help him.

Pearl the Stripper Slips Through the Pearly Gates

Another former floozy who fled to the desert was St. Pelagia. She had been a singer and a striptease artist in decadent old Antioch. Her stage name was Pearl. One day, for some mysterious reason, the Bishop of Edessa caught her act. The next day, he spoke about the stripper in his sermon: "This Pearl is a real lesson for all of us! She takes more time and trouble over her beauty and her dancing than we do about our souls and our fellow Christians." Pearl just happened to hear the bishop's sermon and was moved to tears. She confessed her sins to the bishop, was baptized by him, gave away all her money, and headed for the hills to live as a holy hermit.

Years later, some pilgrims came upon the old exotic dancer to find her wasted and haggard from fasting. No one knew that she was a woman because she had changed her name to Pelagius. Only when she died was her true sex discovered. Because her fellow hermits could not consecrate her as St. Pelagius, they called her St. Pelagia, and she remains the patroness of actresses.

The Desert Is No Place for Harlots in Hair Shirts

With so many women turning from a life of sin to the sanctity of the desert, something had to be done. In every cave and cranny, you could find harlots in hair shirts seeking repentance for their past sins. It wasn't safe. St. Maria, for example, was raped by a lust-crazed monk.

It's a good thing that many of the great saint-confessors had sisters who were equally dedicated to the organization of monastic life. St. Antony's sister formed a shelter for religious women, where they could live lives of prayer and self-denial in preparation for their union with Christ. St. Macrina, St. Basil the Great's sister, also established an early convent, along with the sister of St. Pachomius.

You Get the Wedding Gown When You Die

But the first great "Mother Superior" was St. Scholastica, the twin sister of St. Benedict. She established a monastery for women at Monte Cassino in which "nuns" lived under the same rule as the monks at her brother's monastery.

Women seeking admission to the convent served a *novitiate* for several months to experience the austerities that would be required of them. Only after successfully enduring the trial period could they assume solemn vows and be consecrated as Brides of Christ.

Once they took their vows, the nuns were not permitted to leave the convent for any reason without permission from the Mother Superior. When they died, they were buried in wedding gowns for their mystical union with Jesus.

The Benedictine Rule became the standard means of regulating all aspects of convent life. Later orders of nuns, such as the Cistercians and the Carmelites, were organized by the same standards.

St. Peter Speaks

A **novitiate** is the period of time when one serves as a novice to a religious order. You cannot take vows as a nun or a monk without undergoing a novitiate.

Hagar the Hagiographer

St. Scholastica is the patron saint of rain. If you need her help, say the following prayer: "St. Scholastica, intercede for all women that we may find in our brothers, priests, and other male Christians the complementary wisdom we need for our spiritual growth. Amen."

This Saintly Story Is Really Disgusting!

But this did not stop the saintly excesses of the women—especially those who had been married. St. Hedwig was married at the age of 12 to Henry I the Bearded, King of Silisea. She bore him six children. This, in itself, is a miracle because Hedwig hated sex and (most likely) her husband. She never spoke to Henry in private—and, when she spoke to him in the company of others, Hedwig convinced her husband of the sinfulness of having sex during Lent, on Sundays and holy days, and during her pregnancies. Finally, after 25 years of wedded misery, Henry permitted Hedwig to enter a convent.

As a chaste nun, she spent her time kissing the seats of other members of the convent. She kissed the stools, the chairs, and the pews several times a day. She also enjoyed washing the feet of the other nuns and then drinking the dirty water.

Divine Revelation

The washing of feet is performed on a regular basis in monasteries and convents. It is a sign of true obedience. At the time of the Last Supper, Jesus got up from the meal, took off his outer clothing, and washed the feet of His disciples (John 13:1–5).

This Saint Is One Reason Why You Should Never Complain About Your Wife

The excesses are also evident in the legend of St. Etheldreda, also known as St. Audrey. After the death of her husband, with whom she lived in perfect chastity, Etheldreda spent day and night in prayer, until her knees became like "the knees of a camel." Her relatives insisted that she remarry Egfried, King of Northumbria. As an eager boy, Egfried immediately consented to Etheldreda's demand for a continent marriage.

When the boy became older, he decided that he wanted a real wife and agreed to allow St. Etheldreda to enter a monastery. The twice-married virgin ate only bread and water once a day, wore rough woolen clothes over a hair shirt, and never went to bed.

Hagar the Hagiographer

St. Etheldreda is called St. Audrey in England. During the Middle Ages, a festival was held for this saint in Ely. Because the merchandise was so crummy, it was called "tawdry," and St. Etheldreda, in no time at all, became St. Audrey.

Everything About St. Etheldreda Remains Intact

After she founded the great abbey of Ely, St. Etheldreda grew a huge and unsightly tumor on her neck that she considered a gift from God to remind her of the jeweled necklaces she had worn in her youth. She displayed it to everyone who came into her presence. Seventeen years after her burial, St. Wilfrid exhumed her body to collect some relics. Her body had not decayed, but the tumor on her throat had disappeared.

She became a favorite saint of other nuns because she had married twice and still managed to become a virginal Bride of Christ.

The Least You Need to Know

➤ Many women in the early Church became consecrated virgins.

➤ Married women could become Brides of Christ by living chaste and holy lives.

➤ Women from all walks of life followed the example of the desert fathers.

➤ The religious orders gave way to religious excesses.

Chapter 11

The Great Christian Missionaries: How the Irish Saints Saved the World

In This Chapter

➤ St. Patrick purifies Ireland

➤ St. Columba converts Scotland

➤ An Irish monk saves England

➤ St. Boniface beatifies Germany

➤ An Irish saint discovers America

By the turn of the fifth century, another way to get to Heaven was found. This way was to go out into the world and convert the heathen. At first, this seems contradictory to the advice of the confessors—they said that the best way to get to Heaven was to get away from it all and live in a cave in a desert. But now, some saints discovered, if you go completely in the wrong direction, you can still end up in Heaven. Instead of leading a contemplative life of prayer, meditation, and self-mortification, you can choose the active life of preaching, teaching, and converting sinners.

Good News! There's a Back Road to Heaven!

You see, Jesus told us that we should deny ourselves and take up a cross and follow Him. He said that we should despise the world as the world despised Him. But Jesus also said that we should preach the gospel to all men so that they, too, might come to know the vanity of all earthly goods and goals.

These Guys Are Enough to Ruin a Nice Christian Neighborhood

The Church Fathers came to this realization after encountering the barbarians who kept invading Rome. They were crude! They were unkempt! They were cruel! They were smelly! And, worst of all, they were pagans! *Somebody* had to convert them. *Somebody* had to tell them that clubs should be replaced with crosses. *Somebody* had to inform them that self-denial was much better than rape and pillage. *Somebody* had to turn them from murder to the monasteries. Something had to be done. *Christians* had to take action. A new and terrible threat had appeared, and that threat had to be vanquished.

Not only were the barbarian invaders uninformed about the faith, but so were the people who lived in such pagan lands as Ireland, England, Germania, and, most galling of all, Gaul. New Christian soldiers were needed to put an end to the present evil age so that the entire world would be transformed.

Saints Above! This Can't Be— St. Patrick Is Welsh!

St. Patrick was not the first Christian missionary sent to Ireland—that distinction belongs to St. Palladius—but he succeeded in converting the entire country. In "The Confession of St. Patrick," he tells us that he was originally a guy named Succat, and he wasn't Irish, but Welsh. When he was 16, Patrick was captured by pirates and hauled off to Ireland, where he was sold as a slave.

Just Where Is He Sending All Those Snakes?

For six years, the saint slaved as a swine herder in this barbaric country. During this time, he read the scriptures so faithfully that he could recite them by heart. Every day, he rose before dawn to go out of his humble hut and pray for hours. Finally, Patrick managed to escape from his captors. He walked 200 miles to the coast, where he boarded a ship and, after many adventures on the high seas, finally returned home to Wales.

Knowing that the Irish were a godless race, Patrick decided to bring them the word of God. After being consecrated a bishop, he returned to the old sod and began the difficult task of driving all the snakes—along with the Celtic gods and goddesses—from the Emerald Isle. Snakes, by the way, were symbols of the Druidic religion. Getting rid of the snakes might have meant getting rid of the creepy Druids.

St. Pat's a Cat with Nine Lives!

Patrick established his headquarters in Armagh, where King Laeghaire had his castle. One of his first accomplishments was the conversion of the king's two daughters, Sts. Ethenea and Fidelmia. The daughters managed to convince their father to give Patrick full freedom to conduct his mission throughout the realm.

He then set out to convert the entire nation to Christianity. When he came to a pagan place, Patrick attracted a crowd by performing a miracle or two—giving sight to the blind, healing the deaf, cleansing lepers, casting out devils, and even raising nine persons from the dead. When he told the crowd about Christ, the Celts—by the hundreds—cried out to be saved. Patrick then led them to a nearby watering hole and conducted mass baptisms.

Holy Cow!

The Celtic people were Druids who worshipped hundreds of gods and goddesses. One such god was called the Crum Cruah. The Celts offered their first-born to him as human sacrifice. This, anthropologists believe, helped to put a check on overpopulation.

Divine Revelation

St. Patrick used the shamrock to teach the Irish people about the meaning of the Trinity. For this reason, it became a revered symbol of Ireland.

Saints Alive, It's Friday! Don't Take the Fish!

In his travels, however, St. Patrick encountered many perils. Twelve times his life was threatened by Druidic priests, and several times he was held captive in pagan temples. Even simple folk, at times, became enraged at the saint. One day, while fishing in a stream, St. Patrick had a tremendous catch, while the local fishermen caught nothing. As the saint kept pulling fish from the stream hour after hour, the locals grabbed their shillelaghs and tried to club him over the noggin. The saint hid under a blackthorn bush, where he fell asleep. When he awoke, the bush was covered with flowers. Since it was Christmas day, this flowering was viewed as a miracle. This wondrous event recurred every Christmas, without fail, until the bush was destroyed during World War I.

Hagar the Hagiographer

St. Patrick is the patron saint of Ireland and snakebite. If you want to call upon him, say the following prayer:

Hail, Glorious St. Patrick! We honor thy name,

Tho' Erin may claim thee, the world knows thy fame.

The faith of our fathers is our treasure, too,

Show holy our thoughts that were molded by you.

Through crosses and trials, your image burns bright,

Oh, show us the way, and the truth and the light.

Great Saint, intercede, that we may always be

Devoted and loyal, true children of thee.

Our love and devotion be ever like thine,

Our thought be of Jesus; our hearts be His shrine.

And when to the end of life's path we have trod,

Be near us, great bishop, anointed of God!

Amen.

This Saint Can Get Really Ugly

Second only to St. Patrick in the affection of the Irish people is St. Brigid, the woman who did the most to consolidate his victory. According to legend, Brigid was the daughter of a slave and a king, who were baptized by St. Patrick. After her mother's early death, Brigid was claimed and raised by her father, whom she often annoyed by giving away whatever she found in the palace to the poor. Her most spectacular act of charity involved her gift of her father's jeweled sword to a leper who asked for alms.

Brigid was spectacularly beautiful, and she attracted lusty suitors from every corner of the Emerald Isle. Wanting to be a consecrated virgin, Brigid prayed that she would become hideously ugly. Her prayer was answered. One of her eyes became monstrously huge, while the other shrank to the size of a head of a pin. Realizing that his daughter could never be sold into marriage, the king finally agreed to allow Brigid to enter a convent. As soon as she assumed her vows as a Bride of Christ, her beauty was restored.

St. Brigid's Holy Cow

The good saint established convents for consecrated virgins throughout the country, including the great monastery at Kildare. In time, she became mother abbess of more than 13,000 nuns. Her generosity and hospitality became truly legendary. No sooner did a guest arrive than Brigid would come in from the field, wash their feet, and serve them a meal. If she gave a drink of water to a thirsty stranger, the water was transformed to milk. When she sent a barrel of beer to one monastery, the barrel could be passed on to 17 monasteries before becoming empty. Her cow gave milk three times a day to provide for the steady stream of beggars who showed up at her door.

Brigid was buried at Downpatrick with Sts. Patrick and Columba. In 1283, three knights took the head of Brigid with them to the Holy Land. The knights died in Lisbon, Portugal, where the saint's head is now kept in a special shrine.

Holy Cow!

There persists a legend that St. Mel was completely intoxicated when he administered the vows of consecrated virginity to St. Brigid and, by mistake, ordained her as a Catholic bishop.

And Now a Blurb from Bishop Ibor ...

There is something else you must know about blessed St. Brigid. She is hailed throughout Ireland as "Mary of the Gael." She received this name because Bishop Ibor, during a meeting of the Irish clergy, announced that he had dreamed that the Virgin Mary would appear to the assembly so that they would be encouraged to spread the faith throughout the world. As soon as he said this, Brigid walked into the gathering with several other nuns. The startled Bishop pointed to the beautiful Brigid and cried out, "There is the holy maiden I saw in my dream. Mary has come among the Gael." Upon hearing this, the assembly genuflected before her.

Holy Cow!

Medieval knights looked upon St. Brigid as the perfect woman. She was beautiful, charming, generous, intelligent, and winsome. The word *bride* comes from her name.

How the Irish Saved the World

In time, the nuns and monks of Ireland really changed the world. Irish missionaries traveled throughout much of the medieval world, converting pagan peoples and barbarian hordes to the faith.

Hagar the Hagiographer

St. Brigid, one of our Lord's most beautiful brides, is the patroness of Ireland, New Zealand, milkmaids, fugitives, and poultry raisers. One of the favorite blessings of the Irish people is this: "The protection of God and Colmkille encompass your going and your coming and about you be the milkmaid of the smooth, white palms, Brigid of the clustering, golden brown hair."

St. Columba Starts the First Copyright War

The greatest of these missionaries was St. Columba. We know a great deal about him through a biography that was written by Adamnan, one of his pious monks. From the age of 25, Columba founded a number of churches and monasteries, the most famous being at Derry, Durrow, and Kells. In his spare time, he acted as a scribe, and this got him into trouble. He copied a manuscript of King Diarmuid without permission, which resulted in the first copyright war. The king raised an army to raid Columba's monastery. The saint, in turn, raised his own army. In the ensuing conflict at Cooldrevna, more than 5,000 were killed—all for a book that few people really wanted to read and no one remembers!

After the battle, Columba repented of his Irish temper in confession. As a penance for his sin, his confessor prescribed that Columba must "never again gaze on the face of a man or woman on Irish ground" and that the hot-blooded saint "bring to Christ as many souls as he had untimely sent to Heaven."

Hagar the Hagiographer

According to his legend, St. Columba performed his penance and never again gazed upon a face on Irish soil. But he returned to Ireland to defend the guild of poets, whose works were outlawed by the High King. Columba arrived in the royal court wearing a blindfold to prevent him from seeing the faces of his countrymen. His passionate plea in defense of poetry caused the king to change his mind, and the Irish poets returned to their lyrics. For this reason, St. Columba remains the patron saint of poetry.

Stay Tuned for the Secret of the Loch Ness Monster

And so Columba set off for Scotland, where he established a monastery on the island of Iona. From there, he spread the gospel with a group of disciples throughout Scotland and northern England. Before he died, Columba succeeded in saving more than 5,000 pagan souls, while performing many miracles, including banishing a troublesome dragon from the river Ness into a nearby loch. Periodically, the old Nessie still appears to give the local yokels and American tourists a fright.

The Naked Girls Are a Real Distraction

Equally famous was St. Columban, who was plagued as a lad by sins of the flesh. Small wonder. The saint, it seems, was surrounded by beautiful Irish colleens, who kept shedding their clothes to frolic naked through the woods and streams. He could not keep his eyes away from their bodies and on the holy books. In desperation, St. Columban sought advice from a holy hermit. The hermit suggested that he depart from Ireland for points south, where women were far less beautiful. The saint packed his belongings, gathered a few disciples, and headed off for the wilds of France, where he was—according to his legend—completely free from temptation.

In France, the Irish monk established a monastery at Lixeuil. He was a bit of a disciplinarian. Any monk who coughed during Mass received six lashes. The same punishment was prescribed for anyone who smiled during a church service or clicked their teeth against the chalice at communion. A monk who was late for prayers received fifty lashes. Anyone who spoke with familiarity with a woman received two hundred lashes. The members of this community lived on raw vegetables, bread, and water. They cleared forests, plowed fields, planted and harvested the crops. They fasted and prayed from morning to night. At Lixeuil, St. Columban established the "unending praise" or *laus perennis*—all day and night, every day of the year, monks in relays recited litanies to Jesus, Mary, and the saints.

Talk About Bad Breath!

Eventually, St. Columban got in trouble—not for being too severe—but for refusing to bless the illegitimate kids of the king. He called them a bad breed—"the fruits of adultery and the children of shame." The saint and his monks were ordered to pack up their bags and leave the realm.

St. Columban and his disciples rather traveled through Germany, Italy, and Switzerland—converting the heathen and establishing monasteries. He encountered his greatest frustration in

St. Peter Speaks

St. Columban set the style for monks that has not changed in over 1,400 years. He cut his shoulder length hair close to his head and shaved his dome, thereby creating the *tonsure*. This hair style—that is flattering to no one—is worn as a sign of humility.

Bavaria, where he finally set a vat of beer on fire with his breath and damned everyone in the country to hell. He finally settled in Italy, where he built by hand a library and a monastery.

It's True! An Irish Monk Saved England!

Another Irish missionary almost single-handedly saved northern England. A strapping shepherd lad, St. Cuthbert was the ringleader of the boys of the countryside, all of whom he could beat in "running, jumping, and wrestling."

One day, a waif appeared before him, broke into tears, and said, "Oh, Cuthbert, how can you waste your time in idle play, you whom God has set apart as a priest and bishop?" From that day on, Cuthbert grew grave beyond his years.

St. Peter Speaks

A **See** is the center of jurisdiction for a bishop. It comes from the Latin *sedes*, meaning "seat." It is the place where a bishop keeps his seat or chair. An **episcopate** is the office of a bishop.

When he was 15, while in prayer, the saint saw a host of angels "carrying, as though a globe of fire, a soul to Heaven." Later he learned that St. Aidan, another great Irish missionary who had spent his life trying to convert the wild Brits of Northumberland, had died. Culbert then knew that he had been called to carry out St. Aidan's work.

Upon becoming a priest and a bishop, Cuthbert spread the faith throughout the northern provinces of England and established several monasteries. At Lindisfarne, he established the *See* of his *episcopate*.

Red-Hot Breath Against Ice-Cold Skin

The saint went from hut to hut to convert the Brits. At times, he performed a miracle or two. Once he cured a dying woman's baby of the bubonic plague with a kiss. For this reason, Cuthbert became known as the wonder worker of Britain.

Holy Cow!

Noted hagiographer Sabine Baring-Gould, in her 1917 classic edition of *Lives of the Saints*, writes this: "No saint of his time or country had more frequent and affectionate intercourse with the nuns than St. Cuthbert."

Like all good monks, the holy Irishman loved to be alone. At night, he sneaked out of his cell and disappeared until daybreak. Wondering where he went, a spy followed him on a freezing night in December. Cuthbert walked to the sea, stripped off his clothes, and walked into the icy North Sea, where he chanted and prayed for several hours. At daybreak, Cuthbert turned to the sea and again made the sign of the cross. Immediately, a herd of good otters emerged from the sea, warming the saint by their panting and drying him with their soft fur.

Later, Cuthbert moved from his cell in the monastery to the deserted island of Farne. Here he built a hut of straw with the help of some ravens and was fed by angels. When he died, the patron saint of northern England was buried at Lindisfarne, where his body remained incorrupt for centuries. The monks removed the well-kept cadaver to Durham during the Viking raids. The body radiated miraculous cures until King Henry VIII desecrated the holy corpse in a fit of rage against Catholicism.

No Heathen Wants to Be Alone in Heaven

In 690, St. Willibrord, another Irish monk, set out to save the troublesome pagan tribes of Frisians, who inhabited the Netherlands. Almost immediately, he made an enemy of the Frisian King Rodbod, who thought that Willibrord was an emissary not from the pope, but from his hated enemy, King Pepin the Young. King Rodbod banished Willibrord from his realm and set fire to his churches and monasteries. This greatly annoyed our saint, who retaliated by killing a herd of Rodbod's sacred cows and, even worse, baptizing hundreds of Danes in front of the king's castle.

The king admired the Irishman's guts and agreed to sit down for a civilized chat. Willibrord had the gift of gab and almost succeeded in converting his old nemesis to Christianity. Rodbod stripped off his robes and stood before a stream to be baptized. At that point, he asked the saint one question: "If you must be baptized in order to be saved, what happened to my Danish ancestors?" St. Willibrord simply told him the truth. "Why, they are all roasting in hell," he said. Rodbod answered that he would rather be in hell with the heroes of his country than in Heaven with a group of Irish priests and beggars.

The saint, however, had the last laugh. He converted several members of Rodbod's family so that the king's grandson and namesake, St. Rodbod, succeeded Willibrord as the Bishop of Utrecht. Even for holy saints, such revenge is sweet!

"My God Is Better Than Your God!"

St. Boniface, a disciple of St. Willibrord, became the patron saint of Germany. Upon arriving in Hesse, he found hundreds of dumb Druids dancing around an oak tree that they said was the home of their great

Divine Revelation

The missionary zeal of the Irish saints persisted after the martyrdom of St. Boniface. Their disciples carried the faith to Hungary, Sweden, Finland, and Russia.

Hagar the Hagiographer

St. Boniface is the patron saint of Germany and beer makers. Here's a prayer you can say to him: "St. Boniface, you faced discouragement and failure and learned from them. Help us to hear God's message in our moments of failure and to use what we learn to serve God better. Amen."

god Thor. St. Boniface took an axe, chopped down the tree, and smirked, "My God is better than your god." Amazed that he had not been struck by one of Thor's thunderbolts, the pagans fell to their knees and begged to be baptized.

Boniface then traveled throughout the country, establishing churches and monasteries and creating a host of future residents of the Kingdom of Heaven, including St. Lull, St. Burchand, St. Wigbert, and a bevy of new Brides of Christ, including St. Thelca, St. Walburga, and the saint's beautiful and learned cousin, St. Lioba. By 751, St. Boniface had succeeded in Christianizing the pagan nation and achieved such power and renown that he was able crown his own crony, Pepin, King of the Franks.

Holy Cow!

St. Willibrord is buried in Luxembourg, and his shrine became famous because of a certain ritual that is performed there. Every year, on St. Willibrord's feast day, November 7, the local clergy, city folk, and pilgrims perform a sacred dance that resembles a conga. They take hold of one another by a hip and form a straight line. They then take three steps forward and one step back. The procession dances up and down the aisles of the church, all around the church, until they snake around the tomb of the beloved old saint. This queer dance is supposed to help everything from convulsions to lumbago.

The Book Wasn't Worth It

Having accomplished this monumental chore, St. Boniface and a few of his disciples decided to return to Frisia to complete the work of St. Willibrord. It was an unfortunate mistake. One day, as Boniface was reading about the works of the glorious St. Patrick, a fiendish band of Frisians descended upon his camp and hacked the holy saint to pieces. His body was taken to Fulda, where it still rests. In the chapel, you can also find the book that the saint had been reading—it is dented with sword-cuts. This shows not that St. Boniface was trying to protect himself from the blows, but that he was trying to save the book from being damaged.

Forget About Columbus—St. Brendan Discovered America

By this time, the Irish monks and their disciples had changed the world. Within 200 years, they had created Europe. In addition, they had established the monasteries that came to copy and preserve the great works of antiquity. Almost single-handedly, they had saved Western civilization.

The Irish saints also discovered America. This is verified by the legend of St. Brendan, who set out with 60 fellow monks in search of the mythical Island of the Blessed. They sailed the Atlantic in two huge canoes that contained enough provisions for a month's journey. On the journey, rules of monastic life were strictly observed by all on board so that no harm could come to them.

Judas Iscariot Is Alive and Well and Living on an Iceberg off Greenland

According to *The Navigation of St. Brendan,* one of the most popular works of the Middle Ages, the saint and his monks encountered many beautiful mermaids, whom they piously baptized, and they even encountered Judas Iscariot, taking a brief respite from hell on an iceberg off the coast of Greenland.

Eventually, they arrived either at one of the Canary Islands, the Azores, or the Florida Keys. This claim, of course, was dismissed for centuries as pure blarney. But in 1977, Tim Severin, an expert in ancient navigation, built a long hide-covered canoe or "curragh," following the instructions in the "Navigation," and sailed it from Ireland to Newfoundland by way of Iceland and Greenland, demonstrating the accuracy of St. Brendan's directions and the places he visited during his glorious sea voyage.

A Saint for the Unmentionables

We cannot leave the Irish saints without mention of St. Fiacre, who ploughed thousands of acres with his shillelagh, and erected a beautiful monastery and hermitage—with no help from leprechauns or anyone else. After completing this work, the saint was berated by a neighboring shrew. The woman raised his dander to such a degree that he left a huge imprint of his Irish arse on a nearby stone. The incident confirmed his dislike of women. The saint forbade all women from entering his chapel or visiting his hermitage. When a noblewoman of Paris violated this order, she was transformed into a huge bloated behemoth and went crazy. Another woman peered inside, and her eyes popped out.

St. Fiacre is the patron saint of cab drivers, gardeners, and needle makers. He is the protector against venereal disease and (you guessed it) hemorrhoids.

Hagar the Hagiographer

Saints be praised! I hope you do not suffer from hemorrhoids, let alone some dreadful venereal disease. If you do, recite this prayer to good St. Fiacre: "O glorious St. Fiacre, bless me that I might remain pure and holy throughout the days of my life. Protect me from all unholiness, all impurity, and all occasions of sin. Amen."

The Secret Way to Remain Chaste and Holy

Mention must also be made of St. Flannan, who spread the word throughout Scotland and the Western Isles. He was a handsome lad, and women from far and wide were attracted to him. For this reason, he prayed that he would become physically repulsive. His prayer was answered, and the good saint became covered with hairy warts and seething boils. It is believed that Flannan invented the Irish practice of praying seven times a day while immersed up to the neck in ice water. This, we are told, is a wonderful way to get rid of sexual temptation.

Surprise Quiz

This is a mind-boggling quiz for those of you who are tired of reading about all these Irish saints.

Identify the following:

1. The head of a robber gang who became the patron saint of Africa.
2. The patron saint of America who was the crown prince of Hungary.
3. The Basque monk who became the patron of China.
4. The Italian bishop who became the patron of England.
5. The patron saint of the gypsies, who have no homeland.
6. The Greek philosopher who became the patron saint of France.
7. The son of a ferocious Celtic chieftain and a pure and pious Christian maiden who became patron of Wales.
8. The two brothers, who devised the Cyrillic alphabet, and became patrons of Czechoslovakia and Moravia.
9. The prince, who refused to refused to wed and bed a ravishing princess, and became the patron of Poland.
10. The famous saint and preacher (whose tongue never decomposed) who became the patron of Portugal.

Extra Credit

➤ The saint who had a vision of Christ at the age of six (he was dressed in papal vestments) and became the patron of Italy.

Answers: 1. St. Moses the Black; 2. St. Americus; 3. St. Francis Xavier; 4. St. Augustine of Canterbury; 5. St. Sara; 6. St. Denis; 7. St. David; 8. Sts. Cyril and Methodius; 9. St. Casimir; 10. St. Anthony of Padua. Extra Credit—St. Catherine of Siena.

The Least You Need to Know

➤ Christians became missionaries to convert the barbarians.

➤ St. Patrick converted Ireland and became the greatest Christian missionary.

➤ The Irish saints created Europe and, through a network of monasteries, managed to preserve Western civilization during the Dark Ages.

➤ An Irish saint, St. Brendan, is credited for the discovery of America.

Chapter 12

Popes and Princes: In Heaven, It Pays to Be Rich

In This Chapter

➤ Which saints were born with silver spoons

➤ St. Francis of Assisi and the Poor Clares

➤ Many kings have been canonized

➤ The saints' preferred profession

I hate to break this to you, but few things in life or the afterlife are fair. You might be a very holy person. You might spend day and night in prayer. You might break out in a stigmata or two on occasion. You might spend your summer vacations in leper colonies. You might give all that you possess to the poor. Heck, you might even be able to perform a miracle or two. Still, you don't have much of a chance to enter the communion of saints.

Most Saints Were Fat Cats

To tell the truth, the communion of saints is a rather snobby community. The overwhelming majority of saints are from well-heeled and well-connected families. Very few are from green-collar backgrounds. Even the saints who are known for being very poor were really very rich.

Divine Revelation

The first Christians were from the lowest level of society, including slaves and domestic servants. In his first letter to the Corinthians, St. Paul wrote: "Brothers, think of what you were when you were called. Not many of you were wise by human standards; not many were influential; not many were of noble birth. But God chose the foolish things of the world to shame the wise; God chose the weak things of the world to shame the strong. He chose the lowly things of this world and the despised things—the things that are not—to nullify the things that are, so that no one may boast before him" (1 Corinthians 1:26–29).

St. Peter Speaks

In his Rule of Friars, St. Francis wrote: "The brothers shall appropriate nothing to themselves, neither a house nor place nor anything. And, as pilgrims and strangers in this world, serving the Lord in poverty and humility, let them go confidently in quest of alms. Nor ought they be ashamed, because the Lord made Himself poor for us in this world. This, my dearest brothers, is the height of the most sublime poverty which has made you heirs; poor in goods, but exalted in virtue."

St. Francis Was a Rich Kid

Take St. Francis, for example, who is hailed as the patron saint of Italy and animals. He and his followers—the fabled Franciscans—lived among the poorest of the poor: They begged for their daily bread, they worked at menial jobs, and they preached in the marketplaces. But, let's face facts. This good saint came not from a poor family in a public housing project, but from one of the wealthiest and most influential families in Assisi. He was not a humble serf, but a lordly knight-at-arms. His father was a leading cloth merchant.

Sure, St. Francis walked around in a rough tunic with a cord and spoke of the virtue of apostolic poverty, but he could afford to do it. This guy was born in a castle with the proverbial silver spoon in his mouth. When he wanted to raise money to repair a church, Francis sold bolts of cloth that he removed from his father's warehouse. When his angry father accosted his son for such pilfering before the local bishop, St. Francis took off his clothes and began to run around the palace stark naked. No poor person would act so shameless or so snotty.

His name wasn't even Francis—it was Giovanni de Bernadone. I'm not saying that he wasn't a nice guy.

After all, he gave sermons to the birds, made a peace treaty with a mean wolf, and instituted the custom of a crib in the church at Christmas. But he wasn't a regular guy from the streets, not by a long shot. Upon his death, St. Francis wanted to be buried in a pauper's field, but instead he was enshrined in a huge basilica that bears his name.

The Poor Clares Weren't Poor, Either

The same is true of St. Clare, the founder of the Poor Clares. Yes, this saint and her fellow nuns lived on alms and spent their time making clothing and providing shelter for the poor and homeless. Sure, St. Clare is a great figure of poverty. She, too, was kind and caring. As a matter of fact, St. Clare would literally give you the horsehair shirt off her back.

But St. Clare was the beautiful and rich daughter of the illustrious Offreducio family. She, too, was raised in a castle and was surrounded by wealth and nobility. On Palm Sunday in 1212, she decided to elope. She dressed herself in her most luxurious gown, adorned herself with the most precious family jewels, and slipped off to a small church. Waiting for her in the sanctuary was a fellow member of the local nobility, St. Francis. Clare removed all her clothing and her jewelry and put on a sackcloth robe. St. Francis cut her long flowing hair and married her—to Christ!

Upon entering the cloister, Clare summoned her sister Agnes to join her. Clare's father, Faverone, went crazy. Not only did Clare steal the family jewels, but she also took her sister, who was a kid of 14. Faverone sent a group of hoods to rescue his little girl from the clutches of Clare. The thugs burst into the convent and grabbed Agnes by the hair. Clare immediately prayed for a miracle. Agnes, who was small and slender, suddenly became as heavy as lead so that the tough guys could not make her budge an inch. They left in a huff, and Agnes stayed with Clare.

St. Clare Becomes a Television Celebrity

Clare and her followers wore no shoes, ate no meat, slept on a dirt floor, and lived in absolute poverty. Pope Gregory IX tried to convince the saint of her folly and offered to absolve her from the vow of absolute poverty. Clare replied, "Holy Father, absolve me from my sins, but not from the obligation of following our Lord." Such a statement could be made only by a saint with money. Many of the serfs and commoners of the thirteenth century had no choice but to live on the edge of starvation.

Hagar the Hagiographer

You're not going to believe this, but it's true! In 1958, Pope Pius XII declared St. Clare to be the patroness of television. This title seemed fitting because, when she was old and sick, the saint could not leave her bed to go to midnight Mass one Christmas Eve. But, in her cell, she heard, as if by magic, the singing of angels and saw, as if on a high-resolution television, a scene of the Nativity at Bethlehem.

Oh, No—St. Serf Was Not a Serf

So you still think that a poor slob has a shot at becoming a saint? Then get this: St. Alexis, the patron saint of beggars, was a rich Roman noble who made a pledge to the Virgin Mary that he would live a life of chastity. Forced by his rich parents to marry a rich princess, Alexis escaped breaking his pledge in the wedding bed by escaping from the castle in the disguise of a poor beggar. He remained dressed as a beggar and suffered all kinds of indignities for 17 years. Just before he died, Alexis revealed his true identity and received a lavish funeral.

What's more, St. Wendon was the son of a sixth-century Scottish king, and St. Serf was not a serf, but the son of a sixth-century Arabian princess. It just goes to show that some things never change—not even in the realm of the eternal.

It's Easy to Get Canonized ... If You're a King

Here is just a short list of the kings and rulers who became saints:

➤ Charlemagne is the first holy Roman emperor hailed as a saint, along with the poor and humble apostles. His canonization was purely political. As all hagiographers know, this "holy" Roman emperor was not holy. He once tried to sexually assault the chaste St. Amalburga (circa 800).

➤ King Eric IX of Sweden, who conquered Finland in 1150, is not only a saint but also a martyr because several of his subjects succeeded in beheading him. By the way, this righteous king told the Finns that they could choose between baptism and death. Strange to say, many chose death.

➤ Elizabeth of Portugal (born 1271) and Elizabeth of Hungary (born 1207) were both queens who lived in lavish palaces and went on to inherit a mansion in Heaven. What's more, they were not even virgins because they were married with children.

➤ King Edward I of England is a saint for no known reason. He assumed the throne in 1013 at the age of 13, upon his father's death. When he turned 16, Edward decided to visit his half-brother, Ethelred. There his beautiful but wicked stepmother seduced him "with her female blandishments" and had him butchered by her henchmen. Ethelred became king, and then a series of miracles began to take place at Edward's grave. Ethelred had the decency to have Edward named a saint, and the wicked stepmother joined a nunnery.

➤ King Stephen of Hungary is a saint for his slaughter of an unruly barbarian horde known as the Magyars. The name for Magyars in French is ogres, and they seemed to be ugly giants.

➤ King Oswald of Northumbria is a saint, even though his greatest accomplishment was defeating King Cadwallon in battle. When King Oswald died in battle, King Oswin became king and a saint. Upon gaining the throne, King Oswin declared war on his brother Oswy. In the whole bloody mess, no one appeared to be particularly good or saintly.

➤ King Richard of England is a saint, but his only saintly accomplishment, other than having money and power, was giving birth to three saints: Sts. Willibold, Winebold, and Walburga.

➤ King Wencelaus of Czechoslovakia is a saint and the subject of a popular Christmas carol. At royal banquets, he forced his guests to recite the Lord's Prayer. Those who refused were struck with a club. King Wencelaus hated his mother, whom he exiled, and his brother, who tried to seize his throne. His happiest moment came when Emperor Henry (discussed next) gave him the arm of St. Vitus as a present.

➤ Henry the Emperor is a saint, despite the fact that he used the church to solidify his political power. In 1014, he took the throne from the hands of the pope and declared himself holy Roman emperor. He lived in chastity with his queen, St. Cunegund, but, in truth, Henry never found her very attractive. On his deathbed, he returned his bride to her parents with this note: "Receive back again the virgin you gave me."

➤ King Sigebert of Austrasia is a saint, despite the fact that he gained the crown at the age of 12 and did little to distinguish himself except establish 12 monasteries.

➤ King Louis IX (born 1214) of France is a saint because he was rich, powerful, pious, charitable, and the unsuccessful leader of a crusade. Come to think of it, Louis X is also a saint.

This is just a very short list of the royalty that inhabits the Kingdom of Heaven, and this book does not contain enough pages to list all the princes and princesses, counts and countesses, barons and baronesses, and other assorted members of the nobility who have been canonized.

Holy Cow!

As a prank, Napoleon had himself proclaimed a saint. He distributed images of himself as an early Egyptian hermit and martyr named St. Neopolus. He even circulated stories about the heroic deeds of this saint. Soon people throughout France were praying to St. Neopolus, and a Masonic lodge was dedicated to him.

Saints Really Pop Out of the Papacy

But being a king or a queen does not ensure sainthood. The best profession for a potential saint is the papacy. There are more popes in Heaven than kings and queens, princes and princesses, abbots and abbesses, soldiers and statesmen, philosophers and poets, or any other professional or vocational group. Of the first 50 popes, 48 are saints. Your chance of being a saint if you are a blue-collar worker is less than 1 in a billion; if you are of royal blood, your chance is 1 in a million. But, if you are a pope, your chances are almost excellent (even though few have been canonized since the sixth century) at 1 in 4.

It Helps to Have Chutzpah

The greatest of the early popes was Pope Leo I (440–461). Pope Leo claimed that it did not matter how immoral or inept an individual pope might be as long as he was the rightfully elected successor of St. Peter. He strengthened the ties between church and state by demanding that the Roman Emperor Valentinian III enforce papal decrees by imperial law. For this reason, if you were believed to be a heretic, you were banished to a remote desert, tossed into prison, or burned at the stake.

Pope Leo played an important part in a controversy in the early Church. Many Christians began to wonder about the nature of Christ. Is Jesus, by His basic nature, God or man? No question had more clergy members scratching their heads. At last, Pope Leo decided the issue by saying that Christ had two natures, one divine and one human, that were combined in one person. When he issued this decision, he signed his decree with these words: "St. Peter has spoken through Leo." Let's face it, the guy had *chutzpah*.

St. Peter Speaks

According to Catholic doctrine, popes can go to hell, despite their gift of infallibility. A few, including Pope Honorius I (625–638), have been condemned as heretics.

How to Ward Off a Barbarian Invasion

Pope Leo had the uncanny ability to scare the hell out of everyone he encountered. The truth of this can be evidenced by the way he handled Attila and the troublesome Huns.

Hagar the Hagiographer

Only three popes have been given the title "Great": Pope Leo I, who reigned from 440 to 461; Pope Gregory I, who reigned from 590 to 604; and Pope Innocent III, who reigned from 1198 to 1216. Innocent III, for some unexplained reason, has never been declared a saint.

In 451, Attila and his horde invaded Italy and slaughtered nearly everybody (men, women, and children) and everything (dogs, cows, horses ... you get the picture) they came upon. After sacking Milan, the Huns, with skulls on their spears, set out for Rome. Helpless to prevent the conquest of the city, the Roman Emperor abdicated all responsibility to the pope. Pope Leo, in full regalia, met Attila at the gates of the city and brandished the cross before the dumbfounded barbarian. This act, for some mysterious reason, filled Attila with horror. He and his horde turned from the city, forever altering the course of human history.

Unfortunately, Pope Leo was less successful in dealing with Genseric and his horde of vandals, who sacked Rome for 14 days before the pope was able to chase them away.

If You Can't Convert 'Em, Then Kill 'Em!

As Pope Leo I saved Rome from the Huns, Pope Gregory I, another holy saint, saved Rome from the Lombards. When these unwashed and unsavory barbarians began to rape and pillage their way through Italy, the imperial government headed for the hills and established headquarters at Ravenna. To make matters worse, famine and plague struck the city. All would be lost, save for our stout-hearted saint.

Pope Gregory took charge of the situation without a moment's hesitation. He collected taxes, provisioned the city, and summoned an army for its defense. The saint dispatched orders to the generals in the field, and, after a series of bloody skirmishes, managed to make a lasting peace with the loathsome Lombards.

St. Gregory's Vision of a Perfect Society

After securing peace, Pope Gregory administered the papal estates and expanded the papal holdings throughout Italy. With these holdings came taxes and tribute money. Money now flowed into the papal coffers as never before.

To top it all, this saintly pope was also a very prolific writer. He wrote a basic textbook (the first of its kind) for the training of the clergy and an incredibly long commentary (more than six volumes) on the Book of Job. In his dialogues, he presented his vision of a Christian society on earth. This society, he said, must be structured in accordance with the Heavenly Kingdom, where every saint and every angel has a proper place and a proper function. Pope Gregory wanted earthly society to be ordered by a chain of command, leading from the local priests to the bishops to the pope.

Holy Cow!

Attila, whom Christians called the "scourge of God," was never quite right after his meeting with Pope Leo the Great. Two years after leaving Rome, he died of a burst artery on his wedding night with a young Gothic woman.

Holy Cow!

Pope Gregory I was the first pope to wage war, the first pope to order bloodshed, and the first pope to command an army.

Freeze Him If He Gives You Trouble

One of the greatest popes is St. Gregory VII (1073–1085), who is also known as St. Hildebrand. During his time, kings possessed the power to appoint all the bishops

Hagar the Hagiographer

Pope Gregory I wrote a great deal about the miraculous power of holy relics. His most cherished relics were the chains that bound St. Peter and St. Paul. He once sent them to a friend with this note: "Let these chains be applied constantly to your ailing eyes, for they possess wondrous power."

Divine Revelation

Pope Gregory IV was a great champion of clerical celibacy. He excommunicated all priests who were married or had concubines. He also forbade Christians from attending a Mass that was celebrated by a priest who kept a woman in his house.

in their realm. Often they appointed relatives or friends who coughed up the right amount of cash. Pope Gregory VII tried to put an end to this practice, claiming that only a pope had the right to appoint a bishop.

King Henry VI of Germany objected to this claim and defied the pope's authority. In retaliation, Pope Gregory excommunicated the king and ordered his subjects not to obey him. Fearing the loss of his kingdom, King Henry knelt in the snow for two days, begging forgiveness, before the good pope finally gave him absolution.

St. Gregory VII was the first pope to send papal legates or representatives throughout Christendom, and he established the Latin Mass so that Christian worship would be uniform and universal or "Catholic."

For Heaven's Sake, Keep the Hookers Happy!

Pope Pius V (1566–1572) lived in the Lateran Palace like a monk. He ate little and threatened his cook with excommunication if he put forbidden ingredients (such as a meat bone on Friday) in his soup. His great goal was to transform the city of Rome into a monastery.

His first act as pope was to outlaw prostitution in Rome. The Roman senate balked at this, saying that it was only natural for the oldest profession to prosper in a center of celibacy. If the prostitutes left, they said, no woman would be safe from the clergy.

No Bull for This Saint

The righteous pope next forbade Christians and residents of Rome from entering a tavern. He almost decided to proclaim adultery a capital offense. In what is called the "last bull," Pope Pius V outlawed bull fighting throughout the Roman Empire.

In 1570, Pope Pius V contributed a large sum of money to aid an uprising against Queen Elizabeth I. When the uprising failed, he issued a decree deposing her from the throne. It was the last attempt by a pope to overthrow the ruler of a land.

You've Got to Admit, the Hat Is Funny

The last pope to be canonized was Pope Pius X (1903–1914), who considered himself a prisoner in the Lateran Palace. Once, when meeting with his old friends from Venice, the humble pope pointed to his hat and robes and burst into tears, saying, "See how they have dressed me up!" He lived frugally and disliked ceremony. When he died, his attendants found in the pockets of his white soutane what might have been found in the pockets of a schoolboy: a pen knife and the stump of a pencil.

Pope Pius X was a great enemy of modernism, the belief that truth changes and that all things are relative to time and place. Up until 1967, priests were required to take an oath that they always would remain in opposition to this false teaching. The pope also believed in a literal interpretation of the Bible and said that any attempt to treat sacred scripture as a human document must be condemned.

Warning of Things to Come

In 1985, Pope Pius IX was beatified (not to be confused with Pope Piux X, who was canonized). Pius IX was the first pope to affirm that he was infallible when he spoke as Bishop of Rome on matters of faith and morals. His first infallible pronouncement was the dogma of the Immaculate Conception of Mary. What's that? You'll find out in Chapter 14, "You've Tried the Rest, Now Here's the Best: Blessed Virgin Mary."

Hagar the Hagiographer

Several popes who became saints were married. According to Mark 1:30, St. Peter was married. St. Hormisdas (514–523) enjoyed the pleasures of connubial bliss and was the father of another pope who became a saint, St. Silverius (536–538). The last married pope appears to have been Adrian II (867–872).

Holy Cow!

The ring of a pope is used to authenticate official papal pronouncements. Because any decree from the papal throne must be accepted with intense solemnity, the pope's ring is immediately removed from his right hand at the time of his death and is destroyed by the papal chamberlain. During the Middle Ages, the pope's entire hand was hacked, and, while the ring was cast into a fire, the hand was saved as a holy relic.

St. Peter Speaks

Pope Pius X is a favorite saint of conservatives in the Catholic Church. He has a cult following, and a standardized prayer is offered to him. Want to say the prayer? Recite this: "Glorious Saint Pius X, blessed model of the priesthood, obtain for us holy, dedicated priests, and increase vocations to the religious life. Dispel confusion and hatred and anxiety, and incline our hearts to peace and concord so that all nations will place themselves under the sweet reign of Christ. Amen."

The Least You Need to Know

➤ Most saints came from nobility.

➤ St. Francis, the champion of apostolic poverty, was the son of a wealthy merchant.

➤ St. Clare, who founded the Poor Clares, was also from a wealthy family.

➤ Many saints were powerful kings and queens.

➤ The papacy is the greatest supplier of saints.

Chapter 13

The Church Gives Doctoral Degrees to Some Dead Saints

In This Chapter

➤ Patrons have preferred status

➤ Saints have cults

➤ The true story of Santa Claus

➤ The real Valentine

➤ The Church Doctors

We'd like to think that the community of the saints is a democratic society, where all saints are equal before the throne of God. We would like to think that in Heaven there is no distinction of rank and class. Unfortunately, this is not the case. Some saints have special status. Some saints are venerated more than other saints. Some saints have been singled out as patrons.

Some Saints Are More Special Than Other Saints

In the early Church, certain Christian heroes who went to their death in an exemplary way were held in such honor that they became the centers of devotion and veneration. These saints developed cult followings. They had their own fans, who held them in highest reverence. Some developed large *cults*, some minor cults (just as some sports figures have many fans, and some few fans).

The True Story of Santa Claus

Certain groups of people—painters, carpenters, stone workers, bricklayers, farmers, furriers, gravediggers, and grocers—turned to the same saint or hero for protection. This came about in a logical way. The stirring deed of the saint, a significant miracle the saint performed, or even the date of the saint's death came to determine how, and even by whom, the saint would be held in veneration.

St. Peter Speaks

Cult comes from the Latin *cultus*, meaning "worship" and "veneration." Before they were proclaimed saints in the early Church, every saint had a group of devotees who saw him or her as an object of pious devotion—in other words, as a "cult" figure.

Let's take the case of St. Nicholas, or Santa Claus, as he is known by his Dutch name. We really don't know much about St. Nicholas except that he was a bishop of Myra, a city in southwest Turkey, and that he may have attended the Council of Nicea in 324. Pious folklore, however, tells us that this saint was a particularly holy infant. From the time of his birth, he refused his mother's breasts on feast days and holy days. After his parents died of plague, he went around performing charitable deeds.

When he learned that three young women were about to enter brothels because they had no money, he left bags of money on their doorstep and even dropped gifts down their chimney. In times of famine, he went from house to house, leaving loaves of bread on the doorsteps. For these reasons, St. Nicholas became the patron saint of bakers, brides (the virgins eventually became happily married), and children.

Hagar the Hagiographer

Let me give you another example of how a saint becomes a patron saint. By mistake, a woman of ill repute was buried in a Catholic cemetery outside Paris in 400. The results of this were disastrous. A huge black serpent emerged from her grave with the corpse of the wanton woman in his claws. He chewed on the corpse, spitting her grisly remains on anyone who walked by. The bishop of Paris, St. Marcel, was summoned to the scene. Ignoring the serpent's evil hisses, he clobbered it with his staff, wrapped it in his robe, and cast it in a fire. For this reason, St. Marcel is the patron saint of vampire killers.

St. Valentine's Story Is a Heart-Breaker

Let's cut to another case. We don't know anything for certain about St. Valentine. It was kind of a common name among early Christians. Three different saints named Valentine were killed on the same day during the same period of persecution (circa 269). As a matter of fact, eight complete bodies of St. Valentine can be found in Roman churches, along with an additional head. It was not any detail of his life that resulted in St. Valentine becoming the patron saint of lovers, but the date of the martyrdom of this mysterious saint is significant. According to legend, he was put to death on February 14. This was the pagan holiday of Lupercalia, in which birds were believed to choose their mates and when pagan boys courted pagan girls with presents.

There are more than 10,000 saints in Heaven, and fewer than 500 are singled out with feast days and Masses held in their honor. Most of the saints are forgotten figures who get no attention. In fact, standardized prayers have not even been formulated to say to them. Many of these saints were wonderful, brave, and holy figures, but they get no respect. It doesn't seem fair.

Holy Cow!

Some saints deserve to be patrons, and yet they are sadly neglected. One such holy one is St. Vitalis of Gaza. In 500, this holy hermit left his cave in the desert to save the harlots of Alexandria. With the money he earned every day by hard labor, Vitalis purchased the company of fallen women, telling them, "I pay you this sum so that you will spend one night without sin." Once alone with the hooker, the saint fell on his knees and prayed with her until the break of dawn. He visited every whore and whorehouse in town, raising a lot of eyebrows. One day, after leaving a house of ill repute, a prude struck him over the head and killed him. Vitalis's funeral was attended by hundreds of former harlots, who had become good wives and mothers. Shouldn't St. Vitalis at the very least be venerated as the patron saint of hair tonic, if not harlots?

A Ph.D. for Saints?

Not only are certain saints singled out as patrons, but a very select few are singled out as doctors. This means that what they have to say is of particular significance and importance. If you need the right prescription for salvation, you should turn to them rather than the saints who are lacking this angelic degree. Who are the doctors? The list, along with the dates of their distinction and the name of the presiding pope, is as follows:

➤ St. Albert the Great (1932, by Pope Pius XI)

➤ St. Alphonsus Liguori (1871, by Pope Pius IX)

➤ St. Ambrose (1295, by Pope Boniface VIII)

➤ St. Anselm of Canterbury (1720, by Pope Clement XI)

➤ St. Anthony of Padua (1946, by Pope Pius XII)

➤ St. Athanasius (1568, by Pope Pius V)

➤ St. Augustine (1295, by Pope Boniface VIII)

➤ St. Basil the Great (1568, by Pope Pius V)

➤ St. Bede the Venerable (1899, by Pope Leo XIII)

➤ St. Bernard of Clairvaux (1830, by Pope Pius VIII)

➤ St. Bonaventure (1588, by Pope Sixtus V)

➤ St. Catherine of Siena (1970, by Pope Paul VI)

➤ St. Cyril of Alexandria (1882, by Pope Leo XIII)

➤ St. Cyril of Jerusalem (1882, by Pope Leo XIII)

➤ St. Ephraem the Syrian (1920, by Pope Benedict XV)

➤ St. Francis de Sales (1877, by Pope Pius IX)

➤ St. Gregory the Great (1295 by Pope Boniface VIII)

➤ St. Gregory of Nazianzus (1568, by Pope Pius V)

➤ St. Hilary of Poitiers (1851, by Pope Pius IX)

➤ St. Isidore of Seville (1722, by Pope Innocent XIII)

➤ St. Jerome (1295, by Pope Boniface VIII)

➤ St. John Chrysostom (1568, by Pope Pius V)

➤ St. John of Damascus (1890, by Pope Leo XIII)

➤ St. John of the Cross (1926, by Pope Pius XI)

➤ St. Lawrence of Brindisi (1959, by Pope John XXIII)

➤ St. Leo the Great (1754, by Pope Benedict XIV)

➤ St. Peter Canisius (1925, by Pope Pius XI)

➤ St. Peter Chysologus (1729, by Pope Benedict XIII)

➤ St. Peter Damian (1828, by Pope Leo XII)

➤ St. Robert Bellarmine (1931, by Pope Pius XI)

➤ St. Teresa of Avila (1970, by Pope Paul VI)

➤ St. Thomas Aquinas (1567, by Pope Pius V)

➤ St. Therese of Lisieux (1997, by Pope John Paul II)

The Saint Who Hated Sex

St. Jerome (340–395), whose real name is Eusebius Hieronymus Sophronius, was the most highly educated of the Church Fathers. One day, after reading Cicero, Jerome took a nap and dreamed that he was summoned to appear before the throne of God to give an account of his existence. "I am a Christian," Jerome declared. "No, you're not," God responded. "You are a Ciceronian!" The dream scared the daylights out of Jerome, and he cast aside Cicero and devoted his time and attention to the holy scriptures. This resulted in the first Latin translation of the Old and New Testaments in a version of the Bible that we call the Vulgate.

After spending some time as a hermit in the desert, where he was burned black, Jerome became the pope's personal secretary and a spiritual adviser to several wealthy Roman women. He was the most puritanical of all Puritans and thought that sex, even among married couples, was sinful and that any man who loved his wife too much was guilty of adultery. "I praise marriage," he wrote, "but only because it produces virgins." He even attacked St. Peter for his lack of chastity and said that the leader of the apostles managed to cleanse himself from "the filth of his marriage" only by his martyrdom.

All Feminists Are Not Eunuchs

St. Jerome penned an attack on the Roman women of his age that is ageless:

> The old women paint their cheeks with rouge and their eyes with belladonna and cover their faces with powder. No number of years can convince them they are old. They behave like trembling schoolgirls before their grandsons. Gentile widows, who should be praying for a happy death, flaunt silk dresses, deck themselves in gleaming jewelry, and reek of musk. Other women put on men's clothing, cut their hair short, blush to be women, and prefer to look like eunuchs.

St. Peter Speaks

Why are there so many doctors in God's heavenly house? It all began in 1295, when Pope Boniface VIII said that Sts. Ambrose, Jerome, Augustine, and Gregory the Great should be singled out among the saints as outstanding doctors of Christian thought. Throughout the years, more names were added to the list. The latest saints to receive this honor were Sts. Teresa of Avila, Catherine of Siena, and Therese of Lisieux.

Holy Cow!

St. Jerome provides insight into the morality of Rome at the turn of the fifth century. He speaks of unmarried women who prevent conception by the use of evil potions, and women who secure abortions from midwives in the marketplace.

This saint was highly influential in the development of the doctrine of the Virgin Mary. He broke with other Christians who held that Mary had had other children after she gave birth to Jesus. He maintained that her hymen remained intact and that she had never had sex with St. Joseph or anyone else.

There is a softer side to this strict saint that is revealed in his legend. One day, a lion came limping to St. Jerome on three paws. Jerome examined the fourth paw and removed a sharp thorn. The lion remained grateful for the saint's kindness and walked by his side every day to protect him and his donkey.

Hagar the Hagiographer

St. Jerome is one of the least popular saints in the Kingdom of Heaven. For centuries, the only group who would claim him as a patron were librarians. They had little choice because he had formed the first Christian library in his monastery at Jerusalem. There are no standardized prayers you can say to him.

A Saint Saved by His Mother's Love

St. Augustine (354–430) remains one of the most influential thinkers in the history of Western civilization. In his *Confessions,* St. Augustine tells us that he had been less than a model for sainthood in his youth. "Like water I boiled over," he writes, "with the heat of my fornications." He settled down with a mistress, and the couple had a son, whom St. Augustine called Adeodatus, meaning, "gift from God."

After a torturous religious pilgrimage, Augustine at last became a Christian, thanks to the tears of his mother, St. Monica, and the sermons of St. Ambrose. When his mother died, Augustine sold his property, gave the proceeds to the poor, and established a monastery. Eventually, he became the Bishop of Hippo in North Africa.

Hagar the Hagiographer

St. Ambrose, a Doctor of the Church, was a great defender of celibacy. He is often depicted in art as wielding a whip. This signifies the time when he had a rival bishop flogged for saying that marriage was just as pleasing to God as virginity. St. Augustine thought that this saint was the smartest man in the world because he could read without moving his lips. St. Ambrose is the patron saint of geese and orators.

St. Augustine Originates Original Sin

Augustine believed that all of us inherit an evil will because of the sin of Adam. We can't help ourselves. Everything we do is for our own satisfaction. Even when we help old ladies cross the street or give bucks to beggars, we perform these acts of kindness to demonstrate to ourselves, as well as to others, that we are model citizens. We can't do anything without self-interest. Our thoughts are centered on ourselves, and nothing but grace can change this. St. Augustine described this condition as original sin. He maintained that the basic nature of man is not good (as humanists presume) and not a blank tablet (as philosophers assume), but evil (as scripture shows). "If you want to see original sin," he wrote, "look at the children in a nursery."

Before the fall of Adam, St. Augustine said that man and woman could completely control their sex organs. They were totally free of animal instinct. He said that proof of this original power of mind over matter resides in the ability of some people to wiggle their ears and of others to expel gas in a musical manner.

No Saint Belongs in Brooklyn

St. Augustine came up with the first philosophy of history in his efforts to explain the fall of Rome in 410. He wrote in *The City of God* that there are two cities, two human societies. The one city is the temporal city (personified by Rome) that is controlled by the devil. The other city is the eternal Kingdom of Heaven that is governed by God. The inhabitants of the temporal city are motivated by love of the flesh. The inhabitants of the eternal city are motivated by the love of the spirit. The followers of Cain belong to the earthly city; the followers of Abel belong to the city of God. One is headed for destruction; one is headed for glory. The city of man is represented by Rome; the City of God is represented by the Catholic Church.

St. Thomas Chases a Floozy with a Firebrand

The greatest Doctor of the Church is St. Thomas Aquinas (1225–1274). When he was a young noble in the Italian village of Aquino, Thomas told his parents of his wish to become a Christian monk. They were horrified by this career choice. His mother (Countess Theodora) had him kidnapped from the monastery (to which he had retreated) and locked him up in a tower of the family castle. His brothers (both good military men) sent a luscious harlot to his room in the middle of the night. The saint managed to drive away the strumpet with

Hagar the Hagiographer

St. Augustine believed that God, in His infinite goodness, calls all men and women into fellowship with Him. The problem is that we don't listen to His call. "You have made us for yourself," he writes of God in his *Confessions*, "and our hearts are restless until they rest in you."

Divine Revelation

St. Augustine's notion of the two cities comes from the letter to the Hebrews that speaks of Christians longing for and belonging to a city that is not of this world. It says that "the people of faith were longing for a better country— a heavenly one. Therefore, God is not ashamed to be called their God, for He has prepared a city for them" (Hebrews 11:16).

Hagar the Hagiographer

St. Albert the Great, another divine doctor, was the mentor of St. Thomas Aquinas. He traveled from place to place in wooden clods and was called a "clodhopper." He said that frequent sexual congress (an act that man "shared with beasts") could cause sickness, body odor, and baldness, and, when really excessive, could cause the human brain to shrink to the size of a pomegranate.

St. Peter Speaks

In 1880, Pope Leo XIII pronounced St. Thomas Aquinas not only the "doctor of the angels," but also the patron of all Catholic schools and Catholic students. He made it mandatory for all seminarians to study the thought of St. Thomas Aquinas as the official philosophy of the Church.

a blazing firebrand. When she fled, he fell into a swoon and had a vision of two angels securing a tight girdle around his loins. The good saint never again was troubled by sexual temptation.

His writings represent a response to the rediscovery of the writing of Aristotle in the thirteenth century. The Arabs managed to save the works of this Greek philosopher, and these "lost" works fell into the hands of the holy crusaders. When they reappeared in the West, eventually the writings of Aristotle created a sensation and a greater challenge to Christianity than the theory of evolution. Aristotle shocked the medieval mind by his claims that the world is eternal, that God is an impersonal Being with no knowledge of individual people or particular events, and that the soul is not immortal. The Church immediately banned the reading of the philosopher's works and ruled that his writings should be burned.

What's This About a Woman's Water Content?

In his hundreds of writings, St. Thomas managed to make Aristotle into a Christian thinker. He spoke of God in philosophic terms as the Creator of all beings, goodness, and truth; as a Being present in every living thing by His power and essence; and as the uncaused cause, in whom essence and existence, being and becoming, are and the same. (Does this make you scratch your head? It should! You can't understand Thomas without understanding Aristotle.)

On a more basic level is St. Thomas's take on women, whom he called "misbegotten men." The saint believed that women are more easily seduced by sexual pleasure than men because they have a higher water content in their bodies. He further wrote, "Nothing drags the mind of man down from its elevation so much as the caresses of a woman and the bodily contacts without which a man cannot possess his wife."

Forget the Head, How About a Toe?

During his lifetime, St Thomas established a reputation for holiness. On his deathbed, he beheld a vision and said, "All that I have written is straw." As soon as he gave up the ghost in 1274, his fellow monks cut off his head and boiled it so that it could be sold as a sacred relic.

Of course, these doctors are great—they are among the highest saints in Heaven. But for the highest saint, the greatest saint, and the most holy saint, you'll have to turn the page.

The Least You Need to Know

➤ Patron saints have privileged status.

➤ Cults are centers of saintly veneration.

➤ Only 500 saints have feast days on the liturgical calendar.

➤ Several saints have been designated as divine doctors.

➤ The greatest Doctors of the Church are St. Jerome, St. Augustine, and St. Thomas Aquinas.

Part 4

The Queen of Heaven

All studies of the saints must come to center on the Virgin Mary. She remains the most venerated member of the communion of saints. In fact, she is not simply a member of this community, but she is its Queen. St. Peter and St. Paul, along with all the other saints, bow before her. St. John and St. Joseph do her bidding, and all the other saints are at her command. She can appear as anything, anywhere, and can make demands on the faithful. She can order devotions to be held, shrines to be built, and countries to be consecrated.

More Catholics pray to Mary than to her divine Son. More than two billion Hail Marys are said every day. People travel throughout the world—to the most remote locations—to catch a glimpse of her. Every year, more than 1,000 Polaroid pictures are presented to the Vatican as proof of her appearances. Her shrines are major tourist attractions. More than 10 million people visit her basilica at Guadalupe every year, and five million visit her shrine at Lourdes. There are five bleeding statues of the Madonna in Italy alone, and hundreds of thousands of people come to see them. In recent years, Mary has made appearances in such places as Conchabamba, Bolivia, and Brooklyn, New York. Before you go to Heaven, you should get to know her. After all, she is your mother.

Chapter 14

You've Tried the Rest, Now Here's the Best: Blessed Virgin Mary

In This Chapter

➤ Mariology versus Mariolatry

➤ Veneration versus supreme veneration

➤ Mary's pious parents

➤ Mary's joys

➤ Mary's seven sorrows

You can almost hear the conversation in the early Church: "Sure, we should venerate Valentine, even though no one knows much about him, and we should create a cult for Clement—after all, he was thrown into the Black Sea with an anchor around his neck. St. Mathurion, even although he is associated with clowns, became a marvelous martyr, and St. Viviana (also known as St. Bibiana), although she is associated with hangovers, proved to be a very virtuous virgin. Sure, the saints were holy and inspirational, and they make great role models for everyone who wants to go on in glory. But, let's face it, there's just something about Mary."

There's Something About Mary

It's not just something special—it's something *very* special. After all, Mary is the Mother of God. Just think about that! If the saints have a high place in Heaven, then Mary must have a higher place—higher than anyone else. A good Jewish boy like

Jesus would always honor, respect, and obey His mushka. This only makes sense. Therefore, if the saints deserved *dulia* or "veneration," Mary must deserve *hyperdulia* or "supreme veneration."

Hagar the Hagiographer

We don't know a great deal about St. Zechariah. According to legend, St. Zechariah became a holy martyr because he refused to turn over his son, John the Baptist, to be put to death by King Herod during the slaughter of the Holy Innocents.

St. Peter Speaks

Mary is a subject in herself. The study of Mary is called **Mariology.** Throughout the years, many theologians have come to specialize in this subject. One of the foremost Mariologists of our time is Marina Warner, author of *Alone of All Her Sex: The Myth and the Cult of the Virgin Mary.* The veneration of Mary is called **Mariolatry.**

Zechariah Becomes Speechless and Sex-Starved

According to the gospel accounts, Mary's story begins with the conception of John the Baptist. Zechariah, a priest, was married to an old and barren woman named Elizabeth. While performing his temple duties, the angel Gabriel appeared to tell him that a son would be born to him who would be called John. Zechariah, knowing that he was long past his prime, asked for a sign that this wondrous prophecy was true. The angel gave him a sign by striking the perplexed priest speechless (Luke 1:8–25). Without saying a word, Zechariah returned home, had sex with his wife, and shouted with joy.

If You're a Saint, It's Never Too Late

When Elizabeth, who was post-menopausal, became pregnant, she spent five months in seclusion before parading around the marketplace in a maternity dress. "The Lord has done this for me," she told her friends and neighbors. "In these days he has shown his favor and taken away my disgrace among my people" (Luke 1:23–25).

Gabriel Says a Hail Mary

St. Luke then turns his attention to the Virgin Mary and the conception of Jesus. In the sixth month of Elizabeth's pregnancy, the angel Gabriel was sent on another mission from God. This time he was sent to Nazareth, a town in Galilee, to give a message to a young maiden named Mary, who was the fiancée of a man named Joseph. This event is known as the Annunciation.

When St. Gabriel the Archangel appeared before her, he said, "Hail Mary, full of grace, the Lord is with you!" Quite naturally, Mary was startled to find an angel before her and, according to Luke, wondered what in the world the strange creature was talking about. St. Gabriel then said to her, "Don't be afraid! You will be with child and give birth to a son, and you are to give him the name Jesus. He will be great and will be called the Son of the Most High" (Luke 1:26–30).

Oh, Stop It! I'm a Virgin!

Mary asked the angel the pressing question that has come down through the ages: "How will this be," she asked, "since I am a virgin?" Gabriel answered, "The Holy Spirit will come upon you, and the power of the Most High will overshadow you. So the Holy One to be born will be called the Son of God." The angel also informed Mary that, as a sign of God's power, her cousin St. Elizabeth had also conceived a son. Hearing this, Mary accepted her destiny with these famous words, her so-called "fiat": "I am the Lord's servant. May it be as you have said" (Luke 1:34–38).

The Annunciation represents the first solemnity (or very holy day) for Mary. Celebrated March 25, it is much higher than a normal feast day like the other saints are treated to during the liturgical year. If you are a real devotee of Mary, you will attend Mass that day and offer a series of prayers to her in honor of this event.

Unwed Mary Hits the Road

When the good Gabriel flew away, Mary immediately packed her bags and went to her cousin Elizabeth's house. Upon seeing the Blessed Virgin, St. Elizabeth felt her baby "leap with joy" in her womb. This caused the good woman to blurt out, "Blessed art thou amongst women and blessed is the fruit of thy womb" (Luke 1:42).

Elizabeth proceeded to call Mary "mother of my Lord" (Luke 1:43) and said, "Blessed is she who has believed that which the Lord has said to her will be accomplished!" These words provide the basis for the doctrine that Mary, as the Mother of God, is the Queen of Heaven. The Feast of the Visitation, a solemn day on the Roman Catholic liturgical calendar, is celebrated on May 31.

St. Peter Speaks

St. Gabriel and St. Michael are the two greatest archangels in the Kingdom of Heaven. Gabriel's legend informs us that he led the chorus of heavenly angels when they sang to the shepherds in Bethlehem. In 1952, Pope Pius XII declared St. Gabriel the Archangel to be the patron saint of the telecommunications industry. In 1972, Pope Paul VI placed all postal workers (and stamp collectors) under his protection.

Divine Revelation

The name Jesus is the Greek form of the Hebrew name *Yeshua*, which, in turn, is a variation of *Yehoshua* (meaning "God saves"), or Joshua, in English. Although the name in ancient Palestine was rather common, it would prove significant because Jesus came "to save His people from sin."

The Virgin's trip to Elizabeth's house is called the Visitation of Mary. It is not a solemnity—that is, a very holy day, but rather it's a very special feast day that is celebrated on May 31. May, by the way, is the month of Mary, even though, as all devotees of Mariolatry know, the Blessed Virgin was born on September 8, which is another very special feast day.

The Skinny on Mary

The real story of Mary begins not with the Annunciation (as non-Catholics think) but with the legend of her parents, St. Anne and St. Joachim, a story that is completely un-Biblical.

According to "The Apocryphal Gospel of the Nativity of Mary" (circa 140), the barren St. Anne was married to a rich merchant named St. Joachim. When St. Joachim was told that it was unfitting for him to present offerings at the temple because of his childlessness, the saint fled into the wilderness, where he fasted for 40 days.

Sure, They Did It, but They Really Didn't Have Fun

As a reward for their piety and prayers, an angel appeared separately to each of Mary's parents, telling them that the womb of St. Anne would be miraculously opened "so that which is born may be acknowledged to be not of lust, but of the gift of God." The angel proclaimed that the child should be called Mary and that she would be consecrated to the Lord from the moment of her conception. Hearing this, St. Anne said, "If I bear this child, I will bring her as a gift to the Lord, my God, and she shall serve Him all the days of her life."

This pious legend provides the basis for Mary's title as "the Immaculate Conception." Most people think that the Immaculate Conception refers to Mary's miraculous conception of Jesus, but this is not the case. The title comes from St. Anne's conception of the Virgin Mary. For centuries, theologians debated over the words of the angel to Sts. Anne and Joachim that their child would be conceived "not of lust, but of the gift of God."

Many learned Doctors of the Church, including St. Thomas Aquinas and St. Bernard of Clairvaux, said that Mary's parents, being mortal, must have derived some carnal pleasure in the act of Mary's begetting, thereby infecting her with original sin. But, in 1870, the Blessed Pope Pius IX decreed that St. Anne and St. Joachim experienced not the least pleasure (let alone orgasm) during the conception of their daughter, and that Mary had been conceived without sin—that is, in an immaculate manner. Just what that manner was is a matter for your imagination!

The Sanctified Womb, or, How Mary Escaped the Sin of Adam

The Feast of the Immaculate Conception is celebrated on December 8. It the second of Mary's sacred solemnities and a holy day of obligation. This means that it is a day in which Catholics must attend Mass to honor the Blessed Virgin.

Before flying away, the angel also informed Mary's parents about God's plan for their daughter: "When she has grown up, just as she herself shall be miraculously born of a barren woman, so in an incomparable manner she, a virgin, shall bring forth the Son of the Most High, who shall be Jesus."

Mary Enters the First Kosher Convent

As soon as Mary was born, St. Anne and St. Joachim honored the promise they made to the angel. They gave their daughter to the Temple, where she lived with the high priests in perfect obedience until she was 12. At 12, she was returned to her parents because the priests believed it was high time for Mary to be married. Upon returning the virgin to St. Anne and St. Joachim, the high priests set about to find the perfect spouse.

St. Peter Speaks

The Virgin Mary as "the Immaculate Conception" is the patroness of the United States of America. If Americans want to invoke her in this capacity, they should say this prayer: "O Mary, conceived without sin, pray for us. O Mary, conceived without sin, pray for us who have recourse to thee. Amen."

Frank Sinatra Was Right: "Fairy Tales Can Come True"

Hold on, you're thinking! We started with a discussion of Mary in the Bible, and now you are talking about St. Joachim and St. Anne, Mary's early years in a Temple (the Jewish equivalent of a convent), and high priests hunting for the right husband for her. These stories that you're telling us are completely and utterly unscriptural. To make sense, you should separate the testimony of scripture from the stories about the saints, but you're not doing that! You're dissolving the distinction between scripture and folklore! And it's downright annoying!

When you turn to the lives of the saints, testimony from scripture and historical facts become intermeshed, if not interwoven, into folklore and pious

Hagar the Hagiographer

St. Anne's entire head, a priceless relic of Christianity, is now on display at Lyons, Apt, Aix-la-Chapelle, and Chartres in France, in Bologna, in Sicily, and in Germany. Parts of her body, for some unexplained reason, have ended up in Scranton, Pennsylvania.

Divine Revelation

The popes have made infallible pronouncements (statements on faith that must be accepted without question) only on two occasions. The first was the declaration of the dogma of the Immaculate Conception on December 8, 1854, by Pope Pius IX. In order with this pronouncement, all Catholics are compelled to believe that the Virgin Mary was the only human being ever conceived without original sin.

Holy Cow!

In many parts of the world, including the United States, images and even small statues of St. Joseph are buried in the front lawns of people who want to sell their houses when the real estate market is slow. Because Joseph was looking for shelter for his family in Bethlehem, it is believed that he will lead good Christians to a good Christian home.

tradition so that it is, at times, extremely difficult to separate one from the other. In the legend of a saint, the elements of scripture and tradition are meant to combine, although, at times, the combinations form more of a mixture (that quickly dissolves into separate parts) than a true compound.

There's something else you must know about this intermeshing of Biblical testimony and tradition. When it comes to Roman Catholicism, both elements are equally valid and true. For this reason, even though the Immaculate Conception comes strictly from noncanonical sources, it must be accepted as unquestionable truth.

Great Choice for a Groom: Eighty-Nine, Crippled, Poor, Forgetful, and Impotent!

The man finally chosen by the chaste priests in the temple to be Mary's husband was a widower named Joseph, who was 89 years old and had six grown kids. It wasn't that this old man really wanted to marry the 14-year-old virgin. As a matter of fact, he balked at the idea by saying, "She's a girl! I fear I should become the laughing stock of Nazareth!" But the high priests informed him that the marriage was the will of God. They informed Joseph that he would not really serve as Mary's chosen husband. After all, as the priests knew all too well, Joseph was not only past his prime, but also (like Bob Dole and so many other hapless senior citizens) a victim of erectile dysfunction.

Another thing that we know about St. Joe is that he was crippled and walked with a staff. When he left his staff in the temple and hobbled off absent-mindedly to his hovel, the old man's staff magically transformed into a bouquet of flowers. When the high priests saw this, they knew that the senile senior citizen was a perfect match for Mary.

Mary Submits to a Really Strange Pregnancy Test

Joseph, Mary's fiancé, was very unhappy to discover his wife-to-be in the holy family way. He thought that she must have fooled around with some Philistine, if not the proverbial milkman. For this reason, he thought about dumping her, or, as it says in scripture, "getting a divorce."

While Joseph was considering his options, an angel (we don't know which one) appeared to the befuddled carpenter in a dream and said, "Joseph, son of David, do not be afraid to take Mary home as your wife, because what is conceived in her is from the Holy Spirit" (Matthew 1:20).

The legend of Mary and Joseph embellishes the gospel account by telling us that the couple became the subject of gossip and that they were dragged before the high priests. To decide whether Mary had committed an act of fornication, they ordered her to submit the dreaded test of the bitter water. If the water caused her to puke or gag, she would betray her guilt and would be subjected to a stoning. If she could drink the water, she would show her innocence. Mary quaffed the liquid as though it were a refreshing glass of lemonade.

Mary and Joseph did not stay very long in their comfortable little hut. The emperor Augustus issued a decree that each man was to be taxed in the city of his birth. So Joseph left for Bethlehem with his bride, "who was great with child," on a three-day trek across the wilderness.

Holy Cow!

In ancient Palestine, betrothal (getting engaged) was just as binding as marriage. If a woman's fiancé died before the wedding, she was considered a widow. Betrothal lasted about a year, and an act of unfaithfulness was viewed as an act of adultery.

Hagar the Hagiographer

Although dominant tradition, including the testimony of St. Epiphanus, maintains that St. Joseph was 89 at the time of his marriage to Mary, another legend says that he was 33 (the perfect age) at the time of Christ's birth. This tradition is captured in a work called *The Mystical City of God* by a fifteenth-century nun named Sr. Mary of Agreda. In this work, Joseph is a virile but celibate carpenter who eats meat, unlike his wife, who is depicted as a devout vegetarian. He can also perform feats of Herculean strength that would put Samson to shame.

The Christmas Story, with a Touch of Science Fiction

At Bethlehem, the Blessed Virgin gave birth to her Son in a place that could have been a cave or a barn. We know only that the place contained a manger—a feeding trough for domestic animals—and that the holy family could not find a room at the inn or nearby caravansary. According to such early Christian works as *The Proto-Gospel of James,* the entire world came to a screaming halt the moment Jesus was born. St. Joseph, who was wandering around the streets of Bethlehem looking for a midwife, noticed that everything had stopped moving, even the bats and birds in the sky. According to this apocalyptic account, "Sheep were being driven by shepherds and yet they did not come forward. The shepherds tried to strike them but their staffs remained suspended in the air. And then, all at once, everything went on as before."

That night the shepherds in their fields were told of the blessed birth by a heavenly choir of angels and went to the barn to visit the baby Jesus in adoration. The shepherds proceeded to tell Mary and Joseph what they had seen in the Heavens, but Mary, we are told, "kept all these things and pondered them in her heart" (Luke 2:19).

Divine Revelation

Bethlehem, the town where King David and Jesus were born, is situated on a low but steep ridge just south of Jerusalem. Since the time of David, Bethlehem was the site of a large caravansary or inn because it was situated on the main route between Jerusalem and Egypt.

St. Peter Speaks

Mary is celebrated by more solemnities, or very holy days, than anyone else, except Jesus. Only seven other saints are celebrated with such profound devotion: St. Joseph (solemnity on March 19), St. John the Baptist (whose birth is celebrated by a solemnity on June 24), Sts. Peter and Paul (who are celebrated with a joint solemnity on June 29), and Sts. Michael, Gabriel, and Raphael (the archangels) who are celebrated on September 29. All the saints, of course, are treated to a solemnity on November 1 (party day in Heaven), which is another holy day of obligation.

Mary Gets Slapped with Seven Sorrows

After the birth, according to Jewish law, Mary had to remain separate from all religious ceremonies for 40 days, the first 7 of which she would have been considered "unclean." The end of this period marks the Solemnity of Mary, another holy day of obligation. It is celebrated on January 1. Because Jesus was circumcised on this day, the first of the year used to be celebrated as the Feast of the Circumcision. This third of the four solemnities of Mary is not meant to signify that the Blessed Virgin became ritually clean. She needed no cleansing because she was born without sin and was conceived without sex. It is rather celebrated to remind us that she is not just the mother of a human being named Jesus, but rather the one and only Mother of God.

When the 40 days were over, the holy family traveled five miles north to Jerusalem for the rites of purification and the sacrifice at the Temple. For this rite, Mary was required to sacrifice two pigeons, or doves, that Joseph bought for a few shekels in the courtyard. After this ritual was performed, an old priest named Simeon took the baby Jesus in his arms, said a prayer over the child, and turned to Mary and said, "This child is destined to be the downfall of many in Israel, a sign that will be opposed—and you yourself will be pierced with a sword—so that the thoughts of many hearts may be laid bare." These words are the source for the Catholic devotion to Mary as Our Lady of Sorrows, a devotion that is represented by a sword piercing the Blessed Virgin's breast. Her seven sorrows, according to Mariologists, are as follows:

1. The prophecy of St. Simeon (Luke 2:32–34)

2. The flight into Egypt (Matthew 2:13–21)

3. The three-day separation from Jesus (Luke 2:41–50)

4. Her meeting with Jesus on His way to Calvary

5. The Crucifixion

Hagar the Hagiographer

In the early Church, there was a fierce debate concerning Mary's true status. Some, like Nestorius, said that Mary was the mother of Christ. Others, like St. Cyril of Alexandria, maintained that Mary must be venerated as the Mother of God. At the Council of Ephesus in 430, Nestorius and his followers were cast into prison, and Mary's title as the Mother of God became official.

St. Peter Speaks

Just as Mary received seven sorrows, the Church affirms that she also received these seven joys: the Annunciation, the Visitation, the Nativity of our Lord, the Adoration of the Magi, the Finding of the Child Jesus in the Temple, the Apparition of the Risen Christ to His Mother, and the Assumption and Coronation of the Blessed Virgin in Heaven.

6. The removal of Christ's body from the cross
7. The burial of Jesus

No Limbo for These Kids: The First Christian Martyrs

Having already received her first sorrow, Mary's second sorrow struck when King Herod, knowing that the Messiah had been born, issued an order that all boys two years and under be put to the sword. Warned of the impending "slaughter of the innocents" in a dream, the holy family headed for Egypt, where they stayed in hiding until Herod was dead.

Thank Heaven He Didn't Have Toy Soldiers!

The scriptures don't tell us much about the childhood of Jesus, let alone the weird relationship between Mary and Joseph. The noncanonical gospels are the only sources for this material. In the apocryphal Gospel of Thomas, we are told that the child Jesus loved to make clay sparrows and to bring them to life. He also worked in the carpenter shop, where Joseph allegedly got a good government contract: to make crosses for public executions.

The canonical gospels recorded only one incident, which took place when Jesus was 12. The holy family settled in Nazareth when Jesus was three, and, like good Jews, journeyed to Jerusalem every year to celebrate the Feast of the Passover. On their way home, Mary and Joseph discovered that their son (in Joseph's case, "adopted son") was missing. The frantic parents returned to the holy city and looked for Jesus for three days in every nook and cranny. Finally, Mary and Joseph found Him sitting among the teachers in the Temple and asking them questions. When his parents scolded Jesus for taking off without telling them where He was going, He said, "Why were you searching for me? Didn't you know I had to be in my Father's house" (Luke 2:41–49). Mary and Joseph, we are told, didn't understand what He was saying, but Mary "treasured all these things in her heart."

Hagar the Hagiographer

The male children who were slaughtered by King Herod are celebrated as the first Christian martyrs. They are the patrons of babies and choirboys. On the feast day for "the Holy Innocents," English parents whipped their children as they lay in bed. This ceremony was known as Childermas.

By the three days of separation from Jesus, Mary's heart was pierced by the third of the seven swords of sorrow. The reunion of the holy family in Jerusalem is celebrated as the Feast of the Holy Family, with Joseph and Mary as models of domestic life and Christian holiness.

Okay, Mary, What About the Seven Other Kids?

The next years of Mary's life are lost to us, but, according to hagiography, Joseph remained ever chaste and Mary remained ever virgin. This assertion appears to be contradicted by a passage in Mark's gospel that states that Jesus had brothers and sisters, and mentions the names of His brothers as James, Joseph, Judas, and Simon. But tradition holds that these brothers were Joseph's children from his previous marriage. And they were not kids—they were old men (in their 70s and 80s) with grandchildren.

Despite this troublesome reference in scripture (Mark 3:31–45) to Jesus having brothers and sisters, the belief in Mary's perpetual virginity persisted in primitive Christian communities. In 649, Pope Martin V said that the belief in Mary as "Ever Virgin," must be received as matter of faith. Mary, the Pope said, was a virgin at the time of her conception and afterward.

Wrap Joe's Soul and Take It Away

Pious tradition, rather than scripture, tells us that Joseph died when he reached the age of 111, several years before Jesus began His public ministry. According to *The History of Joseph the Carpenter*, the old man was in remarkably good health at the time of his death. His sight never failed, he had no noticeable weaknesses (except his lameness), and he still had all his teeth. Before he died, Joseph saw Jesus at the side of his bed and cried out, "O Jesus, my Savior, the deliverer of my soul! O Jesus, my protector!"

Having said these words, the archangels Michael and Gabriel appeared to remove St. Joseph's soul from his body. They placed the soul in a "shining wrap" (aluminum foil or cellophane?) and took it to Heaven. He is hailed as the patron saint of a happy death because the old man died in the company of Mary and Jesus.

He'd Rather Be Dead Than Red

In 1933, St. Joseph became hailed as the "patron of those who combat atheistic communism" by Pope Pius XI—after all, he was a carpenter, a blue-collar

Hagar the Hagiographer

St. Jerome, the great Doctor of the Church, objected to the depiction of St. Joseph as a hoary-headed old widower. He preferred to think of him as a robust, middle-aged carpenter. He wrote, "He who was worthy to be called the father of the Lord remained a virgin." The names of the brothers and sisters of Jesus were the names of cousins or friends. The Jews, he said, had a limited vocabulary for close relationships.

Holy Cow!

In medieval plays and pageants, St. Joseph was depicted as a comic figure, who is benign, good-natured, and absent-minded. He was called "the Divine Cuckold."

worker. The feast day of "St. Joseph, the Worker" was set for May 1, as a sort of Christian counter-demonstration to the godless celebration of May Day in Red China and the USSR.

With the death of St. Joseph, the early life of St. Mary comes to an end. The next time we encounter the Virgin is at a wedding party in Cana of Galilee, where, at her request, the good Lord performs His first miracle.

The Least You Need to Know

➤ The study of Mary in Christian thought is called Mariology.

➤ The veneration of Mary is Mariolatry.

➤ Mary is the only saint who is supposed to receive "supreme veneration."

➤ Many teachings and doctrines about Mary come from folklore.

➤ Mary is hailed not as the mother of Christ, but as the Mother of God.

Chapter 15

Mary II, the Sequel: How the Blessed Virgin Captured the Throne of Heaven

In This Chapter

- ➤ Mary, the Intercessor
- ➤ Ways to win the Virgin's attention
- ➤ Mary's Dormition
- ➤ Mary's Assumption
- ➤ The Mary craze

One of the most significant stories in the Bible for the study of the saints is the account of the wedding feast at Cana, where Jesus changed water into wine. This is not one of the Lord's great miracles, like walking on water, raising the dead, or calming a tempest at sea. As a matter of fact, it might be one of the least impressive, but, when it comes to hagiography and Mariology, it's the most important.

Mary Gets Her Way with Jesus

Most of us know the story. Jesus attended a wedding in Galilee with His mother and His disciples. Everybody had a good time, including St. Simon, the Zealot, who, according to tradition, was the groom. Then a problem occurred. The parents of the bride and groom ran out of wine. They turned to Mary for help. Mary, in turn, went to Jesus and said, "They have no wine." Jesus answered, "Dear woman, why do you involve me? My time has not yet come." But Mary persisted and told the servants to follow her Son's instructions. Jesus told the servants to fill six stone water jars, each of which could hold 20 to 30 gallons, with water. When the jars were filled, Jesus transformed the well water into Manischevitz, or some other kosher wine (John 2:1–11).

Come On, Do It for Your Mother!

This story might not seem significant until you really think about it. Jesus did not want to perform this miracle. He said that the time wasn't right. And yet His mother said, "Listen, Jesus, do this for me." And, guess what? He did. Jesus changed His mind for the sake of His mother. She interceded and succeeded! That's why the story is so important. It shows that Mary can get Jesus to do things for her, simply because she's His mother!

According to Mariolatry, Mary is still His mother, and He still listens to her. She is with Him in Heaven just as she was with Him on earth. She is alive, just as He is alive, and she communicates with Him. Mary can still intercede and succeed!

Jesus Would Have Probably Told Anyone Else, "Forget It!"

Think about the lesson of this story a bit more. If the parents of the bride and groom went directly to Jesus, He might not have performed this miracle. He might have said, "I can't do anything about your problem right now." Everybody would have been served water, and the celebration would have come to a screeching stop. But the parents went to Mary, and she got the job done because she has influence over Jesus—more influence over Him than anyone else.

Sure, you might go to one of your favorite saints to obtain a divine favor for you. If you are Spanish, you can turn to St. Emillion; if you are Welsh, you can turn to St. David; if you are Italian, you can turn to St. Catherine of Siena or St. Francis of Assisi. That's all well and good. These saints are good friends and close companions of Jesus and He very well might perform favors for them. But, if you are really in need of an urgent favor, as all hagiographers know, it is best to turn to Mary.

Divine Revelation

The wine that Jesus made from water was of an extraordinary vintage. When the master of the banquet tasted it, he called to the bridegroom, took him aside, and said: "Everyone brings out the choice wine first and then the cheaper wine after the guests have had too much to drink; but you have saved the best until now" (John 2:9–10).

St. Peter Speaks

St. Jerome said that Jesus complies with His mother's wishes because the Lord upholds the fourth commandment: "Honor thy father and thy mother."

Three Ways to Win Mary's Heart

How do you establish a good relationship with Mary? There are three ways:

1. Pray to her on a regular basis.

2. Honor her on her feast days, especially her solemnities.

3. Praise her to others.

The next time we meet Mary in John's gospel, she is standing at the foot of the cross, where, upon seeing His mother with His beloved disciple St. John, the dying Jesus says to her, "Dear woman, here is your son." Then, turning to St. John, Jesus says, "Here is your mother" (John 19:26–27). From that day on, the gospel says, the disciple took Mary into his home.

Mary Is Your Real Mama, No Matter Who You Are

This scene at Calvary is the source for the affirmation of Mary as the Universal Mother. Vatican II spoke of this position, declaring: "Mary shared her Son's sufferings as He died on the cross. Thus in a wholly singular way, Mary cooperated by her obedience, faith, hope, and burning charity in the work of the Savior in restoring supernatural life to souls. For this reason, Mary is mother to us in the order of grace."

This means, whether you like it or not, that Mary is your mama. Maybe you are a Methodist and you don't want Mary as your protector. Maybe you are a Buddhist and you don't believe in the Virgin Mary. Maybe you are an atheist and think that all this talk about Mary is sheer poppycock. It doesn't matter. Mary is your mother, and she will remain your mother, even if you are in hell for all eternity. This means that you can shun St. Anne. You can disregard St. David. You can shuck St. Nick. But you can't abandon Mary, not even by denying her. Every person on the planet, according to papal decree, remains under her care as her children.

Hagar the Hagiographer

St. Emillion, the patron saint of Spain, lived in holy happiness as a hermit until the bishop ordered him to serve as a parish priest. He was dismissed from this position after he gave all the church's goods, including the gold chalices, to the poor. St. David, the patron saint of Wales, established monasteries throughout his country and ate nothing but bread, salt, and leeks.

St. Peter Speaks

What, you don't know the "Hail Mary"? Get on your knees. It goes like this: "Hail Mary, full of grace, the Lord is with thee. Blessed art thou among women, and blessed is the fruit of thy womb, Jesus. Holy Mary, Mother of God, pray for us sinners now and at the hour of our death. Amen."

Divine Revelation

The final mention of Mary in the New Testament is this passage from the Book of Acts: "Then the apostles returned to Jerusalem from the hill called the Mount of Olives, a Sabbath day's walk from the city. When they arrived, they went upstairs to the room where they were staying. Those present were Peter, John, James, and Andrew; Philip and Thomas, Bartholomew and Matthew; James, the son of Alphaeus and Simon the Zealot, and Judas son of James. They all joined together constantly in prayer, along with the women and Mary, the mother of Jesus, and with His brothers." (Notice the troublesome mention to the brothers again).

Mary Became Den Mother to the First Disciples

The final appearance of Mary (by name) in the scriptures is in the "upper room" in Jerusalem, where the disciples had gathered after the Ascension of Jesus into Heaven. Her presence with the disciples on this occasion is the basis for the belief and legend that she was present at the feast of Pentecost, when the disciples received the gift of tongues.

Mary Really Knew the Way to Go

For the rest of the story of Mary, we have to return to noncanonical works that were circulated in the early Church. According to these sources, Mary remained with St. John until the time of her strange demise—or, as we say, "Dormition." Because she was born without original sin, Mary was not subject to the penalty of death. For this reason, when it came time for her to leave the world, the Holy Virgin simply fell asleep. When this happened, Jesus miraculously appeared before St. John and the weeping apostles—who had gathered at the foot of the Virgin's bed—to carry His mother bodily into Heaven, where she awoke from her sleep to the applause of the saints.

Divine Revelation

In the Gospel of Luke, a woman, seeing Jesus, cries out from a crowd: "Blessed is the womb that bore you, and the breasts that nursed you." Hearing this, Jesus replied: "Rather, blessed are they who hear the Word of God and keep it" (11:27–28).

This story of Mary's Assumption has no basis in scripture. It comes from several sources that have been condemned as heretical. Yet this teaching must be accepted—along with the teaching of the Immaculate Conception—as unquestionable, even if not gospel, truth.

Mary's Life in Heaven

Mary lives with a corporeal body in Heaven, along with Elijah, who was transported to Heaven by a fiery chariot, and, of course, Jesus, who ascended into Heaven. The other saints have noncorporeal, spiritual bodies. For this reason, Mary can do things that the other saints are unable to do. For example, she can bleed real blood and shed real tears.

You might think that after 2,000 years Mary might be a bit of a fright, with no hair, flesh falling from her face, and no teeth in her mouth. But this is not the case. Her body is incorruptible. She remains forever young and lovely, just as she was when she became the mother of Jesus. There's something else about Mary: She doesn't smell of death and corruption. She smells of ethereal perfume, like the frankincense that had been given to her so long ago by one of the Magi.

One more thing you must know: Mary can appear in the flesh to anyone at anytime. What's more, she is likely to appear at the most unlikely places, such as a small town in Portugal and a village in Yugoslavia. Recently, she has even been spotted in Peoria, Illinois.

Mary Gets Crowned in Heaven

But the story of Mary's life (not to mention her afterlife) did not end with her Assumption into Heaven. Once she arrived in the celestial kingdom, she was crowned Queen of Heaven. This, too, is a teaching that, within the confines of Roman Catholicism, must be believed.

Holy Cow!

The feast of Mary's "Dormition," or falling asleep, was celebrated in eastern churches in the fifth century. The Assumption was not declared an official Catholic dogma until 1946; it was the second infallible pronouncement of a pope. Both pronouncements, as you now know, concerned Mary.

Divine Revelation

The Second Book of Kings in the Old Testament gives this account of the prophet Elijah's miraculous assumption into Heaven: "As Elijah and Elisha were walking along and talking together, suddenly a chariot of fire appeared and separated the two of them, and Elijah went up to Heaven in a whirlwind. Elisha saw this and cried out, 'My father! My father! The chariots and horsemen of Israel!' And Elisha saw him no more" (2:11–12).

Holy Cow!

The Blessed Virgin Mary is, far and away, the most popular of all the saints. More than two billion "Hail Marys" are said throughout the world every day.

St. Peter Speaks

Exegetes are scholars who interpret the Bible. The first exegete to provide this interpretation of the Book of Revelation was St. Jerome.

St. Peter Speaks

Why is the Virgin Mary called Our Lady? The answer lies with St. Jerome, who said that Mary should be properly addressed as "Lady" because, in the Syrian language, Mary means "lady."

Some might think that the idea of Mary being Queen of Heaven is totally off the wall. But Mariologists say that this teaching has a scriptural basis. Specifically, they say that this teaching is contained in the following passage from the Book of Revelation:

> A great and wondrous sign appeared in Heaven: a woman clothed with the sun, with the moon under her feet and a crown of twelve stars on her head. She was pregnant and cried out in pain as she was about to give birth. Then another sign appeared in Heaven: an enormous red dragon with seven heads and ten horns and seven crowns on his head. His tail swept a third of the stars out of the sky and flung them to earth. The dragon stood in front of the woman who was about to give birth, so that he might devour her child the moment it was born. She gave birth to a son, a male child, who will rule all the nations with an iron scepter. And her child was snatched up to God and to his throne (12:1–5).

According to the interpretation of pious Catholic *exegetes,* the woman clothed in the sun is Mary, the dragon is the devil, and her son is Jesus. The fact that the woman has the sun and the moon at her feet shows that she is the Queen of Heaven. Protestant *exegetes* don't buy this interpretation.

If Not the Queen, How About the Queen Mother?

The tradition of Mary as the Queen of Heaven stems from the fifth century. St. Gregory Nazianzen called Mary "the mother of the king of the universe." Similarly, St. Andrew of Crete hailed Mary as "the Queen of the entire human race, faithful to the exact meaning of her name, who is exalted above all things, save for God Himself."

When you think about it, the arguments of the early Church Fathers in favor of Mariolatry make sense (kind of). Mary has to be the Queen of Heaven who is referred to in the Book of Revelation because all Christians celebrate Christ as king. After all, Jesus told

Pilate that He was a king and that His kingdom is not of this world. Now, if Christ is the King of Heaven, then Mary must be the Queen of Heaven—if not, then, at the very least, the Queen Mother of Heaven. Because this is true, all Christians must venerate Mary with even more devotion than they display to worldly monarchs.

Forget Elvis and the Beatles: The Mary Craze Sends Christians into a Frenzy

Mariolatry erupted in full force after Mary was declared the Mother of God by the Council of Ephesus. It was like the outbreak of Beatlemania times a thousand. To understand what happened, we have to go back to 421, when a fierce controversy was raging between two Christian bishops: Bishop (St.) Cyril of Alexandria and Bishop Nestorius of Constantinople.

When Nestorius came into Constantinople after living in the desert as a hermit, the newly appointed bishop was shocked to find Christians fighting with words and fists among themselves over the question of Mary. The argument centered on this issue: "How should we speak of Mary? Should we hail her as the Mother of Christ or the Mother of God?" For Nestorius, the matter seemed perfectly clear. Mary, he said, had given birth to a man because the mere idea of a woman giving birth to God was downright ridiculous.

Don't Split Jesus into Two

But this answer did not settle the issue; it heightened it by raising another issue that was equally disturbing and equally volatile. By saying that only the human nature of Jesus was born of the Virgin Mary, Nestorius, according to St. Cyril of Alexandria, had divided Christ into two separate and distinct beings: One being was a finite character with a human

Divine Revelation

When He appeared before Pilate, Jesus said, "My kingdom is not of this world. If it were, my servants would fight to prevent my arrest by the Jews. But now my kingdom is from another place." When Jesus said this, Pilate queried: "Are you a King?" Jesus answered by saying, "You are right in saying I am a king. In fact, for this reason, I was born, and for this I came into the world, to testify to the truth. Everyone on the side of truth listens to me" (John 18:36–37).

Hagar the Hagiographer

The debate between Nestorius and St. Cyril was so furious that, after the close of the Council of Ephesus in 432, Emperor Theodosius had both bishops cast into prison. St. Cyril managed to get out of his cell by bribing several prison guards.

189

Holy Cow!

In the minds of the Protestant reformers, the words of St. Cyril of Alexandria seemed highly ironic because, through Mary, they believed, the human race really became shackled by the so-called "bonds of idolatry." John Calvin told his flock in Geneva: "There is no idol more detrimental to true belief than the Virgin Mary."

Hagar the Hagiographer

The depiction of Mary as the Second Eve is contained in the writings of St. Irenaeus (circa 180). He came up with the doctrine of recapituation, by saying that the deeds of Eve were undone by Mary, just as the sins of Adam and his progeny were balanced by the atoning work of Jesus.

nature who grew in wisdom, suffered, and died (just like everybody else); the other being was the divine Son of God who performed miracles, imparted spiritual truth, and rose from the grave. "You cannot divide Jesus in half!" St. Cyril screamed.

This terrible dilemma was finally resolved at the Council of Ephesus, where it was decided that Jesus had two natures that were combined into one person. Because they were combined in a miraculous way, you cannot say that Jesus has a split personality.

St. Cyril Becomes the President of Mary's Fan Club

This ruling decided something else, too. It decided that Mary is, in fact, the true Mother of God because she gave birth to both the human and divine natures of Christ. The effects of this decision were incredible. Shrines were built to Mary on the sites of ancient temples to such pagan goddesses as Artemis and Cybele. The feast of Isis, the popular goddess of the mystery religions, overnight became the feast of the Assumption of Blessed Virgin. The craze over the real Madonna, who wasn't just *like* a virgin but was the real thing, created the greatest of all Christian cults, the Cult of the Virgin Mary.

St. Cyril of Alexandria, the saint who, more than anyone else, gave rise to this cult, wrote of Our Lady in highly rapturous prose:

> Mother of God, who contained the infinite God under your heart, which no space can contain. Through you, the most Holy Trinity is adored and glorified, demons are vanished, Satan is cast down from Heaven and into hell, and our fallen nature again assumed into Heaven. Through you, the human race, held captive by the bonds of idolatry, arrives at the knowledge of the truth.

Mary Enters the Garden of Eden

As soon as she was acknowledged as the Mother of God, Mary became a major celebrity in Christendom. She received a host of other titles, including Co-Redeemer and Co-Mediator before God with her son. In medieval art, Mary came to sit at the right hand of God, with Jesus on the left.

Soon she became proclaimed not only as Immaculate Conception, Mother of God, and Queen of Heaven, but also as Second Eve. The argument by Mary lovers went this way: Eve was a virgin, and Mary was a virgin. Eve was visited by a bad angel, and Mary was visited by a good angel. Eve initiated the Fall of man, and Mary initiated man's Redemption.

If You Won't Help Me, I'll Tell Your Mother!

Stories about the Madonna circulated throughout Christendom. St. Caesarius of Heisterbach says that a youth was persuaded by Satan on the promise of great wealth to deny Christ, but he could not be coaxed to deny Mary. When Satan left, the youth repented and the Virgin forgave him. St. Caesarius also writes of a fellow Cistercian brother who offered this prayer to Jesus: "Lord, if You will not free me from carnal temptations, I will complain about You to Your Mother."

By the early Middle Ages, Christians prayed so much to Mary that popular folklore depicted Jesus as jealous. In one legend of Mary, Jesus appeared to a monk who deluged Heaven with Ave Marias from morning to night and said, "My mother thanks you for all the prayers you have been reciting to her, but, now and then, it wouldn't hurt for you to say a word to Me."

Mary had become so popular that the prophet Mohammed said that she was really the third person of the Trinity. It was just about this time when Mary started making widespread appearances throughout the Western world. We'll cover these in the next chapter.

Holy Cow!

In the closing cantos of *The Divine Comedy*, Dante writes this about the Virgin Mary: "Look now upon the face that is most like the face of Christ, for only through its brightness can you prepare your vision to see Him."

The Least You Need to Know

➤ Of all the saints, Mary is the most powerful intercessor.

➤ There are three ways to establish a spiritual relationship with Mary: pray to her, honor her feast days, and praise her to others.

➤ Mary did not die, but she was assumed into Heaven.

➤ The Council of Ephesus gave great impetus to the cult of the Blessed Virgin.

➤ Mary is hailed as the "Second Eve" because of her work in the Redemption of mankind.

Chapter 16

In the Flesh: Mary Begins to Pop Up Everywhere

In This Chapter

➤ Mary as Co-Mediator

➤ Mary as Co-Redeemer

➤ Mary visits merry ol' England

➤ *The Golden Legend* arrives

In January 1993, an ordinary guy named Ray Doiron, who spent his life as a bread truck driver, was getting ready for bed in his modest home in Renault, Illinois. Just as he was preparing to take off his boxers, lo and behold, a beautiful young woman appeared to him. She was dressed in white, and she spoke English without the slightest trace of an Aramaic accent. He felt a breeze as she spoke. She told him to pray for peace, to reject evil, and to welcome God. Then—poof!—the woman vanished into thin air.

Mary Makes Many Appearances

A few days later, the beautiful young woman appeared again out of the blue to the retired bread truck driver with the same message. "I came to you as a loving mother," the beautiful vision said, still wearing her white dress. "Why me?" Ray asked. "I picked you," the woman said, "because you are the least apt instrument. Therefore, people that know you will know this is not your word."

In the past, Ray had been a frequent visitor to Our Lady of the Snows shrine in Belleville, just a few miles down the road, and he knew the Madonna when he saw her, just as any other red-blooded, rosary-saying, bread truck deliveryman would. Realizing that the Virgin wished to keep in close contact with him, Ray began to visit her shrine again on a regular basis.

St. Peter Speaks

For hundreds of years, Catholics have viewed Mary as the Co-Mediator with her son, Jesus, for man's salvation. A **mediator** is a person who goes between two parties to resolve a problem. Catholics say that Mary goes between God and man to resolve problems, to plead cases, and to present petitions.

Madonna Wows Crowd in Illinois

The news that the Blessed Virgin Mary had appeared to the bread truck guy spread like crazy from Illinois to Kalamazoo. In no time at all, hundreds appeared at the shrine to kneel next to Ray to get a peek at the Madonna. Soon thousands were cramming the shrine. In a matter of months, Ray was kneeling before the statue with 6,000 tourists and pilgrims behind him.

This goes to prove a point that the real Madonna draws a large crowd whenever she appears and wherever she appears. Take the case of the six children in Medjurgorje, Yugoslavia, of all places. On June 24 and 25, 1981, the Blessed Virgin appeared to six children on the hillside of this remote village. These appearances might have been forgotten, but the youngsters, who ranged in age from 10 to 16, continued to have visions. It got to the point that the Holy Mother would stop by almost nightly for a chat.

St. Peter Speaks

Mary has been proclaimed a Co-Mediator in the plan of salvation for these reasons:

➤ She cooperated with God by knowingly and willingly consenting to serve as the virgin vessel for His Son's conception.

➤ She gave birth to Jesus, thereby bringing redemptive grace to mankind.

➤ As a mother witnessing her Son's death, she took an active part in Christ's act of atonement.

The Blessed Virgin Can Fly Without Wings

Whenever Mary appeared, she always hovered a few inches above the ground, even though she didn't have wings. She wore not her usual white dress, but a dress that was kind of drab and gray, with a white veil. The children guessed her age at 20 and said that she had black hair and blue eyes. There was something, however, that was very peculiar about her appearance: She wore a halo with bright stars around her head. And, guess what—she spoke perfect Croatian.

At that time, few people in the world had ever heard of Medjurgorje, and practically fewer wanted to go there. The place was located on the top of a rocky mountain that visitors had to climb by foot. There was no public transportation. There were no nice restaurants and no comfortable hotels. For years, the only thing new to appear in this place was an occasional mountain goat.

Let's Hope She Shows Up in Scranton

Word of the Blessed Virgin's visitations spread like wildfire, and tourism went through the roof in Medjurgorje. All inns were booked within a 50-mile radius of the mountainous village. The taverns and teashops were packed to overflowing. The shops were mobbed with customers. Suddenly, cottage industries popped up all over the place. The peasants, living under a communist regime without the proverbial pee pot, became thriving capitalists, selling rosaries, statues, miraculous metals, and religious souvenirs.

By 1990, more than nine million pilgrims had made their way up the rocky mountain to stand on the hillside with the kneeling children. Although few, if any, of the tourists caught an actual glimpse of the Virgin, several said that they smelled her, and the smell was of fragrant flowers.

People throughout the world are willing to spend their life's savings to catch a sight of her, and Mary sightings are now more frequent than reports of UFOs.

Holy Cow!

Mary is hailed as Universal Mother, Immaculate Conception, Second Eve, Queen of Heaven, and Co-Mediator. Soon she might be proclaimed (to the dismay of Protestants) Co-Redeemer of Mankind. Unofficially, she already received the title of Co-Redeemer more than 500 years ago. Lately, a papal commission has been established to examine the Virgin's status in this regard.

St. Peter Speaks

Holy days of obligation are days in which all Catholics must attend Mass. There are six holy days of obligation in the United States; three of them are feast days for Mary.

Divine Revelation

St. Salome, also known as Mary Salome, was the wife of Zebedee and the mother of the apostles John and James. She asked Jesus to allow her sons to sit next to Him in His kingdom (Matthew 20:22). She was present at the Crucifixion (Matthew 27:56) and was one of the women who discovered the empty tomb (Mark 16:1ff.).

St. Peter Speaks

Iconoclasts were religious extremists who went about the eastern regions of Christianity destroying the images of the saints as false idols. St. John Damascene believed that such acts were not only blasphemous, but also traitorous because a Christian's destruction of the images of Mary represented the same crime as a subject's defacement of an image or icon of the queen.

The Blessed Virgin's First Post-Assumption Appearance

The first appearance of the Virgin occurred shortly after she ascended into Heaven. St. James the Greater, one of the original 12 apostles, traveled to Spain to spread the Gospel. His mission was very unsuccessful, and the saint became greatly disheartened. As St. James sat by the road with his head in his hands, the Mother of God miraculously appeared to him. She gave to the saint an image of herself and a small column of jasper wood. The Virgin then instructed him to get busy and construct a church at that very site. "This place is to be my house," she said, "and this image and column shall be the title and the altar of the temple you will build." St. James obeyed the Holy Mother's instructions and created the first shrine in her honor. If you visit this church in Compostella, you'll find the image of the Virgin and the white column still on display.

Why did the Madonna single out St. James for her premiere appearance? St. James the Greater was the brother of St. John, the Beloved Disciple, who took care of the Virgin until the time of her Dormition. In other words, Mary was a close family friend. In addition, tradition tells us that St. Salome, the mother of James and John, was a close relative of the Blessed Virgin.

She's a Real Help: Mary Gives a Saint a Hand

The visitations of the Virgin were few and far between during the first Christian centuries. After the outbreak of the Mary craze with the Council of Ephesus in 431, appearances became more common.

One of her most famous visitations concerned St. John Damascene, the great opponent of *iconoclasts*. Brought up in the court of the Islamic ruler of Damascus, St. John became the chief financial officer for the caliph, Abdul Malek, in 810. Falsely accused of forging a letter, the caliph ordered his guards to cut off the saint's right hand. The guards carried out the order. In his agony, St. John cried out to the Virgin, who appeared to restore his hand to his body. When the caliph caught sight of the restored hand, he fell to his knees and became a Christian.

St. Peter Speaks

One of the most famous prayers to Mary is "Hail! Holy Queen." It goes like this: "Hail! Holy queen, mother of mercy, our life, our sweetness, and our hope. To you we cry, poor banished children of Eve. To you do we send up our sighs, mourning and weeping in this valley of tears. Turn then, O most gracious advocate, your eyes of mercy toward us, and after this our exile, show unto us the blessed fruit of your womb, Jesus. O clement! O loving! O sweet Virgin Mary! Pray for us, O holy mother of God, that we may be made worthy of the promises of Christ. Amen."

Humble Mary Visits an Uppity English Lady

In 1061, the Blessed Virgin made three visits to the Lady Richeldis de Farerches in Walsingham, England. During one of her visits, the Madonna treated Lady Richeldis to a visit of her old home in Nazareth, which was still standing. The Virgin showed the noble woman the exact spot where Gabriel had stood to make his Annunciation. Mary then instructed Lady Richeldis to build an exact replica of the small but quaint hut in Nazareth on the widow's estate at Walsingham. The Madonna gave these instructions: "Let all who are in any way distressed or in need seek me there in that small house that you will maintain for me at Walsingham. To all who seek me there, I shall give succor."

Holy Cow!

Every year, more than five million pilgrims visit the shrine of Lourdes, where Our Lady appeared in 1858. More than 10 million visit the shrine of Our Lady in Guadalupe, Mexico, where the Madonna made an appearance in 1754.

Horrors! Henry VIII Destroys the Blessed Virgin's Home

The Lady Richeldis did as she was told, and the replica of the Virgin's dwelling place became one of the greatest pilgrim sites in Europe. By 1200, a large church was built around the cottage to protect it from the elements. Many kings and queens came there to pay their respects to the Virgin.

The last king to make an appearance was Henry VIII, who loved to pay his respects to Mary with flowery poems and hymns. After he broke with the Roman Catholic Church, Henry ordered the destruction of the church and Mary's holy little house in 1534. In 1924, Alfred Patten, an Anglican priest, rebuilt the church, but the Virgin failed to appear to give him exact specifications.

Holy Cow!

The Bollandists, who check the accuracy of the lives of the saints, have questioned the veracity of the story of St. Dominic and the rosary. They point out that the first mention of this legend occurred 250 years after the saint's death.

Hagar the Hagiographer

St. Simon Stock is celebrated as the father of the Carmelites. The Carmelites originally were a group of hermits who lived in the desert regions of Palestine. When the Moslems conquered the Holy Land, these hermits were driven from their caves and huts. They migrated to Mount Carmel, France, where the first of many Carmelite monasteries was established.

Take Time to Count the Roses—Even If You Can't Smell Them

Of all the visitations during the Middle Ages, the most significant one occurred in Prouille, France, in 1208. On that occasion, Mary appeared to St. Dominic and taught him to pray the rosary and to use the rosary as a remedy for sin, especially the sin of heresy.

The first rosary appeared in the form of a wreath of roses—50 roses that were separated into groupings of 10. Upon touching each rose, St. Dominic was told to say a Hail Mary. Upon the completion of 10 Hail Marys or one "decade," the saint was instructed to say one Our Father and one doxology ("Glory be to the Father, the Son, and the Holy Ghost). For each decade, the preacher was told to meditate on one mystery of the life of Jesus and Mary.

Mary Takes Stock of St. Simon with a Scapular

The next significant appearance of the Blessed Virgin occurred to St. Simon Stock in 1251. Driven from the Holy Land by the Muslim hordes, St. Simon returned home to England, where he became the prior of a Cistercian monastery at Mount Carmel. One day as he was praying the rosary, Mary appeared to him with something called a scapular in her hand. No one had ever seen a scapular before. It consisted of two pieces of brown cloth—each with an embroidered image of the Virgin—tied together with a string. The cloth seemed to come from a monk's cloak that hangs from the shoulders. *Scapula* is the Latin word for "shoulder." Maybe that's why Mary called it a scapular.

In any case, the Virgin told St. Simon that this rather ordinary and cheap-looking scapular was more priceless than the most exquisite DeBeers necklace. "My beloved son," she said to the saint, "receive this scapular for your order. It is a special sign of a privilege that I have obtained for you and for all God's children who honor me as Our Lady of Mount Carmel. Those who die devotedly clothed with this scapular shall be preserved from eternal fire. The brown scapular is a badge of salvation. The brown scapular is a shield in time of danger. The brown scapular is a pledge of peace and protection until the end of time."

Introducing a No-Risk, 100 Percent Guaranteed, Very Inexpensive After-Life Insurance Policy

St. Simon Stock and his fellow Carmelites began to make and distribute scapulars for Christians throughout the world. The saint died in 1265 and immediately became the patron saint of tanners.

Are you wearing a scapular? If not, then you need your spiritual head examined. Think about it: They are very inexpensive—less than $5 in any religious gift shop—and they can keep you and your loved ones from going to hell. No After-Life Insurance is available at such a low price.

Holy Cow!

You've never seen a scapular? They look like two oversized postage stamps connected by a string for you to wear around your head. Because the cloth is taken from a monk's robe, a scapular is supposed to remind you that you are called to a life of prayer.

She Still Gives Milk to Her Good Children

During this time, when Mary was in her heyday, a French prior, Gautier de Coincy, collected many of the existing legends into a tremendous poem of 30,000 lines that he dedicated to the Virgin. In these lines, we find the Madonna curing a sick monk by having him suck milk from her breasts; a robber who prayed to her before being hanged, only to be supported from strangling by her invisible hands; and a nun who left the convent for a life of sin, returned years later in broken repentance, and found that the Virgin had taken her place so that the other nuns had never noticed her absence.

In 1290, Iacopo de Voragine, Archbishop of Genoa, compiled stories of Mary and the other saints for a collection called *The Golden Legend*. This marvelous book contains a lesson and a legend about a saint

Divine Revelation

Because the reading of scripture often gave rise to heresy, such as the Cathari, the Church taught that the Old and the New Testaments are not self-explanatory and should not be read without official permission. The most widely read books by nuns and priests during The Middle Ages were *The Romance of the Rose*, *Reynard the Fox*, and *The Golden Legend*.

for every day of the year. For centuries, it was read aloud daily to monks and nuns as they dined in silence. Many of the most famous stories of Mary are contained in these pages.

One story concerns a widow who permitted her only son to go off on a holy crusade. The boy was captured by the Turks and cast in a cell. The widow prayed daily to the Virgin to obtain her son's release. When months passed by without a response, the widow stole a statue of the infant Jesus from a chapel and hid Him under her bed. That night, the Virgin opened the door to the prison, released the youth, and told him: "Tell your mother to return my Son now that I have returned you."

The Least You Need to Know

➤ Mary is called the Co-Mediator of man's salvation.

➤ St. James beheld the first apparition of the Blessed Virgin.

➤ St. Simon Stock was told of the secret of the scapular.

➤ The lives of the saints were compiled into *The Golden Legend*.

Chapter 17

More Mary Sightings

In This Chapter

➤ St. Teresa of Avila's mystical vision

➤ Our Lady of Guadalupe

➤ The Miracle at Fatima

➤ Mary's television debut

I know what you're thinking: "Why four chapters on Mary?" It's not fair. The 12 apostles are compressed into one chapter. St. Patrick gets merely a few pages. St. Agnes is passed over in a paragraph or two. And St. David is dismissed in a sentence. And here we have another complete chapter on the Queen of Heaven. Give us a break.

Mary's on the Move

But the other saints are quite content to remain in Heaven. Few people receive a visit even from St. Peter—one of the last times he popped up was in St. Agatha's prison cell. Speaking of St. Agatha, where has she been for the past 1,800 years? And St. Paul was one of the greatest apostles, but one rarely sees him. He stays in Heaven with the other saints.

Come See Us, St. Zita

All of the 10,000-plus saints can do us a favor. They can put in a good word for us with God. But they don't materialize before our eyes. As a matter of fact, they don't even speak to the people who venerate them as patrons. Their statues don't come alive and bleed. And only rarely do their relics liquefy (St. Januarius being an exception). They don't pop up in hillsides and hotel rooms to sing hymns or recite prayers—not even to scare the hell out of sinners. Even the Irish on St. Paddy's day can't catch a sight of the great saint—unless, of course, they've had a bit too much green beer.

Hagar the Hagiographer

The relics of St. Januarius are preserved in Naples. Eighteen times a year, a flask containing a few of his bones is placed near his severed skull. When this happens, the bones begin to liquefy, becoming bright red in color. At certain times, the liquid bubbles and froths. This is a popular attraction for relic lovers.

Holy Cow!

In the East, Mary is depicted as Asian. In Africa, she is depicted as an African. In Latin America, she appears as Hispanic. In Europe, she remains a pale white Caucasian.

One reason for the lack of sightings of the other members of the heavenly host is that the other saints—from St. Abdan, the patron of barrel makers, to St. Zita, patroness of housemaids—are reluctant to leave Heaven for any reason. They are happy just to remain before the throne in the eternal thrall of the Beatific Vision.

You Can Always Count On Mary

Another reason is that the other members of the community of saints aren't nearly as powerful as the Virgin Mother. Remember that Mary alone is worthy of extreme veneration. This means that she simply can't get enough respect, attention, and devotion. No other saint can command another saint to build a church in his or her honor. Only Mary can make such demands and receive immediate obedience.

A third reason is that Mary is the Queen of Heaven, not just one of the subjects or a member of the choir. She is a Co-Mediator and Co-Redeemer. This means that she is almost as exalted as Jesus. Because she is one of the two saviors of mankind, it only makes sense that Mary should leave her throne now and then to see what's happening on planet Earth.

The White Dress Is Really a Uniform

On rare occasions, the Blessed Virgin makes appearances with close friends, including her old and impotent husband and St. John the Evangelist, with whom she lived for many years after the Ascension of her Son. When St. John shows up, he is usually dressed as a bishop.

Throughout history, Mary has appeared to the high and mighty and the poor and lowly in churches and chapels, but also at some of most unexpected spots. And she hasn't always looked like a lily white Caucasian in a Holy Communion dress.

Divine Revelation

Mary's name has been said to come from the Hebrew word meaning myrrh and from the word for "bearer of the light." St. Jerome called her "Stella Maris," meaning a "drop from the sea." This name evolved into one of her many titles, "Star of the Sea." Other sources say that the name Mary comes from "Marah," the place of bitter water in the Old Testament.

St. Teresa Meets St. Mary

In the sixteenth century, Mary appeared before the great Christian mystic St. Teresa of Avila. As a young child in her native Castile, Teresa read the lives of the saints in *The Golden Legend* and ran away from home with the hope of being martyred by the Moors. At the age of 20, she entered a Carmelite convent and began to live a life of fasting, prayer, and self-flagellation.

After going for several days without food and drink, St. Teresa often fell in a swoon and had spiritual encounters with the Lord. These experiences caused either deep despair or complete ecstasy.

She Seemed So Young and Shy ...

One of her greatest spiritual adventures was an encounter with the Blessed Virgin. St. Teresa described her as a young and kind of shy teenager:

> The beauty which I saw in Our Lady was wonderful, though I could discern in her no particularly beautiful detail of form: it was her face as a whole that was so lovely and the whiteness and the amazing splendor of her

Hagar the Hagiographer

St. Teresa's heart is kept on display at her old convent in Avila. It appears to have been sliced several times (a miracle called transverberation), and it wears a small crown. One of her breasts, by the way, is in safekeeping at the Church of St. Pancras in Rome.

vestments, though the light was not dazzling, but quite soft. Our Lady appeared to me quite like a child, and I was struck by this.

Mary Makes Demands in Mexico

A radically different Mary appeared in 1531 to a converted Indian named Juan Diego on a mountain near Tepayac, outside Mexico City. The Virgin appeared once again out of nowhere, which struck Juan Diego with complete surprise. He fell to his knees before her and saw that she was "of exceeding great beauty, with garments that shone like the sun." Mary gave the humble Indian the same instruction she gave to St. James the Greater and dozens of others: "Instruct the bishop to build a church at this spot in my honor."

Like any normal person who received a direct order from an apparition, Juan Diego went to Bishop Zumarraga and informed him of the Virgin's demand. The bishop refused to believe the poor peasant's story and rudely dismissed him.

The Flowers Become a Photograph

Some time later, the beautiful Virgin again materialized before Juan, this time telling him to gather roses from a bush on top of a nearby mountain. Although it was December, the faithful Indian climbed the mountain and found the roses in full bloom.

Gathering the roses, Juan Diego returned to the doubtful bishop and let the roses fall from his cloak to the floor. As soon as he did this, the image of the Virgin miraculously appeared on Juan's humble cloak. The bishop became a believer and built a church, in accordance with Mary's wishes, in honor of Our Lady of Guadalupe.

In commemoration of this visitation, Mary was named patroness of Mexico in 1754 by Pope Benedict XIV, of Latin America in 1910 by Pope Pius X, and of all the Americas in 1945 by Pope Pius XII. As patroness of all

Hagar the Hagiographer

St. Teresa of Avila is the patroness of Spain. She is to be invoked against headaches and heart disease. If you have a problem of the heart or head, say this prayer: "Dear wonderful Saint, model of fidelity to vows, you gladly carried a heavy cross following in the steps of Christ who chose to be crucified for us. You realized that God, like a merciful father, chastises those whom He loves, which to people of the world seems silly indeed. Amen."

Holy Cow!

Scientists from MIT have examined the image of Mary on Juan Diego's cloak, which remains at the shrine in Guadalupe. They note that Mary's eyes appear to have captured the reflections of the people who were present when the miracle occurred. The cloth, made of woven grass, is in remarkable condition. Experts agree that the cloak should have disintegrated hundreds of years ago.

Americas, her image, dark-skinned like an Indian with lustrous black eyes, appears as a magnetized ornament on the dashboards of cars.

For some reason, Juan Diego, the simple peasant to whom Our Lady appeared and who was responsible for the creation of the Basilica of Our Lady of Guadalupe, has not been proclaimed a saint. This appears to be a gross oversight because he seemed to be much nicer than St. Catherine Laboure, whom you will meet later in this chapter.

At Heart, Mary Is a Parisian

For some unexplained reason, the Virgin Mary spent the nineteenth century in France. In the summer of 1830, St. Catherine Laboure, a member of the Sisters of Charity convent in Paris, was awakened in the middle of the night by a five-year-old girl dressed in white, who said, "Catherine, Catherine, wake up and come to the chapel: the Blessed Virgin is waiting for you."

Catherine followed the child to the chapel and found all the candles blazing and a beautiful young woman surrounded in white light sitting in the Father Director's chair. The child said, "This is the Blessed Virgin." Catherine fell on her knees and placed her hands in Mary's lap. The two women chatted for several hours about world conditions and the problems in France.

The Virgin Balances on a Ball

Five months later, the little girl again appeared long after midnight to summon St. Catherine to the chapel. This time the Virgin appeared holding a large ball that was topped by a small cross. "The ball," Mary said, "is the world, especially France." Performing a marvelous feat of balance, the Virgin stood upon the ball, and a green serpent appeared beneath her feet. An oval shape appeared around the Virgin with these words in gold: "O Mary, conceived without sin, pray for us who have recourse to thee." Still standing on the ball, Mary posed and said: "Have a medal struck after this model. Those who wear it will receive great graces."

Hagar the Hagiographer

When asked the identity of the little girl, St. Catherine said that she was her guardian angel. Every Catholic schoolgirl is taught that she is accompanied through life by a personal angelic protector. In 1670, Pope Clement IX proclaimed October 2 to be the feast day of the guardian angels. These heavenly bodyguards are the patron saints of the police.

After the spiritual authorities were told of the Virgin Mary actually modeling in the chapel, they authorized the medals to be made. News of the apparition was reported in the press, and the medals sold like hotcakes. So many cures were reported that the medals were called "the miraculous medals."

Did They Really Have to Hack Off Her Hands?

After her visions, St. Catherine Laboure returned to her life as a religious sister, cleaning the chicken coops and caring for the infirm. She spoke to no one, except the priest in confession. Her superiors, who knew nothing of her identity, found her to be cold and aloof. She predicted that she would never see January 1, 1877, and, sure enough, she died a few minutes before midnight on December 31, 1876.

Her body now reposes under glass, and her clear blue eyes remain open and stare at humble pilgrims who bow before her. Her hands, however, have been severed from her body and now remain in her old convent, along with the chair on which the Blessed Mother sat. Visitors to the chapel scribble messages bearing their needs and intentions, and leave the notes for the saint to read before her small shrine.

Hagar the Hagiographer

If you want to call upon Our Lady of the Miraculous Medal, say this prayer: "O Virgin Mother of God, Mary Immaculate, we dedicate and consecrate ourselves to thee, under the title of Our Lady of the Miraculous Medal. May this Medal be for each of us a sure sign of your affection for us, and a constant reminder of our duties to you. Ever while wearing it, may we be blessed by thy loving protection and preserved in the grace of thy Son. O most powerful Virgin, Mother of our Savior, keep us close to you every moment of our lives. Obtain for us, your children, the grace of a happy death so that in union with you, we may enjoy the bliss of Heaven forever. Amen."

It Was Mary, Not the Lord, Who Appeared at Lourdes

Twenty-eight years later, the Madonna appeared before a 14-year-old girl named Bernadette Soubirous, who could neither read nor write. St. Bernadette, who, besides being illiterate was also small and asthmatic, saw the Virgin 18 times in a grotto by a river near her home in the southern French village of Lourdes.

This sighting became one of Mary's most popular sightings and gave rise to a novel called *The Song of Bernadette* and a wildly successful movie (with a running time of two-and-a-half hours) that was released by 20th Century Fox in the midst of World War II.

If You Can't Smoke It, Eat It!

The Virgin ordered the sweet but simple Bernadette to do many strange things. On one occasion, the young girl scraped the ground to uncover a spring and ate some grass, in obedience to the Lady who imposed this unusual penance on the child.

As the visitations continued, the local bishop pressed St. Bernadette to discover the Lady's name. On the Feast of the Annunciation, Bernadette finally popped the question, and the Blessed Virgin replied: "I am the Immaculate Conception." This was in 1858, four years after the official definition of the Immaculate Conception was proclaimed by the pope.

Today, 27,000 gallons of water flow each day from the creek that St. Bernadette uncovered. Five million pilgrims visit Lourdes each year to buy some vials of this water that has been the cause of many cures. At the site is an underground church that seats more than 20,000.

Other apparitions of Mary in nineteenth-century France are as follows:

➤ 1836, Our Lady of Victories, Paris, to Father Genettes

➤ 1840, Blangy, to Sr. Justine Bisqueyburu

➤ 1846, La Salette, to Melanie Calavat and Maximum Giraud

➤ 1871, Pontmain, to Eugene and Joseph Barbadette and their five children

➤ 1876, Pellevoisin, to Estelle Faguette

Hagar the Hagiographer

By the time of the last apparition of the Virgin Mary to St. Bernadette at Lourdes, 25,000 people had gathered to see the young shepherdess pray to the Virgin.

Holy Cow!

When St. Bernadette first beheld the apparition, Mary was reciting the rosary to herself. This seems strange and makes you wonder how the Virgin said the prayers. Think about it. Did she say, "Hail Me, full of grace! The Lord is with me"? Sad to say, this pressing question was never answered.

Mary Visits Three Kids in Fatima

The most significant appearance of the Virgin Mary during the twentieth century occurred on May 13, 1917, at Fatima, a small village in Portugal. At this time, Mary materialized before three children: Lucia dos Santos, 9, and her two cousins, Francisco Marto, 8, and Jacinta Marto, 6.

When she appeared, Mary was floating on a cloud and fingering a rosary. "Don't be afraid," the Holy Mother told the children. "I won't hurt you." Lucia, who was the bravest of the group, approached the apparition and asked the beautiful woman where she came from. "I came from Heaven," the Virgin answered.

Let's Hope Francisco Said His Prayers!

The Blessed Virgin told the children to come to the same spot at the same hour on the thirteenth day of every month for the next six months. During one of these scheduled visits, Lucia asked if she would go to Heaven. The Lady said, "Yes, you will." Lucia then asked if Jacinta and Francisco would go to Heaven. The Blessed Mother said, "Also. But Francisco will have to say many rosaries."

On July 13, the Virgin Mary gave the children this instruction: "Sacrifice yourselves for sinners and repeat often, especially when you make a sacrifice for them, 'Jesus, I do this for love of You and for the conversion of sinners and in reparation for the sins committed against the Immaculate Heart of Mary.'"

Mary's Miracle Is a Scream

During one of her visits, the Holy Mother told the children three secrets:

➤ All sinners will go to hell. God will save the world only if the planet devotes itself to the Sacred Heart of Mary.

➤ A second world war will occur as a sign that God will punish the world for its crimes.

➤ God is coming to punish the world unless Russia is converted and dedicated to Mary's Sacred Heart.

On her final visit, Mary revealed herself as Our Lady of the Rosary. By this time, more than 70,000 people had gathered in hope of catching a brief glimpse of her. That's when the miracle of the sun took place. The clouds parted in the sky, and the sun appeared in a psychedelic manner. It appeared to spin faster and faster, shielding concentric silver light through the heavens. By the time the sun stopped spinning, it shed a yellow light over everyone and everything. The people cried out with alarm and then fell to their knees on the muddy ground.

Hagar the Hagiographer

Before Mary made her appearance, an angel visited the three children at Fatima and urged them to pray to the hearts of Jesus and Mary. Some hagiographers think that the angel must have been Gabriel because he remains Mary's favorite messenger.

Holy Cow!

In the past 30 years, Mary has made more appearances than all the previous centuries combined. She has been seen in such diverse locations as Akita, Japan; Toowoomba, Australia; Ninh Loi, Vietnam; Ballinspittle, Ireland; Naju, Korea; Ohlau, Poland; Terra Blanca, Mexico; Conchabamba, Bolivia; Manila, Philippines; Mozul, Iraq; Litomanora, Slovakia; El Escorial, Spain; Milan, Italy; San Nicolaus, Argentina; Damascus, Syria; Betania, Venezuela; Kibeho, Rwanda; Dozule, France; Rome, Italy; and Vladimir Prison in Russia.

The Two Newest Saints

The story of Fatima didn't end with this miracle. On May 31, 1981, Pope John Paul II was seriously wounded by a would-be assassin's bullet. The pope was saved from death because he turned to look at a young girl waving a picture of Our Lady of Fatima.

Holy Cow!

When Mary appeared at Fatima, she asked for Russia to be consecrated to her Immaculate Heart. Four months after this warning, the Russian Revolution erupted and the so-called "evil empire" of communism came into existence.

Divine Revelation

Pope Pius XII said that Fatima represents the greatest intervention of God through an apparition of Mary in world history.

St. Peter Speaks

The Virgin Mary has not appeared in Egypt since the lukewarm reception of her television debut in 1969.

The pope spoke several times to Lucia, who had become a nun, from his hospital bed. He read everything about Fatima and became increasingly devoted to Mary. In 2000, he presided over the canonization of Jacinta and Francisco Marto, who had died of influenza in 1919. Sts. Jacinta and Francisco are two of the newest saints in Heaven.

Mary Appears on the Tube

In 1969, the Blessed Virgin made her first television appearance. While Americans were watching reports of the Chicago riots and the war in Vietnam, Mary began appearing on the tube in Egypt. She was viewed by millions, including Egyptian President communist.

The Egyptians were watching their favorite programs when Mary appeared out of the proverbial blue tube. She didn't say anything. She seemed to float above the roof of St. Mary's Coptic Church with a dove on her head. She was bathed in bright light, and her image seemed kind of fuzzy.

It's Interesting but Kind of Monotonous

This was kind of interesting, but it continued. The next night, Mary appeared again in the midst of prime time viewing. She didn't say a word. She just floated silently above the church with her hands folded in prayer. The apparitions continued. One night the appearance lasted for nine hours. The Egyptians, who wanted to see "Gilligan's Island," became very upset. The local officials conducted a search of every property within a 15-mile radius of the station in Zeitun to see if the broadcast was a hoax. But they found no cause of the weird broadcasts.

The television appearances continued into 1970. The Coptic Patriarch Kyrellos VI said that there was no doubt in his mind that the Mother of God was appearing on the roof of his church. After all, the church was the site of the home of the holy family when they lived in Egypt. Even the Moslems were proclaiming the visions as miraculous from their minarets.

Finally, the apparitions stopped and programming returned to normal. Strange to say, these weird occurrences never captured the mass media attention. Everyone agrees that it would have been a better show if she had said a few words or wiggled her nose.

Mary Keeps Popping Up All over the Planet

The twentieth century was an incredibly busy time for the Madonna. She made more than 1,000 reported visits, including several stops in the Orient. In 1950, Mary Ann Van Hoof caught a sighting of the Virgin in Necedah, Wisconsin. It was her first reported appearance in the United States. Since then, the Blessed Mother has been spotted in Brooklyn, New York; Cleveland, Ohio; Wilmington, California; Conyers, Georgia; Marlboro, New Jersey; Lincoln, Nebraska; Hillside, Illinois; Endfield, Connecticut; Cincinnati, Ohio; Bayside, New York; Rochester, New York; Emmitsburg, Maryland; Belleville, Illinois; Massillon, Ohio; and Millbury, Massachusetts.

As a woman from the Middle East, Mary appears to be very partial toward desert heat. For this reason, she has made more appearances in Arizona than any other state. Phoenix and Scottsdale have become her favorite haunts.

Hagar the Hagiographer

In the past 150 years, the Virgin Mary has loved to visit the Emerald Isle. Her first appearance in Ireland took place on August 21, 1879, when she appeared to 14 startled women in the town of Cork in County Mayo. Since then she has been spotted in such Irish locations as Achill, Carns Grotto, Ballinspittle, Tyrone, and Bessbrook.

Holy Cow!

Of the individuals who have seen Mary in the past 30 years, 20 have been stigmatics. Stigmatics are individuals who manifest the five wounds of Jesus on the cross and bleed from the hands, the feet, and the side.

The Least You Need to Know

➤ Apparitions of saints, other than Mary, are very uncommon.

➤ Mary has more power and authority than other members of the communion of saints.

➤ Mary has materialized on every continent.

➤ More than 1,000 sightings of the Virgin Mary have been recorded in the twentieth century.

Part 5

Saints in the Twenty-First Century

It's tough to become a saint in the twenty-first century. You have a group of tight-lipped Jesuits called the Bollandists who keep expelling saints—very popular saints—from the celestial kingdom. And now you have all these restrictions to keep people—good people like you and me—from gaining entrance to the pearly gates. You have to live a chaste and holy life. You have to display heroic virtue. And get this: You have to perform some miracles. You might not think that this last part is tough until you realize that you have to perform miracles after you're dead. What's worse, you have to allow people to dig you up and examine your bones after you have been buried for many years. But, if you are really determined to become a saint, there is a way. Save your money, say your prayers, and turn the page.

Chapter 18

Heavenly Horrors! Saints Get Kicked Out of God's Kingdom

> **In This Chapter**
>
> ➤ Early basis for sainthood
>
> ➤ Medieval canonization process
>
> ➤ Lives become fairy tales
>
> ➤ Buddha gets canonized
>
> ➤ Bollandists expose bogus saints

The community of saints had gone insane. Heaven was becoming an asylum. It was filled with phony saints who had no respect for the holy martyrs, no awareness of Almighty God, and no knowledge of Jesus Christ, let alone the eternal mystery of the Blessed Trinity. And yet the bogus saints received the same reverence and veneration as the real heroes of the faith. It was enough to make even the most meek and mild member of the communion of saints scream with righteous rage and indignation.

How Saints Went Crazy

In the beginning, any Christian congregation could proclaim one of its departed members a saint. The criterion was simple: A saint had to be someone who died for his or her faith. That was it. When the early Christians were fed to the lions, members of their congregation removed their bones from the arena and placed them in the catacombs, which were the Christian underground burial sites. Over 750,000 bodies were buried in tunnels along the Appian Way and other roads around Rome. These tunnels were vast and measured more than 90 miles. The early Christians often could walk from tunnel to tunnel, or catacomb to catacomb. The labyrinthine passageways were often beautifully decorated with murals and sculpture. They contain the earliest examples of Christian art.

Smell Decay, Start to Pray

The 42 catacombs around Rome were not only the first Christian cemeteries, but also the sites of worship services. When they sang hymns, offered prayer, and read the "good news," the early Christians were surrounded by thousands of dead bodies. The stench of decay was often offset by the burning of perfumed candles and incense.

When a new victim of the persecution was buried in the catacombs, his or her name was recorded in the congregation's Book of Martyrs. Every congregation maintained such records. These books contained the dates of the deaths of the holy martyrs. At the anniversaries of their passing into glory, the names of the martyrs were read and their deeds was recalled, and the congregation piously proclaimed their sainthood.

Hagar the Hagiographer

The bodies of early Christians were buried outside the city of Rome. It was against the law for anyone—even an emperor—to be buried in the eternal city. Romans were buried in vaults above the ground or, if they were poor, cremated. Christians forbade cremation because they expected their bodies to be raised at the last judgment.

There's Something Funny About St. Philomena

This was all well and good, save for the fact that a few Christians looked around the catacombs and saw names inscribed above bones and thought that some good martyrs might have been overlooked or forgotten. And so, names were added to the Book of Martyrs that never should have been recorded with the lists of holy ones.

In fact, some names that came to be added to the Book of Martyrs were not names at all, but rather pious greetings. For example, someone found a vial in a catacomb with this inscription *"Lumena–paxte–Fi."* This was mistranslated to read: "Lumena, peace be with you." Gradually, an elaborate biography evolved around St. Philomena. It wasn't until 1968 that scholars found the source of the error. *Lumena*, as it turned out, was a common inscription in Roman cemeteries. It simply meant "dear one."

St. Peter Speaks

The word **cemetery** comes from the Christian use of the Greek word *koimeterion*, which means "bedchamber."

We Always Knew Bibiana Was Full of Something!

Another case in point is St. Bibiana (also known as St. Viviana). One inscription above the remains of a person buried in the catacombs was Viviana. Gradually, St. Viviana became depicted as a young virgin who had been put to death on a pillar during the reign of Emperor Julian. In reality, *viviana* means "full of life." The inscription merely bears witness to the fact that the dearly departed was someone who was probably a lot of fun.

But it gets even crazier. Because the Spanish pronounce the letter V and the Romans pronounced the letter B, The name of this saint in Spain became "St. Bibiana." *Bibiana* does not mean "full of life," but rather "full of drink." And so, St. Bibiana became the patroness against hangovers!

It got worse. After Christianity became the official religion of the Roman Empire, pious Christians found inscriptions above bodies in shrines, such as Hermes, Mercury, and Dionysus. In no time at all, many pagan gods got canonized and took their place along with the real heroes of the Christian faith.

Hagar the Hagiographer

As the burial places of favorite martyrs drew large crowds to certain catacombs for memorial services, vents were provided to let in light and air from the surface. People vied for the honor of being buried next to a martyr's tomb, hoping to share the martyr's happiness in Heaven.

Sometimes It Pays to Be Well-Dressed

In the fourth century, a man died during religious services at a church in Cremona, Italy. No one knew his name or anything about him, except that his cloak had been finely tailored. No one knew his family or any of his friends. Nobody knew where he came from or where he worked. But, what the heck, this guy died during the Gloria of the Mass. What's more, he died with his arms stretched out like someone who had been crucified, and the guy fell face down before the altar. Surely, this unknown Christian must have been a good man or "homo bonus." In no time at all, Christians were offering prayers to St. Homonbonus, who was depicted as a happily married cloth maker. He went on to become the patron saint of tailors.

Hagar the Hagiographer

By the seventh century, it was believed that St. Homonbonus worked solely to feed the poor and the needy. His head is preserved in the Church of St. Giles.

Sure, He's Dead, but He Should Do Something!

By the fifth century, the church decided that saints could no longer be canonized by popular acclaim—only by official recognition by a bishop. Bishops were told to gather testimony about the personal holiness of a Christian's life before granting him or her entrance into the heavenly kingdom. What's more, the dearly departed should not be proclaimed a saint unless he or she performed a miracle during his or her lifetime or, better yet, after death.

And so, as soon as a supposed saint died, bishops asked people questions about the person's life. People responded by telling stories they had heard from other people. This hearsay evidence, coupled with pious folklore, became the new basis of canonization.

St. Martin Gets Goosed

This new criterion for sainthood is evident in *The Life of St. Martin of Tours,* by Sulpicius Severus, a work that became a model for medieval hagiography. Written in 401, the book is filled with page after page of mind-boggling testimony to St. Martin's wonder-working ability, so much so that the reader easily loses sight of the fact that St. Martin was one of the Church's greatest missionaries to rural France.

In the biography we are told that Martin, who sought to live as a holy hermit, cured lepers with a kiss and raised several people from the dead. He exposed several falsely proclaimed saints with visions of the sanctified ones in hell. When the people of Tours sought St. Martin to serve as their bishop, the saint, not wanting the position, hid in a cave until his hiding place was revealed by a honking goose. The biography also contains accounts of Martin's own method of exorcism, whereby he expelled demons from the bodies of good Christians by administrations of holy water enemas.

According to Sulpicius Severus, Martin died in 400 on the pagan feast of Vinalia, when new wine is tasted. For this reason, he became the patron saint of drunkards, innkeepers, and, of course, geese.

The intended reform to canonization only made things worse. Gullible bishops proclaimed elves and fairies as saints. This can be witnessed by the life of St. Ia, a cute little pixie who sailed from Ireland to Cornwall on a leaf. At Cornwall, we are told, the pixie established a monastery that became known as St. Ives.

Holy Cow!

Every nation, city, church, craft, soul, and crisis in life had its patron saint; as in pagan Rome every aspect of life had its god.

St. Peter Speaks

Before becoming a convert, St. Martin of Tours was a celebrated soldier. He offered a prayer to God that has become a Christian classic: "Lord, if Your people still have need of my services, I will not avoid the toil. Your will be done. I have fought the good fight long enough. Yet if You bid me continue to hold the battle line in defense of Your camp, I shall never beg to be excused because of failing strength. I shall perform Your work You entrust to me. While You command, I shall fight beneath Your banner."

St. Dymphna and Her Dad

The lives of the saints often became as lurid as tales from the crypt. Take the story of St. Dymphna. This saint, according to her legend, was the cute teenage daughter of an Irish chieftain named Damon. When Damon's wife died, the distressed chieftain sought high and low to find a fitting woman to replace her. Then his grief-crazed eyes fell upon his nubile daughter. As soon as he revealed his depraved desires, Dymphna fled from Ireland with the help of a priest, St. Gerebernus, and a court jester.

After searching several months for a perfect hiding place, Dymphna and her companions settled in Belgium. Damon sent out spies who managed to locate her. The crazed chieftain crossed the sea, broke into his daughter's cell in a convent, and demanded that she commit a heinous act of incest. When Dymphna refused, her hopelessly insane father drew his sword and slew her where she stood. At her grave, miraculous cures of mental disorders, including epilepsy, began to occur.

St. Bee and Her Bracelet

Another strange saint's tale concerned a beautiful Irish princess, St. Bee, who became engaged to Jesus when she was an infant. As an engagement present, Jesus sent her—by means of an angel—a beautiful bracelet marked with the sign of the cross. When the king of Norway attempted to force Bee to marry a mere mortal, the beautiful princess slipped away from her castle and sailed to Ireland on a piece of sod, wearing nothing but her birthday suit and the beautiful bracelet.

Holy Cow!

St. Bee's beautiful bracelet is kept in a monastery at Bega, where it remains on display. For centuries, novices and newlyweds held it while making their vows.

219

Upon landing in the land of leprechauns, Bee was fed for years by sea gulls, gannets, and the little people. Eventually, the beautiful princess got some clothes, became a nun, and mended the clothes of anyone who would work to build her monastery. She became the patroness of laborers and the great friend of St. Oswald, who appears to have been a real person.

How Snow White (Along with Rip Van Winkle) Became a Saint

The stories of several saints became the basis not only of folk traditions but also of fairy tales. An early version of Rip Van Winkle can be found in the saintly account of the Seven Sleepers of Ephesus, who are the patron saints of insomnia. The story of Cinderella has its roots in the story of St. Germaine, Rapunzel in St. Barbara, and Snow White in St. Aldegund.

St. Aldegund was the beautiful daughter of Frankish nobility. Her parents, Walbert and Vertilia, were saints, along with her sister, Waudru. St. Aldegund's wicked step-mother, who was a sorceress, wanted this dedicated virgin to marry so that she herself could become the fairest in the land.

Before the arranged wedding day, Aldegund slipped away from her stepmother's cas-tle by crossing a raging river without getting wet. She ran into the enchanted woods, where she lived in a hermitage with several chaste and holy monks. Her stepmother and her jilted fiancé set out in search of her, but the Lord, in His goodness, granted Aldegund the gift of invisibility. True to the spirit of Walt Disney, this saintly fairy tale has a subplot, involving lovable cartoon characters. Aldegund had a pet fish who was attacked by a mean raven. The raven was finally frightened away from the cute little fish, who bubbled prayers in a pond by a ferocious, but truly Christian, lamb.

Hagar the Hagiographer

The Seven Sleepers of Ephesus were seven boys from Ephesus who escaped persecution under the reign of Decius by taking refuge in a cave. They walled up the entrance with heavy stones and proceeded to fall asleep for 363 years. When they finally awoke, one of the boys journeyed into Ephesus, now completely Christian, to buy a loaf of bread. He paid a merchant with an old coin that the locals believed came from a treasure chest. They followed the boy to the cave, where they found his companions yawning and stretching after a nice long nap.

According to her legend, Aldegund finally became a nun in a Benedictine convent in the wilds of Flanders. She became a disciple of St. Amand, the patron saint of beer, and had a number of supernatural visions. Aldegund developed cancer of the breast. She bore this agonizing affliction, including repeated incisions and probings with red hot pokers, with complete patience and trust in the Lord. She died in 684 and became the patroness against cancer and childhood diseases.

Proof That People Really Stink

Few of these stories are stranger than the legend of St. Christina the Astonishing. Orphaned at age 15, Christina became a consecrated virgin.

One night, the young saint suffered a cataleptic fit and was pronounced dead. She was placed in a coffin and prepared for burial. At her funeral Mass, Christina flew out of her coffin and squatted in the rafters. The mourners fled in horror, leaving only one of her sisters and the parish priest in the chapel. They coaxed her to come down. Christina related the story of her death and out-of-body experience.

She had visited hell and purgatory, saw friends and loved ones in both places, and was finally transported to Heaven. As soon as she entered the pearly gates, she heard the priest delivering her eulogy and caught a whiff of the people in the congregation. Their odor was so rancid that it aroused her from her coffin and deprived her of an immediate place in the celestial kingdom.

For the rest of her life, Christina found the smell of people so offensive that she spent most of her time perched on the tops of towers and weathervanes. She hid in ovens and cupboards, climbed trees, and even levitated to avoid anyone who came near her. The stench of men was particularly noxious. People couldn't help but notice her bizarre behavior and decided that Christina was bonkers. They attempted to confine her, but she could pass miraculously through locked doors.

According to legend, St. Christina the Astonishing lived in a way that was considered holy. She slept on rocks, wore rags, and ate wild roots in the forest. She often stood for hours in freezing water in the middle of winter, spent long stretches of time

Hagar the Hagiographer

The terrible stench of humanity, according to the legend of St. Christina, came from the corruption of sin. Everyone whom the saint encountered stunk to high heaven. Even the stench of venial sinners, such as monks and nuns, was barely tolerable.

Hagar the Hagiographer

St. Christina the Astonishing spent the last years of her life in St. Catherine's convent at Saint-Trond, Belgium. She was attended by pious nuns but always had to hold her nose when they entered her cell.

in tombs, and frequently rolled in fires without being burned. Moreover, she often allowed townsfolk to tie her to a mill wheel so that she could be continuously dunked for hours without suffering bodily harm. This truly astonishing saint is the patroness of madness.

How Buddha Became a Catholic Saint

More figures of folklore were becoming canonized until a truly terrible and utterly embarrassing mistake was made. Catholic bishops unknowingly proclaimed Buddha a Christian saint. The story of Buddha was carried by crusaders and merchants from the East and passed into the annals of the Church as the life of St. Josaphat.

According to legend, St. Josaphat was the son of an Indian king, who kept him under constant supervision to prevent him from becoming a Christian. Astrologers had forecast that Josaphat would be led to the truth and would become a great saint. Despite all the king's precautions, a holy hermit by the name of St. Barlaam disguised himself as a merchant and managed to convert the boy to the faith. Eventually, Josaphat resigned his throne to live a life of meditation with St. Barlaam.

This story is the story of Siddharta Buddha, and the name Josaphat is a corruption of "bodhisattva." Strange to say, even after this truth was uncovered, Christians continued to venerate St. Josaphat and to visit his shrine in India.

Holy Cow!

Buddhists believe that Siddharta Buddha was kept in confinement by his father, the raja, to prevent him from leading a life of prayer and meditation. The Buddha was enlightened by a pious ascetic who came to him in disguise.

Bollandists Expose Bogus Saints

But, with Buddha in Heaven, the Church had to take action to protect the communion of saints. By the fourteenth century, it was decided that only a pope, as the *Vicar of Christ,* could pronounce a deceased Christian (let alone a fairy, fey, or imp) a saint. By the seventeenth century, a group of Jesuit scholars, called the Bollandists, were commissioned to separate fact from fiction in the lives of the saints.

St. Peter Speaks

The Bishop of Rome is called the **Vicar of Christ** because he is the vicarious representative of Jesus Christ on earth. This means that the pope stands in place of Christ when he makes official announcements.

Thousands of saints were purged from official hagiographies, including St. Josaphat, St. Ursula, St. Catherine of Alexandria, St. Alexis, and St. Wildefortis, the bearded virgin.

By debunking the blessed ones, the Bollandists soon ran amok of Church authorities. When this group of Jesuits said in 1700 that the Carmelite order had not been founded by the Old Testament prophet Elijah in 875 B.C., furious Carmelite officials demanded an immediate retraction. But the Bollandists produced documents to prove that the order really had been created by a group of hermits in 1200 A.D.

St. Christopher Uncovered as a Giant Fraud—And a Cannibal

As the rules for canonization were altered and re-altered, more bogus saints were given the boot from Heaven by the Bollandists. In 1968, one of the most popular saints, St. Christopher, was removed from official *litanies* of the church, causing thousands of pious Catholics to scream to high heaven.

For hundreds of years, Catholics wore St. Christopher medals that came to serve as Catholic identity tags. If you wanted to know whether somebody was a Catholic, you looked to see if that person was wearing a St. Christopher medal or, at least, a scapular. If you didn't see the medal, you presumed that the person was a non-Catholic. It was believed that anyone who beheld the image of St. Christopher on a medal would be free from harm that day, so St. Christopher became the patron saint of travelers.

The real St. Christopher was an obscure martyr from Asia Minor who died during the reign of Diocletian. Medieval hagiographers developed the scant facts of this martyr's life into a full-blown fiction concerning a terrible giant named Reprobus who ate anyone who came his way. Reprobus was a blacksmith's son who wanted to serve the most powerful king in the world.

The 20-foot giant first joined the mercenary army of a tribal chieftain. He thought that this chieftain must be the most powerful king in the world until he saw his master tremble before a wicked sorcerer. Reprobus next sought to serve mighty Satan. Satan seemed all-powerful until Reprobus saw the devil scream in horror before a crucifix worn by a holy

Hagar the Hagiographer

St. Wildefortis was a beautiful virgin who consecrated her virginity to Jesus. When her father, the king of Portugal, pressed her to marry, St. Wildefortis prayed that the Lord would make her unattractive. Her prayer was graciously answered. Overnight, she sprouted a full beard and mustache. The wedding plans, of course, were cancelled.

St. Peter Speaks

Litanies are lists of the names of the saints that were included in the closing prayers of the Mass. The priest would intone the name of a saint in Latin, and the congregation would respond by chanting: *Ora pro nobis* ("Pray for us").

hermit. The giant next bound himself in service to the hermit, who became known as St. Babylas of Antioch and was given the task of helping people cross a treacherous river.

Hey, This Kid Weighs a Ton!

One day, a child appeared at the river and asked Reprobus to carry him across. Reprobus hoisted the child on his shoulder and almost buckled under the small kid's tremendous weight. The giant barely made it to the other side. Later it was revealed to Reprobus that the child was Christ Himself, burdened by all the sins of the world. Reprobus planted his staff by the side of the river, where it instantly transformed into a palm tree.

Hagar the Hagiographer

One legend of St. Christopher maintains that he had the head of a dog before his conversion.

Henceforth Reprobus became known as Christophorus, or "Christ-bearer." The giant then set out on a career of preaching and brothel closing. Eventually, Christopher was arrested by the wicked St. Dagon and sentenced to execution, but the arrows of his executioners remained suspended in midair. This story gave rise to the belief that anyone who beheld an image of St. Christopher would not die that day.

As the patron saint of travelers, St. Christopher's popularity soared in the age of the airplane and automobile. Until he fell into disgrace as a pious fiction, St. Christopher metals dangled from the rearview mirrors of cars that were even owned by non-Catholics.

Hagar the Hagiographer

St. Christopher is the patron saint not only of travelers but also of bachelors, bus drivers, ferryboat men, horsemen, police officers, skiers, and truck drivers. If you want to invoke him, say this prayer: "Dear saint, you have inherited a beautiful name—Christ-bearer—as a result of a wonderful legend that, while carrying people across a raging stream, you also carried the Child Jesus. Teach us to be true Christ-bearers to those who do not know Him. Amen."

The Least You Need to Know

➤ Popular acclamation produced the first saints.

➤ During the Middle Ages, bishops held the right of canonization.

➤ The lives of saints gave rise to fairy tales.

➤ Bollandists separated truth from fiction in the lives of the saints.

➤ St. Christopher was exposed as a pious legend.

Chapter 19

Sainthood Made Easy: A Step-by-Step Guide to Your Canonization

---

In This Chapter

➤ The rules of sainthood

➤ Making a case

➤ The position paper

➤ Beatification

➤ Canonization

So you want to become a saint, eh? Well, then, you've got to meet some criteria first.

Are You a Saint? Let's Check and See

Are you a saint? Answer the following questions to find out:

➤ If you have ever had an illicit sexual relationship with a member of the opposite sex, forget it!

➤ If you have ever belonged to some weird religious group like the Rosicrucians, forget it!

➤ If you have ever committed a crime, including not paying a parking ticket, forget it!

➤ If you have ever been involved in radical political action of any kind, including demonstrations during the Vietnam War, forget it!

➤ If you have ever spread a mendacity (in other words, told a lie), forget it!

➤ If you have ever absented yourself from Mass and the sacraments when you were not on your deathbed, forget it!

➤ If you have ever advocated an anti-Catholic position, forget it.

➤ If you have ever used birth control, forget it!

➤ If you have ever supported a pro-choice candidate for public office, forget it!

St. Peter Speaks

Certain acts merit immediate excommunication from the Roman Catholic Church. One such act is submitting to an abortion. Another is joining a Masonic Lodge. Such sins can be absolved only by a bishop.

➤ If you have ever joined a secret society of any kind, including a Masonic Lodge or a college fraternity, forget it!

➤ If you have ever openly criticized the pope, forget it!

➤ If you have ever watched morally objectionable movies (anything with an "R" rating), forget it!

➤ If you have ever advocated cultural diversity or the acceptance of alternative lifestyles, forget it!

➤ If you have ever received Holy Communion in a non-Catholic church, forget it!

➤ If you have ever sought the public spotlight for a purpose that was not parochial, forget it!

➤ If you have lived the good life and lived the American dream, forget it!

Make Sure You Perform a Miracle or Two

If you still think you qualify, then it's time to consider your accomplishments. Have you furthered the work of the Church? Have you been an outspoken critic against permissiveness and the spirit of this secular age? Have you performed acts of charity? Have you denied yourself for the good of others? Have you advanced the gospel in your workplace, in the marketplace, and in the world about you? Have you worked to promote the virtues of poverty and obedience? Have you maintained your virginity? Or, if you are married, have you kept your marriage chaste like Joseph and Mary did?

Hagar the Hagiographer

To avoid the excesses of medieval bishops, Pope Gregory IX in 1234 reserved the right of canonization to the papacy alone. This right was reinforced by Pope Urban VIII in 1642.

And, last but most important, did you ever perform a miracle? I don't mean a small miracle like healing a toothache or a headache. I'm talking about a full-fledged miracle or miracles: curing third-degree burn victims, giving sight to someone who was blind, restoring hearing to someone who was born deaf, or raising to life a dead body.

Before You Can Begin, You Have to Die

Even if the answer to all these questions is a resounding "yes!" you still have much work to do. First, you have to attract attention to your work so that the Church will notice your Christian charity. You must become a very public defender of the faith, writing letters to editors, appearing on television programs, and even standing on soapboxes. You have to gather a group of friends and admirers around you—people who will spread word of your saintliness. You have to distribute all your worldly goods to the poor and the needy. You have to suffer from a terrible malady in silence. And, finally, you must die.

It's that easy. Your chances for *canonization* are greater now than any time in the past 600 years. Pope John Paul II has canonized more saints than all of his twentieth-century predecessors combined. Almost 300 have been canonized in the past 25 years. It's almost a return to the time when sainthood was in flower.

The problem now is that the process is so extensive, so long, and so very expensive. But let me take you through the process step by step so that you will be sure to end up with a crown in Heaven.

St. Peter Speaks

Canonization is the declaration of sainthood upon a departed holy one. When a person is canonized, his or her name is written in the book or "canon" of saints.

How to Become a "Servant of God"

The canonization process begins a minimum of five years after a person's death. At this time, friends and admirers can present a petition to Rome, pleading that a "clause" (the Vatican word for "case") be opened. Such petitions are never approved quickly. An initial examination of the merits of the petition must be conducted, simply to make sure that you merit your reputation for holiness. Some cases are not opened for more than a hundred years, as is the case of Father Michael J. McGivney, the founder of the Knights of Columbus.

Holy Cow!

St. Augustine, who lived with a woman out of wedlock, probably would not make it to canonization today. Many think that Dorothy Day, founder of The Catholic Worker movement, will never be canonized because of her sexually permissive youth and her outspoken pacifism.

Hagar the Hagiographer

In the eighteenth century, Pope Benedict IV produced the definitive book on canonization. Called *The Beatification of the Servants of God and the Canonization of the Beatified,* the four-volume work laid down requirements for sainthood that remain in effect to the present day. These are the three requirements:

➤ Doctrinal purity

➤ Heroic virtue

➤ Miraculous intercession after death

Once the Vatican declares that the "clause" can proceed, you, or the proposed candidate, are granted a temporary title of "Servant of God." That's when the real research begins. Every aspect of your life is inspected in excruciating detail. A large part of this research involves reading everything you ever wrote—every note, every letter, every document, every essay. This work is conducted by a team of Vatican censors who look for any inconsistency with the official teachings of the Church. Because of this high level of scrutiny, not many candidates for sainthood have engaged in theological or philosophical speculation. Instead, most are candidates who have never uttered a controversial word or penned a questionable line.

Divine Revelation

In the Old Testament, the Israelites were forbidden to touch dead bodies for fear of being ceremonially unclean and defiled. They were even forbidden to enter a house that contained a dead body for fear of spiritual and physical contamination. Many Christians, however, believe that they can be blessed by being touched by the remains of the saints.

Make Sure the Skeletons Have Been Removed from the Closet

If your witnesses are still alive, they will be called upon to testify before a tribunal. In the case of Mother Teresa McCrory, founder of the Carmelite Sisters for the Aged and Infirm, more than 70 witnesses were summoned. Mother McCrory died in 1984, and many of those who were called to testify in recent years were old and ailing. Still, they were required to make the trip to Rome to face weeks of interrogation.

The tribunal must reconstruct your life by sifting through mounds of paper, everything from your school records to statements of members of the clergy.

In the case of Father McGivney, the tribunal scoured every single newspaper article published in New Haven, Connecticut, from 1875 to 1990 to make sure that no question about the priest's conduct was ever raised for any reason.

Hagar the Hagiographer

Mother Teresa McCrory, a candidate for sainthood, was extremely devoted to another Carmelite nun, for whom she was named, St. Therese of Lisieux, the "Little Flower." Forbidden because of her fragility to perform acts of self-mortification such as self-flagellation and extreme fasting, the "Little Flower" developed the "little way" to subdue the flesh. She would not brush away a mosquito or scratch an itch. She would sleep under heavy blankets throughout the summer and without blankets throughout the winter. She died of tuberculosis in 1897, at the age of 23. She is one of Heaven's most popular saints.

Make Sure You're an Attractive Corpse

Once all this information is gathered and inspected, the Vatican will appoint someone to write a "positio" or "position paper" about you. This isn't easy. Writing a "position" is like writing a doctoral dissertation. The first section of this paper will consist of a biography about you. The second section will entail presenting evidence attesting to your faith, piety, and charity.

Now comes the good stuff. Examiners must exhume your body to study your remains. In the case of Pierre Toussaint, a nineteenth-century New Yorker famous for his work with orphans and cholera victims, forensics experts spent 15 days studying his skeletal remains, using computer technology to match the skull to an antique photograph of the subject.

Being Beatified Is the Next Best Thing

The position paper, along with the forensic evidence, is then submitted to the Vatican's Congregation for the Causes of Saints, a committee consisting of 25 cardinals and bishops. This committee will determine whether you really have lived a life of heroic virtue. If the committee approves, your name is presented to the pope, who must offer his agreement with the findings. If all goes well, you will receive the title "Venerable." But, you have yet to be beatified.

To receive *beatification,* you have to perform a real, honest-to-goodness miracle. "But wait," you're probably thinking, "I'm dead, long dead, before they ever get around to this stage." That's true. You must perform the miracle from your place in Heaven as proof that you are among the blessed.

St. Peter Speaks

Beatification is a papal decree that permits Catholics to venerate a person after his or her death. It is a preliminary step to canonization, although it does not guarantee sainthood. Such a decree bestows the title "Blessed" to a departed soul.

Holy Cow!

Regarding proof of a miracle, Father Peter Gumpel, a member of the Vatican's saint-making commission, said, "We do not accept any cure as a miracle unless we are scientifically, humanly certain that the cure has been instantaneous, not expected, and complete. If God intervenes and works a miracle, He doesn't do it halfway."

This means that a public relations campaign must be conducted on your behalf. People must be encouraged to pray to you for a cure, a healing, or a wonder. After you perform a miracle, written testimony must be presented to the committee. Make sure that the miracle is mind-boggling, such as straightening a curvature of the spine or curing complete blindness.

Modern Miracles Are Harder to Perform

This part is difficult. The Vatican standard for miracles, in this day and age, is rather high. A board of five very exacting physicians must establish the miracle as valid. That's why the cure must have been instantaneous and complete. That's why you have to shy away from terminal illness when performing your miracle. In cases involving cancer, for example, the team of physicians waits a minimum of 10 years to make sure that the disease will not return. Cancer, after all, can go into remission.

Now, if you're satisfied with beatification, you need go no farther, but if you are opting for sainthood, you must perform more than one miracle to show that you really have the power of intercession. Four or 5 miracles are good, but 10 or 12 are better.

Don't Forget to Be the Right Race or Color

Now we get to sensitive areas. In this day of equal opportunity, it is best to be something other than white if you want to be canonized. The current pope has been attempting to change the lily-white complexion of the community of saints. During his reign, Pope John Paul II has added 117 Vietnamese martyrs to the heavenly host, along with the first saints from New Guinea and Nigeria.

Finally, Have Plenty of Cash

For canonization, you also will need a lot of cash. Your supporters must have money for regular trips to Rome, for the services of a canon lawyer, and for the publication of newsletters and circulars about you. They will need money to pay for the services of the 25 members of the Vatican's Congregation for the Cause of the Saints, for the preparation of the position paper, for the services of scientists to exhume and examine your body, and for the Vatican medical team of five physicians to authenticate your miracles. The entire process should cost between $500,000 to $1,000,000, if you're lucky (or should I say blessed?).

The Least You Need to Know

➤ The first step toward sainthood is becoming a Servant of God.

➤ The second step is presenting a position paper.

➤ The third step is exhumation and examination of a candidate's body.

➤ The fourth step is securing the title "Venerable."

➤ The fifth step is beatification.

➤ The final step is the papal pronouncement.

Chapter 20

Hallelujah, It's True! A Few Saints Are Red, White, and Blue

In This Chapter

➤ America's sainthood shortage

➤ Mother Cabrini's mission

➤ The Baltimore Catechism

➤ Nuns among Native Americans

➤ The patroness of parochial schools

➤ Sainthood and political correctness

The United States has a severe shortage of saints. Only five Americans in the past 500 years have been canonized! It's a crying shame. With all the power, wealth, and Yankee ingenuity Americans possess, there should be 5,000 American saints, if not 50,000. Let's face it: According to sociologists, the United States is the most religious nation on earth. More than 60 percent of the Catholics in America go to Mass on a regular basis. This exceeds the percentage in any European nation. There are more religious institutions, charitable organizations, parochial schools, and church-related hospitals in the United States than anywhere else. What's more, the missionaries to the remote regions of the world are, by and large, Americans. And yet, when it comes to sainthood, the people of the United States are getting the short end of the stick.

You might think that five saints in 500 years isn't really too bad, until you realize that three of the five weren't really American. They were born in Europe. We have only two real, red-blooded American saints. It makes you think that the people in the Vatican might have an anti-American bias.

American Saint Abused by Sister Superior

The first American saint to be canonized was Mother Frances Xavier Cabrini in 1946. Mother Cabrini was born not in the Bronx, but in the old Lombard town of Santangelo, Italy. A bout of smallpox prevented this saint from entering a convent at the age of 13, so she became a chaste schoolteacher in an orphanage managed by an insane nun named Antonia Tondini.

The working conditions at the school were really substandard because Sister Antonia used to slap, kick, and insult our saint on a weekly basis. Things got worse when the bishop of Todi, knowing that Antonia was a nutcase, told Mother Frances Cabrini (then known as Francesca) to turn the orphanage into a religious community. Antonia threw a fit and actually began to foam at the mouth, after taking a stick to the back of our tiny saint.

The good bishop finally closed down the place. At that time, Francesca expressed a desire to become a missionary in China. Instead, the bishop told her to establish a community of missionary sisters, along with an orphanage, at an abandoned Franciscan monastery in Codogno. As a good test of her faith, he gave her no money or provisions.

When You Have Mother Cabrini, You Don't Need a Cow

Mother Cabrini, of course, could produce miracles. When there was no money for food, Mother Cabrini said a few Hail Marys, and money miraculously appeared. When there was no milk for the orphans, the empty containers in the barn were filled to the brim with milk from real "sacred cows." Every time a nun was sent to the empty breadbox, the breadbox would contain a fresh loaf of manna from Heaven.

Having created a religious community with no resources, the pope became duly impressed with her managerial skills and asked her to establish a school and an orphanage in New York. At age 39, the tiny nun arrived in the Big Apple in 1889 with six of her religious sisters.

Hagar the Hagiographer

When Mother Cabrini arrived in New York City, she discovered that the priest who had asked for the help of the religious sisters had no means to support them. The saint and her fellow nuns went to the Italian quarter and begged from door to door.

Mother Cabrini Goes Slumming

Mother Cabrini and her nuns lived in a rat-infested room in the Bowery until she managed to obtain money from an Italian countess to build an orphanage on the shores of the Hudson River. Soon she and her fellow sisters were establishing schools and orphanages throughout the country. By 1907, when Mother Cabrini's new religious order, the Sisters of the Sacred Heart, obtained recognition from Rome, the shrewd saint had more than 1,000 nuns in her order in eight countries (including England, Spain, and Latin America) and was the founder of 50 convents, numerous schools, scores of hospitals, and other institutions.

Hey, Mamma, Speaka Da English!

This saint was not without her scoffers. Critics spoke of her rather extreme narrow-mindedness. It seems that the pious nun would not allow non-Catholics into her schools and hospitals, and she refused to accept illegitimate children in her orphanages. It is also true that her mistreatment of workers was the cause of several lawsuits in Italy and even of a riot in Milan.

But why squabble over the details? She became the first American saint in 1946. Strange to say, to her dying day, she never spoke a word of English. Her body is now on display in the chapel of the Mother Cabrini High School in the Washington Heights section of New York City. It is in a glass casket and was proclaimed to be incorruptible. Sad to say, the proclamation was a mistake because Mother is getting kind of moldy.

Hagar the Hagiographer

Mother Cabrini became a naturalized citizen of the United States in 1909. After her death, reports of more than 150,000 miracles flooded the Vatican. She is the patroness of immigrants. If you are an immigrant (or would like to be an immigrant), say the following prayer: "St. Frances Cabrini, intercede for Christians all over the world not to be daunted by difficulties, but instead, as you did, to start worthy initiatives, confident that the ways and means will be given in answer to prayers and requests for assistance. Through Christ our Lord, Amen."

Come on, Johnny, Smile! You're a Saint!

The first American male saint, John Nepomucene Neumann, was from Prachitiz, Bohemia (now the Czech Republic). He came to America as a missionary in 1836 and eventually was appointed bishop of Philadelphia.

St. John Nepomucene shared something in common with the first American female saint, Mother Frances Xavier Cabrini. They were both diminutive (almost dwarfish) in stature, difficult to please, and rather lacking in personality. It was said that this saint never smiled.

The second American saint established 100 new churches in Philadelphia, 80 parochial schools, and a score of orphanages. To staff his schools and orphanages, St. John Nepomucene founded the School Sisters of Notre Dame. He also introduced the devotion of Forty Hours to the Blessed Sacrament. This devotion is important for us because the litanies (the lists of the saints) were chanted as incense was burned before the Eucharist.

During this devotion, all Catholics had to kneel with stiff backs before the altar. Children who did not assume the correct, rigid posture were dragged from the sanctuary by the ear.

One more note about this saint: He gave the world the Baltimore Catechisms that all Catholic school children were obliged to memorize from cover to cover before they could receive the sacrament of Confirmation. It took 112 years to get this hard-working, albeit grim, saint canonized.

Holy Cow!

St. John Nepomucene was educated in the diocesan seminary at Budweis, home of the famous American beer. Because of an overabundance of Catholic priests (hard to believe!), the Austrian government delayed his ordination, forcing him to go to America as a missionary.

Divine Revelation

The Baltimore Catechism became out-of-date by the close of the Second Vatican Council. It was the guidebook for correct moral and religious belief, and it was used in all Sunday school classes. No Catholic publication has been able to replace it.

Hold On! This Saint Is a Protestant!

Now we come to a really American saint. St. Elizabeth Ann Seton was born and bred in the United States, was educated in American schools, and was the cream of the crop in polite society. What's more, she was a WASP. That's right, a White Anglo-Saxon Protestant. Her father was a well-known and wealthy physician who served as professor of anatomy at Columbia, and her mother was the daughter of the Anglican rector of St. Andrew's Church in Staten Island. This family was so prim and proper that they supported King George during the American Revolution.

At 19, the saint, who was a pious Episcopalian, married William Seton, the heir-apparent to a large shipping firm. St. Elizabeth gathered a group of other socialites around her and set about to help the poor. She became so active in social work that she was called "the Protestant Sister of Charity."

Italians Save the American Saint

All did not fare well for the Seton family. When war broke out between England and France, William's business went belly-up, plunging the family into debt. It got worse. William contracted tuberculosis and was told to spend some time in sunny Italy. Due to a yellow fever epidemic in New York (which killed the saint's father), Elizabeth and William were quarantined for four weeks after a seven-week voyage at the docks of Livorno. The miserable conditions aboard the quarantined ship proved too much for William, and he died in Pisa in 1804.

Elizabeth was now alone in the land of the pope. She came under the care of a nice Italian family who gave her comfort, consolation, and Catholicism. Indeed, Elizabeth beheld a Beatific Vision when the priest elevated the Host before her in a church in Florence.

Saint Snubbed by Snotty Episcopalians

When she returned to New York as a Roman Catholic, her snotty Episcopalian friends and relations shunned her and refused to grant her and her children any financial support.

Our undaunted saint reacted to this snub by becoming the very first (former) Protestant Bride of Christ. In time, St. Elizabeth Seton, along with 18 other religious sisters, came to form the Daughters of Charity of St. Joseph, America's very first Catholic order. Since St. Elizabeth was educated and sophisticated, this was a teaching order, and, to the horror of her Episcopalian friends and family, she began to establish parochial schools throughout the land of the free and the home of the brave.

St. Elizabeth Ann Seton is celebrated as the founder of the parochial school system in America. In his canonization allocution for St. Elizabeth, Pope Pius IX spoke of several miracles that this saint performed after her death in 1821, including cures for victims of leukemia and meningitis.

Hagar the Hagiographer

Although St. Elizabeth Ann Seton is the only saint who was born on American soil, Kateri Tekakwitha, a Native American who spread the faith among the Mohawks, was beatified in 1980 and remains a candidate for canonization. Because the process of canonization is so expensive, members of Blessed Kateri's tribe are attempting to raise funds by selling fragments of her bones.

Holy Cow!

Mother Catherine Seton, daughter of the saint, became the first member of the New York Sisters of Mercy. She spent a great deal of her life preparing condemned criminals for death. She died in 1891 at the age of 91.

Hagar the Hagiographer

St. Elizabeth Ann Seton is the patron saint for the death of children, for resolution of problems with in-laws, and for opposition against Catholic authority. This is an excerpt from one of St. Elizabeth's letters to a non-Catholic friend: "Peace, my dear. We will jog up the hill as quietly as possible, and when the flies and mosquitoes bite, wrap the cloak around and never mind them; they can only penetrate the surface. Darling Julia, how I wish you would have such a Catholic cloak also."

Hagar the Hagiographer

Blessed Mother Theodore Guerin, another French woman who served as a missionary to the United States, is a candidate for sainthood. She established St. Mary-of-the-Woods College, the first Catholic institution of higher learning in America, at Terre Haute, Indiana, in 1840. She also opened pharmacies where medicines were distributed to poor settlers and Native Americans.

Really, Rose, the Habit Isn't Flattering for Your Figure

Our next saint, Sister Rose Philippine Duchesne, was born in France and never became an American citizen. Yet Americans claim her as their own because of the severe shortage of American saints.

Known as "the Lady of Mercy," St. Rose Philippine was born in Grenoble in 1940. At 12, she was placed under the care of Visitation nuns at a Catholic boarding school. The young saint was entranced by the religious life and, at term break, announced to her parents that she wanted to enter a convent.

Appalled by the announcement that their charming daughter had decided to become a consecrated virgin, her parents refused to allow Rose Philippine to return to the boarding school, and they kept her at home, where she was tutored with her male cousins until she was 17. But the young saint kept acting stranger and stranger. She insisted on performing the work of domestic servants, emptying chamber pots, scrubbing the kitchen floor, and cleaning the outhouse. What's worse, she refused to wear ordinary clothes and walked about the family house dressed as a pious nun.

Rose Realizes Her Own Wedding Plans

Despite this, the saint's parents made plans for her to marry. Before the day of her betrothal, Rose Philippine secured permission to visit her beloved nuns at the Visitation convent. Once inside the convent, the saint refused to come out and made preparations to become a bride of Christ.

In 1805, St. Rose Philippine became a member of the newly formed Society of the Sacred Heart. When her parents died, she obtained a large inheritance that enabled her to establish more convents and schools for her religious order. She then decided to set out for the New World so that she could embark on the noble task of spreading the Gospel to the "savages."

Bear Grease Is Not Good for French Cooking!

Landing in New Orleans in 1818, our saint, accompanied by four religious sisters, traveled up the Mississippi River and established the first American Sacred Heart house at St. Charles, Missouri, in a log cabin. Rose Philippine didn't find life in the New World pleasing to her sensitive palate. To a friend in France, she wrote, "We have maize, pork, and potatoes, but not eggs, butter, oil, fruit, or vegetables. We should value a case of altar wine and some olive oil—the only edible oil to be had here is bear grease, and it's disgusting."

Still, Rose Philippine persisted, and by 1828 six religious houses were established along the Mississippi River. She also opened several schools in Missouri and Louisiana, where she insisted that students speak French.

Are You Sure She's Not a Statue?

In 1841 and at the age of 71, Rose Philippine finally realized her childhood dream of ministering to the savages. She set up a school for the Pottowatami

Holy Cow!

During the Reign of Terror in 1791, the nuns were expelled from the convent and St. Rose Philippine returned home, where she nursed the sick, taught children, visited imprisoned priests, and gathered a small community. In 1801, Napoleon restored peaceful relations between the Catholic Church and the French government, permitting St. Rose Philippine to return to convent life.

Hagar the Hagiographer

Despite the fact that she was highly educated, St. Rose Philippine was not very good with foreign languages. Although she lived among the Pottowatami tribe, she never could speak one word of the tribe's language. And, although she spent most of her life in the United States, St. Rose Philippine could not speak English.

Indians in Sugar Creek, Kansas. Legend has it that little children approached her as she knelt in prayer in a wigwam and placed small pieces of paper on her habit. When they returned several hours later, they discovered that the bits of paper remained undisturbed and that the stoic saint hadn't moved a muscle. For this reason, the "savages" came to call her "The Woman Who Prays Always."

And Now for Our Newest Saint

And now we come to one of the newest members of the celestial kingdom—Mother Katherine Drexel, who, like most of the other American saints, was born with a silver spoon in her mouth. Her father, Francis Anthony Drexel, was a banker and the partner of robber baron J.P. Morgan. The Drexels lived in a spacious mansion on Rittenhouse Square in Philadelphia, where Katherine was born in 1858. The mansion is now part of Drexel University.

When St. Katherine was in her early twenties, her father died, leaving an estate of $15 million—roughly equivalent to $300 million today—the largest fortune ever recorded in the City of Brotherly Love. Along with her two sisters, Katherine naturally attracted every fortune-hunter this side of the Mason-Dixon line, along with fund-raisers for thousands of charitable causes.

Two priests from the Dakotas traveled to Philadelphia to see Katherine and her sisters, reporting that the federal government was withdrawing its funding for Indian schools. The good saint handed them a check. One year later, in 1878, Katherine was treated to a private audience with Pope Leo XIII. During the audience, our brave saint boldly asked the Pope to send more missionaries to help the poor American Indians. In response, the pope smiled and said, "My child, why don't you become a missionary?"

Jesus Gets a Rich New Bride

That question sealed Katherine's decision to dedicate her life to Christian service. In 1889, at the age of 30, she became a nun and set up her own religious order that was called "The Sisters of the Blessed Sacrament for Indians and Colored People." The front page of the Philadelphia newspaper carried this headline: "Miss Drexel Enters a Catholic Convent—Gives Up Seven Million." Jesus, the poor carpenter from Nazareth, managed to attract yet another incredibly wealthy bride.

Katherine delighted in her new life of poverty, sewing her shoelaces rather than buying a new pair, wearing pencils down to the nib, and traveling third class on trains.

The KKK Won't Mess with St. Katherine!

As the Mother Superior for her new order, Katherine sent a group of nuns to establish her first of 11 schools for Native Americans in Santa Fe, New Mexico. She also committed the resources from her father's trust (around $350,000 in 1900, or $7 million by today's standards) for the education of African-Americans. To this purpose, our saint built nearly 100 schools throughout the South, including Xavier University in New Orleans.

As expected, the Ku Klux Klan did not take too kindly to her efforts. In 1922, Klan members

St. Peter Speaks

To the nuns of her order, St. Katherine said, "Resolve: Generously and with no half-hearted, timorous dread of the opinions of Church and men to manifest my mission. You have no time to occupy your thoughts with that complacency or consideration of what others will think. Your business is simple, 'What will my Father in Heaven think?'"

Hagar the Hagiographer

At Mother Katherine Drexel's funeral, Father Augustus Tolton, who was the only black priest in America at that time, said, "In the whole history of the Church in America, we cannot find one person that has sworn to give her treasure for the sole benefit of the Coloreds and Indians. As I stand alone as the first Negro priest of America, so you, Mother Katherine, stand alone as the first one to make such a sacrifice for the cause of a downtrodden race."

threatened to tar and feather the white priest at one of the saint's schools in Beaumont, Texas, and to burn his church to the ground. As a burning cross was placed before the school, the nuns prayed, and a violent tornado appeared out of nowhere to engulf and carry away the Klan's headquarters. The Klan never bothered our good saint again.

Even in Heaven, It Helps to Be Politically Correct

Mother Katherine had a heart attack in 1935 and, after that, seldom was seen outside the Motherhouse of her order in Philadelphia. But she continued to fight for civil rights, funding the NAACP's efforts to obtain equal rights for black workers. She died in 1955, at the age of 96. Since passing on to glory, our saint has performed several miracles, including the healing of complete deafness. She was canonized in 2000, record time for sainthood in this day and age. But St. Katherine had special appeal to Pope John Paul II. Like him, she was socially liberal and theologically conservative. Even in the Vatican, it can pay (if you have money) to be politically correct.

The Least You Need to Know

➤ Only five American saints have been canonized.

➤ Only two of these saints were born and bred on American soil.

➤ St. Elizabeth Ann Seton established the Catholic school system.

➤ St. Rose Philippine became a missionary to Native Americans.

➤ St. Katherine Drexel devoted her life and wealth to the cause of human rights.

Chapter 21

Saintly Remains: How to Get Rich with a Bag of Bones

In This Chapter

➤ The veneration of blood and bones

➤ The altar stones

➤ The relic craze

➤ The Shroud of Turin

What remains, folks, are the remains: the skulls and bones of the holy ones, swatches of cloth from the clothing they wore, quills that they used to write apologies, chalices they used to celebrate Mass, the staffs and scepters that they held in their hands, the beads that they counted, and the prayer books that they read. Sometimes, little remains of a saint except a strand of hair, a drop of blood, or a trace of a tear.

Little Things Mean a Lot

All these things are worthy of veneration, not simply as souvenirs and mementos of their exemplary lives, but because they can produce cures and healings, they can quicken faith, and they can perform miracles. Saints' *relics,* in a word, are potent. This is clear from the inscription on the tomb of St. Martin of Tours, which says: "Here lies Martin the bishop, oh holy memory, whose soul is in the hand of God; but he is fully here, present and made plain in miracles of every kind."

Get Blessings from Bones

The Catholic Church teaches that because the bodies of the saints were "temples of the Holy Spirit," the physical remains of the holy ones could be the source of many benefits and blessings from God. For this reason, pilgrims throughout the world visit Catholic shrines so that they can touch or be touched by a holy relic.

St. Peter Speaks

Relics are the remains of a saint. Relics such as the bones of St. Polycarp and the blood of St. Januarius were called "first class." The farther the remains were from the person of the deceased saint, the lower in class ("second class," "third class," and so on) they were.

Divine Revelation

The scriptural basis for the veneration of relics is found in St. Paul's first letter to the Corinthians: "Do you not know that your body is the temple of the Holy Spirit? You are not your own; you were bought with a price. Therefore, honor God with your body" (1 Corinthians 6:19–20).

The practice of the veneration of relics seems to have its basis in paganism. In ancient Rome, the blood of executed criminals was credited with special potency, including the ability to cure epilepsy and maladies of the mind. For this reason, the pagans were probably the first to seek the blood-soaked remains of the Christian martyrs. They covered themselves with this blood and allowed the blood to "seep into their system." In time, Christians themselves began to believe in the healing power of the blood and the bones and then continued the pagan practice.

A Great Way to Earn Extra Cash

What's more, the early Christians were accustomed to conducting their worship services in the catacombs, where the bodies of the dead were placed on shelves to decompose. The first Christian altars were adorned with the remains of the holy martyrs. After Christianity became a legal religion, Christians believed that every altar should contain the remains of a martyr. As the new religion spread throughout the Roman Empire, more mortal remains of the martyrs were sought to sanctify new places of worship. For this reason, the precious remains were cut into pieces and sold as "altar stones."

There was a fortune to be made in altar stones, especially those from particularly powerful saints (such as the twelve apostles and members of the holy family). The shrines that housed the remains of these saints became popular pilgrimage sites. And why not? The relics were not only interesting to see for lovers of the macabre, they also possessed the ability to cure what ailed people or to improve the quality of their lives.

The Cathedral of Amiens became a very popular shrine after it gained possession of the actual head of St. John the Baptist. The handsome head was placed on display in a beautiful silver cup. From Amiens you could travel to the Abbey of St. Denis, where you could see the crown of thorns and the decaying body of St. Dionysius the Aeropagite. Three scattered churches in France professed to have the complete corpse of St. Mary Magdalene, and five churches placed on display the one authentic relic of Christ's circumcision.

Drops of Milk from Mary?

If you visit England, you could visit Westminster Abbey to see some of the Lord's blood in a vial and a piece of marble from Pilate's courtroom that contained the imprint of His foot. On view at Exeter Cathedral were parts of the candle that the angel had used to light the tomb of Jesus, along with fragments of the burning bush from which God spoke to Moses. Better yet, you could make a pilgrimage to the monastery at Durham, where you could see St. Lawrence's severed joints, the coals that had been placed on his chest, the shirt of the Virgin Mary, and a stone that was marked with drops of her milk.

Everyone during the Middle Ages was crazy for relics. Even the slightest relic—a sliver of a bone—was great to wear around the neck as a sacred talisman. If you couldn't afford a piece of bone, then you had to settle for a thread from a saint's robe, some dust from a holy tomb, or a drop of oil from a holy body.

Mold Can Be Worth More Than Gold

As relics became more valuable, the bodies of holy men and women were hacked to pieces and "translated," or moved to shrines throughout Christendom. This fate befell St. Thomas Aquinas as soon as he passed on to glory. The right relic drew the crowds and contributions to the offering plate. Small wonder that the Cathedral at Canterbury forked over the equivalent of $6 million for the physical remains of St. Thomas Becket. It was worth the expense: Canterbury became the largest pilgrim attraction in the medieval world.

Hagar the Hagiographer

Some of the earliest Christian texts attest to the healing power of relics. In the "Acts of Thomas," the son of a king in India is cured from a life-threatening disease by dust that blows into the palace from the tomb of St. Thomas.

Holy Cow!

What's this about oil from a holy body? During the Middle Ages, oil was poured over sacred relics and then was kept in vases, sponges, or pieces of cloth to be sold to pilgrims. St. Augustine mentions a dead man who was restored to life by the oil of St. Stephen.

In no time at all, the market for remains gave rise to hundreds of thousands of fake relics that were sold before every shrine. By the twelfth century, St. Guilbert wrote an essay calling for an end to the relic craze. He said that some saints must have been hydras with hundreds of heads, and he cursed relic-mongers who sold moldy bread to pious Christians, saying that it was the very bread from the Lord's Last Supper.

Get a Piece of Mother Teresa Before It's Too Late

The relic craze died down during the Protestant Reformation. The Reformers sacked churches throughout Christendom and destroyed many relics, saying that the remains of the saints had given rise to pagan idolatry.

But relics are still placed in the altars of Catholic Churches, and they are still held in veneration. A good bone, such as the remains of such future saints as Mother Teresa of Calcutta, is still worth a good buck and might produce a blessing.

The Relic of Relics

The most valuable relic in Christendom is the Shroud of Turin. The Shroud is an ancient cloth, measuring 14 feet by 4 feet, that is said to be the burial garment of Jesus. This relic is highly significant because it contains what many believe to be an actual image of Christ. This image, many clergymen and scientists argue, offers positive proof that the body of Jesus radiated an incredible amount of energy after His death.

The Shroud was discovered in 1204, when the crusaders conquered Constantinople. It came into the possession of a French soldier, Otto de la Roche, who noted that it bore marks made by sweat and blood along with the almost indistinct outline of a human body. He claimed it as part of his booty.

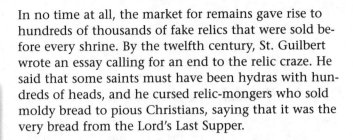

Hagar the Hagiographer

The remains of St. Stephen attracted such noisy crowds to the monastery at Grammont that the monks were prevented from conducting their devotions. The abbot became irate not at the crowds or the monks, but at the body of the dead saint. He told the bones of St. Stephen to stop performing miracles. "Otherwise," he said, "I will toss your bones in the river."

Holy Cow!

If you cannot obtain one of Mother Teresa's toes, or even a toe nail, then, by all means, you must purchase a sliver from the skeleton of Blessed Kateri Tekakwitha that can be yours for less than $10.

In 1357, the Shroud appeared in Europe, when Geoffrey de Charney, a nobleman, purchased it under mysterious circumstances and placed it on public display in Lirey, France. Three years later, Margaret de Charney sold the Shroud for a small fortune to the Duke of Savoy. In 1532, it was slightly damaged by a fire in the Church of St. Chapelle of Chambery.

Hagar the Hagiographer

According to the Gospel of John, Jesus left not just His shroud behind in the tomb, but also a "burial cloth that had been wrapped around his head." St. John says: "This cloth was folded up by itself, separate from the linen" (John 20:7). This cloth is kept in a silver cedar chest in the Cathedral of Oviedo in Spain. Records say that the cloth was removed from Jerusalem in 614, when the holy city was attacked by the Persians. It has been housed in Spain since 1113. No image appears on the cloth, but researchers have concluded that it bears bloodstains similar to the stains on the Shroud of Turin, suggesting that the two pieces of cloth once covered the same head.

Is the Relic Really Radioactive?

In 1889, the first photograph was taken of the Shroud, and something extraordinary happened. The photographic plate converted the impressions on cloth into the black-and-white image of a man who had been crowned with thorns and been whipped, crucified, and lanced by a spear.

It got weird. When submitted to art experts, the image was ruled not to be a forgery. The experts noted that the image was amazingly natural and anatomically correct because, with every human being, the features are not the same on both sides of the face. Medieval artists didn't know this and never painted any dissimilarity between the right and left sides of the face. Even more conclusive proof of the authenticity of the image on the Shroud came from the fact that no artist, medieval or modern, has been able to convert a human face by the process of imagination into a negative image and paint it

St. Peter Speaks

An almost equally important relic is the veil that St. Veronica used to wipe the bloody face of Jesus when He was carrying His cross. The veil contains the imprint of Christ's face and is kept at St. Peter's in Rome. Like the Shroud of Turin, it has had a long and miraculous history. From time to time, the veil glows with supernatural light, and the image of the face assumes lifelike color.

Later studies explained the appearance of the image on the theory that the cloth must have come into contact with an extreme form of radiation.

A Real Mystery for Mystery Lovers

In the 1980s, the Shroud was subjected to numerous scientific tests, including chemical tests, x-rays, gamma rays, and computer analysis. Such research showed that the strange Shroud contained particles of Near Eastern origin and that it probably dated from the time of Christ. What's more, the corpse within the Shroud appears to have been powdered and anointed with oil in the manner described in the Gospel of John.

In 1988, the Church consented to have a swatch cut from the Shroud for carbon dating. The results of these tests conducted at independent laboratories in England, Austria, and the United States concluded that the cloth was made during the Middle Ages.

Five years later, the Health Science Center concluded that the sample of the Shroud that had been used for carbon dating was contaminated by fungi, bacteria, and bioplastic coating that grows on all fibers over the years. The Center argued that the carbon had dated the contaminants, not the linen itself.

At the same time, the Center for Advanced DNA Technologies identified the markings on the Shroud as blood from a human male.

The Least You Need to Know

➤ The first Christians venerated the bones of the martyrs.

➤ Every altar in Christendom was required to contain a relic.

➤ The Reformation dampened the relic craze.

➤ The Shroud of Turin remains the most revered relic.

➤ The mystery of the Shroud remains unresolved.

The Patron Saints

Patrons and Intercessors

Your vocation determines your patron saint. If you are an accountant, turn in your hour of need to St. Matthew, the patron of accountants. Do not turn to St. Genesius, the patron of actors. He's not very good with figures.

Accountants: Matthew

Actors: Genesius

Advertisers: Bernardine of Siena

Alpinists: Bernard of Montjoux (or Menthon)

Altar boys: John Berchmans

Anesthetists: Rene Goupil

Animals: Francis of Assisi

Archers: Sebastian

Architects: Thomas

Armorers: Dunstan

Art: Catherine of Bologna

Artists: Luke, Catherine of Bologna, Fra Angelico

Astronomers: Dominic

Athletes: Sebastian

Authors: Francis de Sales

Aviators: Our Lady of Loreto, Therese of Lisieux, Joseph of Cupertino

Bakers: Elizabeth of Hungary, Nicholas

Bankers: Matthew

Barbers: Cosmas and Damian, Louis

Barren women: Anthony of Padua, Felicity

Basket makers: Antony the Abbot

Beggars: Martin of Tours

Blacksmiths: Dunstan

Blind: Odilia, Raphael

Blood banks: Januarius

Bodily ills: Our Lady of Lourdes

Bookbinders: Peter Celestine

Bookkeepers: Matthew

Booksellers: John of God

Boy Scouts: George

Brewers: Augustine of Hippo, Luke, Nicholas of Myra

Bricklayers: Stephen

Brides: Nicholas of Myra

Brush makers: Antony the Abbot

Builders: Vincent Ferrer

Butchers: Antony the Abbot, Luke

Cab drivers: Fiacre

Cabinet makers: Anne

Cancer patients: Peregrine

Canonists: Raymond of Peninafort

Carpenters: Joseph

Catechists: Viator, Charles Borromeo, Robert Bellarmine

Catholic Action: Francis of Assisi

Chandlers: Ambrose, Bernard of Clairvaux

Charitable societies: Vincent de Paul

Children: Nicholas of Myra

Children of Mary: Agnes, Maria Goretti

Choirboys: Dominic Savio, Holy Innocents

Churches: Joseph

Clerics: Gabriel of the Sorrowful Mother

Communications personnel: Bernardine

Confessors: Alphonsus Liguori, John Nepomucene

Convulsive children: Scholastica

Cooks: Lawrence, Martha

Coopers: Nicholas of Myra

Coppersmiths: Maurus

Dairy workers: Brigid

Deaf: Francis de Sales

Dentists: Apollonia

Desperate situations: Gregory of Neocaesarea, Jude Thaddeus, Rita of Cascia

Dieticians (in hospitals): Martha

Dyers: Maurice, Lydia

Dying: Joseph

Ecologists: Francis of Assisi

Editors: Francis de Sales

Emigrants: Frances Xavier Cabrini

Engineers: Ferdinand III

Epilepsy, motor diseases: Vitus, Willibrord

Eucharistic congresses and societies: Paschal Baylon

Expectant mothers: Raymond Nonnatus, Gerard Majella

Eye diseases: Lucy

Falsely accused: Raymond Nonnatus

Farmers: George, Isidore

Farriers: John the Baptist

Fire prevention: Catherine of Siena

Firemen: Florian

First communicants: Tarcisius

Fishermen: Andrew

Florists: Therese of Lisieux

Forest workers: John Gualbert

Foundlings: Holy Innocents

Fullers: Anastasius the Fuller, James the Less

Funeral directors: Joseph of Arimathea, Dismas

Gardeners: Adelard, Tryphon, Fiacre, Phocas

Glassworkers: Luke

Goldsmiths: Dunstan, Anastasius

Gravediggers: Anthony, Abbot

Greetings: Valentine

Grocers: Michael

Hairdressers: Martin de Porres

Happy meetings: Raphael

Hatters: Severus of Ravenna, James the Less

Headache sufferers: Teresa of Jesus (Avila)

Heart patients: John of God

Hospital administrators: Basil the Great, Frances Xavier Cabrini

Hospitals: Camillus de Lellis, John of God, Jude Thaddeus

Housewives: Anne

Hunters: Hubert, Eustachius

Infantrymen: Maurice

Innkeepers: Amand, Martha

Invalids: Roch

Jewelers: Eligius, Dunstan

Journalists: Francis de Sales

Jurists: John of Capistrano

Laborers: Isidore, James, John Bosco

Lawyers: Ivo (Yves Helory), Genesius, Thomas More

Learning: Ambrose

Librarians: Jerome

Lighthouse keepers: Venerius

Locksmiths: Dunstan

Maids: Zita

Marble workers: Clement I

Mariners: Michael, Nicholas of Tolentino

Medical record librarians: Raymond of Penafort

Medical social workers: John Regis

Medical technicians: Albert the Great

Mentally ill: Dymphna

Merchants: Francis of Assisi, Nicholas of Myra

Messengers: Gabriel

Metal workers: Eligius

Military chaplains: John of Capistrano

Millers: Arnulph, Victor

Missions, black: Peter Claver, Benedict the Black

Missions, foreign: Francis Xavier, Therese of Lisieux

Missions, parish: Leonard of Port Maurice

Mothers: Monica

Motorcyclists: Our Lady of Grace

Motorists: Christopher, Frances of Rome

Mountaineers: Bernard of Montjoux (or Menthan)

Musicians: Gregory the Great, Cecilia, Dunstan

Notaries: Luke, Mark

Nurses: Camillus de Lellis, John of God, Agatha, Raphael

Nursing and nursing service: Elizabeth of Hungary, Catherine of Siena

Orators: John Chrysostom

Organ builders: Cecilia

Orphans: Jerome Emiliani

Painters: Luke

Paratroopers: Michael

Pawnbrokers: Nicholas

Pharmacists: Cosmas and Damian, James the Greater

Pharmacists (in hospitals): Gemma Galgani

Philosophers: Justin

Physicians: Pantaleon, Cosmas and Damian, Luke, Raphael

Pilgrims: James the Greater

Plasterers: Bartholomew

Poets: David, Cecilia

Poison sufferers: Benedict

Policemen: Michael

Poor: Lawrence, Anthony of Padua

Poor souls: Nicholas of Tolentino

Porters: Christopher

Possessed: Bruno, Denis

Postal employees: Gabriel

Priests: Jean-Baptiste Vianney

Printers: John of God, Augustine of Hippo, Genesius

Prisoners: Dismas, Joseph Cafasso

Protector of crops: Ansovinus

Public relations: Bernardine of Siena

Public relations (of hospitals): Paul

Radio workers: Gabriel

Radiologists: Michael

Retreats: Ignatius Loyola

Rheumatism: James the Greater

Saddlers: Crispin and Crispinian

Sailors: Cuthbert, Brendan, Eulalia, Christopher, Peter Gonzales, Erasmus, Nicholas

Scholars: Brigid

Schools, Catholic: Thomas Aquinas, Joseph Calasanz

Scientists: Albert

Sculptors: Claude

Seamen: Francis of Paola

Searchers of lost articles: Anthony of Padua

Secretaries: Genesius

Seminarians: Charles Borromeo

Servants: Martha, Zita

Shoemakers: Crispin and Crispinian

Sick: Michael, John of God, Camillus de Lellis

Silversmiths: Andronicus

Singers: Gregory, Cecilia

Skaters: Lidwina

Skiers: Bernard of Montjoux (or Menthon)

Social workers: Louise de Marillac

Soldiers: Hadrian, George, Ignatius, Sebastian, Martin of Tours, Joan of Arc

Speleologists: Benedict

Stenographers: Genesius, Cassian

Stonecutters: Clement

Stonemasons: Stephen

Students: Thomas Aquinas

Surgeons: Cosmas and Damian, Luke

Swordsmiths: Maurice

Tailors: Homobonus

Tanners: Crispin and Crispinian, Simon

Tax collectors: Matthew

Teachers: Gregory the Great, John Baptist de la Salle

Telecommunications workers: Gabriel

Television: Clare of Assisi

Television workers: Gabriel

Tertiaries (secular Franciscans): Louis of France, Elizabeth of Hungary

Theologians: Augustine, Alphonsus Liguori

Throat ailments: Blaise

Travel hostesses: Bona

Travelers: Anthony of Padua, Nicholas of Myra, Christopher, Raphael

Universities: Blessed Contardo Ferrini

Vocations: Alphonsus

Watchmen: Peter of Alcantara

Weavers: Paul the Hermit, Anastasius the Fuller, Anastasia

Wine merchants: Amand

Women in labor: Anne

Women's Army Corps: Genevieve

Workingmen: Joseph

Writers: Francis de Sales, Lucy

Yachtsmen: Adjutor

Young girls: Agnes

Youth: Aloysius Gonzaga, John Berchmans, Gabriel of the Sorrowful Mother

Patron Saints of Places

In addition to your vocation, your nationality determines your patron saint. Yes, you can have more than one. If you're Irish, do not pray to St. George, the patron of England. He's very likely to snub you.

Alsace: Odilia

Americas: Our Lady of Guadalupe, Rose of Lima

Angola: Immaculate Heart of Mary

Argentina: Our Lady of Lujan

Armenia: Gregory Illuminator

Asia Minor: Evangelist John

Australia: Our Lady Help of Christians

Belgium: Joseph

Bohemia: Wenceslaus, Ludmilla

Borneo: Francis Xavier

Brazil: Nossa Senhora de Aparecida, Immaculate Conception, Peter of Alcantara

Canada: Joseph, Anne

Chile: James the Greater, Our Lady of Mt. Carmel

China: Joseph

Colombia: Peter Claver, Louis Bertran

Corsica: Immaculate Conception

Czechoslovakia: Wenceslaus, John Nepomucene, Procopius

Denmark: Ansgar, Canute

Dominican Republic: Our Lady of High Grace, Dominic

East Indies: Thomas

Ecuador: Sacred Heart

El Salvador: Our Lady of Peace

England: George

Equatorial Guinea: Immaculate Conception

Europe: Benedict; Cyril and Methodius

Finland: Henry

France: Our Lady of the Assumption, Joan of Arc, Therese

Germany: Boniface, Michael

Gibraltar: Blessed Virgin Mary under title "Our Lady of Europe"

Greece: Nicholas, Andrew

Holland: Willibrord

Hungary: Blessed Virgin, "Great Lady of Hungary"; Stephen; Kinga

Iceland: Thorlac

India: Our Lady of Assumption

Ireland: Patrick, Brigid, Columba

Italy: Francis of Assisi, Catherine of Siena

Japan: Peter Baptist

Korea: Joseph; Mary, Mother of the Church

Lesotho: Immaculate Heart of Mary

Lithuania: Casimir, Cunegunda

Luxembourg: Willibrord

Malta: Paul, Our Lady of the Assumption

Mexico: Our Lady of Guadalupe

Monaco: Devota

Moravia: Cyril, Methodius

New Zealand: Our Lady Help of Christians

Norway: Olaf

Papua New Guinea (including northern Solomon Islands): Michael the Archangel

Paraguay: Our Lady of Assumption

Peru: Joseph

Philippines: Sacred Heart of Mary

Poland: Casimir, Cunegunda, Stanislaus of Cracow, Our Lady of Czestochowa

Portugal: Immaculate Conception, Francis Borgia, Anthony of Padua, Vincent of Saragossa, George

Russia: Andrew, Nicholas of Myra, Therese of Lisieux

Scandinavia: Ansgar

Scotland: Andrew, Columba

Silesia: Hedwig

Slovakia: Our Lady of Sorrows

South Africa: Our Lady of Assumption

South America: Rose of Lima

Spain: James the Greater, Teresa

Sri Lanka (Ceylon): Lawrence

Sweden: Bridget, Eric

Tanzania: Immaculate Conception

United States: Immaculate Conception

Uruguay: Blessed Virgin Mary under title "La Virgen de los Treinte y Tres"

Venezuela: Our Lady of Coromoto

Wales: David

West Indies: Gertrude

Emblems, Portrayals of Saints

Various saints are known by symbols. St. Agnes is identified by the symbol of a lamb. Agnus in Latin means "lamb," so the symbol is fitting. St. Andrew is symbolized by "X," which denotes the transverse cross upon which he was crucified. Why St. Antony is symbolized by a hog remains a mystery.

Agatha: Tongs, veil

Agnes: Lamb

Ambrose: Bees, dove, ox, pen

Andrew: Transverse cross

Anne, Mother of the Blessed Virgin: Door

Antony of Padua: Infant Jesus, bread, book, lily

Antony the Abbot: Bell, hog

Augustine of Hippo: Dove, child, shell, pen

Barnabas: Stones, ax, lance

Bartholomew: Knife, flayed and holding his skin

Benedict: Broken cup, raven, bell, crosier bush

Bernard of Clairvaux: Pen, bees, instruments of the Passion

Bernardine of Siena: Tablet or sun inscribed with "IHS"

Blaise: Wax, taper, iron comb

Bonaventure: Communion, ciborium, cardinal's hat

Boniface: Oak, ax, book, fox, scourge, fountain, raven, sword

Bridget of Sweden: Book, pilgrim's staff

Brigid of Kildare: Cross, flame over her head, candle

Catherine of Ricci: Ring, crown, crucifix

Catherine of Siena: Stigmata, cross, ring, lily

Cecilia: Organ

Charles Borromeo: Communion, coat of arms with word *Humiltas*

Christopher: Giant, torrent, tree, Child Jesus on his shoulders

Clare of Assisi: Monstrance

Cosmas and Damian: Phial, box of ointment

Cyril of Alexandria: Blessed Virgin holding the Child Jesus, pen

Cyril of Jerusalem: Purse, book

Dominic: Rosary, star

Edmund the Martyr: Arrow, sword

Elizabeth of Hungary: Alms, flowers, bread, the poor, a pitcher

Francis of Assisi: Wolf, birds, fish, skull, stigmata

Francis Xavier: Crucifix, bell, vessel

Genevieve: Bread, keys, herd, candle

George: Dragon

Gertrude: Crown, taper, lily

Gervase and Protase: Scourge, club, sword

Gregory I (the Great): Tiara, crosier, dove

Helena: Cross

Hilary: Stick, pen, child

Ignatius of Loyola: Communion, chasuble, book, apparition of Our Lord

Isidore: Bees, pen

James the Greater: Pilgrim's staff, shell, key, sword

James the Less: Square rule, halberd, club

Jerome: Lion

John Berchmans: Rule of St. Ignatius, cross, rosary

John Chrysostom: Bees, dove, pen

John of God: Alms, heart, crown of thorns

John the Baptist: Lamb, head cut off on platter, skin of an animal

John the Evangelist: Eagle, chalice, kettle, armor

Josaphat Kuncevyc: Chalice, crown, winged deacon

Joseph, Spouse of the Blessed Virgin: Infant Jesus, lily, rod, plane, carpenter's square

Jude: Sword, square rule, club

Justin Martyr: Ax, sword

Lawrence: Cross, book of the Gospels, gridiron

Leander of Seville: A pen

Liborius: Pebbles, peacock

Longinus: In arms at foot of the cross

Louis IX of France: Crown of thorns, nails

Lucy: Cord, eyes on a dish

Luke: Ox, book, brush, palette

Mark: Lion, book

Martha: Holy water sprinkler, dragon

Mary Magdalene: Alabaster box of ointment

Matilda: Purse, alms

Matthew: Winged man, purse, lance

Matthias: Lance

Maurus: Scales, spade, crutch

Meinrad: Two ravens

Michael: Scales, banner, sword, dragon

Monica: Girdle, tears

Nicholas: Three purses or balls, anchor or boat, child

Patrick: Cross, harp, serpent, baptismal font, demons, shamrock

Paul: Sword, book or scroll

Peter: Keys, boat, cock

Philip, Apostle: Column

Philip Neri: Altar, chasuble, vial

Rita of Cascia: Rose, crucifix, thorn

Roch: Angel, dog, bread

Rose of Lima: Crown of thorns, anchor, city

Sebastian: Arrows, crown

Simon Stock: Scapular

Teresa of Jesus (Avila): Heart, arrow, book

Therese of Lisieux: Roses entwining a crucifix

Thomas, Apostle: Lance, ax

Thomas Aquinas: Chalice, monstrance, dove, ox, person trampled underfoot

Vincent (Deacon): Gridiron, boat

Vincent de Paul: Children

Vincent Ferrer: Pulpit, cardinal's hat, trumpet, captives

Feast Days of the Saints

The Proper (calendar) of the Saints of the Roman Catholic Church follows the Order of the Civil Year, Nov. 27 to Nov. 26. Care should be taken to consult the Proper of the local diocese, because Feasts are not only celebrated by the Universal Church but also by particular dioceses and different congregations.

Nov. 29   St. Saturninus, Martyr. He died in 304, but did he exist?

Nov. 30   St. Andrew, Apostle

Dec. 2   St. Bibiana, Virgin, Martyr. The poor girl was scourged to death in 363.

Dec. 3   St. Francis Xavier, Confessor. A Jesuit hero. He gave away his money and preached the gospel in India, China, and Japan.

Dec. 4   St. Peter Chrysologus, Bishop, Confessor. "Chrysologus" means golden-worded, but his spiritual works read like lead.

Dec. 4   St. Barbara, Virgin, Martyr.

Dec. 5   St. Sabbas, Abbot.

Dec. 6   St. Nicholas, Bishop, Confessor. This is the day for Santa Claus, not Dec. 25.

Dec. 7   St. Ambrose, Bishop, Confessor. This guy, according to St. Augustine, could read without moving his lips.

Dec. 8   The Immaculate Conception of Mary. Read it again. The Immaculate Conception of Mary—not Mary's Immaculate Conception.

Dec. 10   St. Melchiades, Pope, Martyr. Don't believe the martyr part. This guy died a natural death, but he did suffer under the persecution of Maxmimian.

Dec. 11   St. Damasus, Pope, Confessor. Yes, another pope and we're not even through December.

Dec. 12   Our Lady of Guadalupe. This reminds me: Why wasn't Juan Diego, who beheld this apparition, canonized?

Dec. 13   St. Lucy, Virgin, Martyr. She absolutely refused to relinquish the "incorruptible treasure of her virginity" to the very end.

Dec. 14   St. John of the Cross, Confessor, Doctor. A marvelous day for mystics who want to behold the Beatific Vision.

Dec. 16   St. Eusebius, Bishop, Martyr.

Dec. 21   St. Thomas, Apostle. A day for doubters.

Dec. 22   St. Frances Xavier Cabrini. Go see her body in the Bronx.

Dec. 26   St. Stephen, Martyr. The first Christian to get stoned.

Dec. 27   St. John, Apostle, Evangelist. The only apostle who lived to a ripe old age.

Dec. 28   The Holy Innocents, Martyrs. The only infants before the Ascension who did not end up in limbo.

Dec. 29   St. Thomas Becket, Bishop, Martyr. One of Richard Burton's better roles.

Dec. 30   The Holy Family, Feast.

Jan. 1   Solemnity of Mary. This used to be the Feast of the Circumcision.

Jan. 2   St. Basil the Great and St. Gregory Nazianzen. Proof of nepotism in the divine kingdom.

Jan. 3   Epiphany of the Lord.

Jan. 4   St. Elizabeth Ann Seton.

Jan. 7   St. John Neumann, Bishop.

Jan. 14   St. Hilary, Bishop, Doctor. Please don't confuse with Senator Hillary. This guy wrote books on the Holy Trinity that no one reads today,

Jan. 15   St. Paul, the Holy Hermit. This guy was buried by a devout pride of lions.

Jan. 20   St. Sebastian, Martyr.

Jan. 16   St. Marcellus, Pope, Martyr. He really wasn't killed. He was exiled, but he was a pope.

Jan. 17   St. Antony, Abbot. The man who became the very first monk.

Jan. 21   St. Agnes, Virgin, Martyr. She won her crown at 13.

Jan. 22   St. Vincent, Martyr.

Jan. 23   St. Raymond of Pennafort, Confessor. This guy came up with canon law.

Jan. 25   The Conversion of St. Paul.

Jan. 26   St. Timothy, Bishop, Martyr. St. Paul's good buddy.

Jan. 30   St. Martina, Virgin, Martyr.

Jan. 31   St. John Bosco, Confessor. Founder of the Salesian Society of St. Francis de Sales.

Feb. 1   St. Ignatius, Bishop, Martyr. Thrown to the lions in 107, he said: "May I become agreeable bread to the Lord."

Feb. 2   Presentation of Jesus in the Temple.

Feb. 3   St. Blaise, Bishop, Martyr. Don't forget to have your throat blessed.

Feb. 4   St. Andrew Corsini, Bishop, Confessor.

Feb. 5   St. Agatha, Virgin, Martyr. A saint for the Sopranos.

Feb. 8   St. Dorothy, Virgin, Martyr.

Feb. 7   St. Romuald, Abbot. The "angelic hermit."

Feb. 9   St. Cyril of Alexandria, Bishop, Doctor.

Feb. 10   St. Scholastica, Virgin. St. Benedict's sister.

Feb. 11   The Apparition of Our Lady of Lourdes.

Feb. 14   Sts. Cyril and Methodius, Bishops, Confessors. The Greeks love these guys.

Feb. 14   St. Valentine, Priest, Martyr.

Feb. 15   Sts. Faustinus and Jovita, Martyrs.

Feb. 18   St. Marie Bernadette Soubirous, Virgin. She saw the Virgin and ate grass, go figure!

Feb. 24   St. Matthias, Apostle. The Gerald Ford of the saints.

Feb. 23   St. Polycarp, Bishop, Martyr. His bones were more precious than the rarest jewels.

Feb. 27   St. Gabriel of Our Lady of Sorrows. He devoted himself to Our Lady of Sorrows and died of consumption at 21.

March 4   St. Casimir, Confessor. The son of a Polish king who preserved his chastity against all odds.

March 6   Sts. Perpetua and Felicitas, Martyrs. The most famous saints in the early Church.

March 7   St. Thomas Aquinas, Confessor, Doctor. By proclamation, the "greatest Catholic theologian." Unfortunately, he's no fun to read.

March 9   St. Frances of Rome, Widow.

March 10   The Forty Holy Martyrs.

March 12   St. Gregory the Great, Confessor, Doctor. When this pope died, priest and monks began to sing the Gregorian chant.

March 17   St. Patrick, Bishop, Confessor.

March 18   St. Cyril of Jerusalem, Bishop, Confessor.

March 19   St. Joseph, Spouse of the Blessed Virgin Mary and Patron of the Universal Church.

March 21   St. Benedict, Abbot. St. Scholastica's brother.

March 22   St. Isidore, the Farm-Laborer, Confessor.

March 24   St. Gabriel, Archangel. Proof that some extra-terrestrial beings are saints.

March 25   The Annunciation of the Blessed Virgin Mary. A day in honor of the first "Hail Mary."

March 27   St. John Damascene, Confessor.

March 29   St. John of Capistrano, Confessor. A great military recruiter, he enrolled 70,000 warriors for the crusades.

April 3   St. Isidore, Bishop, Confessor. He restored Catholicism in Spain.

April 5   St. Vincent Ferrer, Confessor. He could speak every language in the world and converted thousands of Jews and sinners.

April 11   St. Leo I, Pope, Confessor. This guy managed to scare the hell out of Attila the Hun.

April 13   St. Hermenegild, Martyr. Put to death for refusing to accept Holy Communion from a bishop who had not been properly ordained.

April 14   St. Justin, Martyr.

April 17   St. Anicetus, Pope, Martyr. Another pope who is venerated as a holy martyr even though he died in bed.

April 21   St. Anselm, Bishop, Confessor, Doctor. The Father of Scholastic Theology.

April 22   Sts. Soter and Caius, Popes, Martyrs.

April 23   St. George, Martyr.

April 24   St. Fidelis of Sigmaringen, Martyr. A holy friar who was fried (literally) by Protestants in 1622.

April 25   St. Mark, Evangelist.

April 26   Sts. Cletus and Marcellinus, Popes, Martyrs. More proof that it pays (in the end) to be a pope.

April 27   St. Peter Canisius, Confessor, Doctor.

April 28   St. Paul of the Cross, Confessor.

April 28   St. Vitalis, Martyr.

April 29   St. Peter of Verona, Martyr.

April 30   St. Catherine of Siena, Virgin, Doctor. She underwent a mystic experience known as the "spiritual espousals."

May 2   St. Athanasius, Bishop, Confessor.

May 3   The Finding of the Holy Cross. The great relic was discovered by the Emperor Constantine's mother, St. Helena. A splinter is worth a fortune.

May 4   St. Monica, Widow. St. Augustine's mama.

May 7   St. Stanislaus, Bishop, Martyr.

May 10   St. Antoninus, Bishop, Confessor.

May 11   Sts. Philip and James, Apostles

May 12   Sts. Nereus, Achilleus, Somitilla, and Pancras, Martyrs

May 12   St. Robert Bellarmine, Bishop, Confessor, Doctor. He wrote against Protestant heresies.

May 14   St. Boniface, Martyr.

May 15   St. John Baptist de la Salle, Confessor. The "father of modern pedioagogy."

May 16   St. Ubaldus, Bishop, Confessor. The goombah of Gubbio.

May 17   St. Paschal Baylon, Confessor.

May 19   St. Peter Celestine, Pope, Confessor. He gave up the papacy to live as a hermit in a cave.

May 20   St. Bernardine of Siena, Confessor.

May 26   St. Gregory VII, Pope, Confessor. The pope who made a king beg for mercy.

May 26   St. Philip Neri, Confessor.

May 27   St. Bede the Venerable, Confessor. "The Father of English History."

May 28   St. Felix I, Pope, Martyr.

May 31   The Queenship of the Blessed Virgin Mary.

June 1   St. Angela Merici, Virgin. Founder of the Ursulines.

June 2   Sts. Marcellinus and Peter, Martyrs.

June 6   St. Boniface, Bishop. Martyr. The first bishop of Germany.

June 9   Sts. Primus and Felician, Martyrs.

June 10   St. Margaret, Queen of Scotland, Widow.

June 11   St. Barnabas, Apostle. According to the Book of Acts, this guy was really good-looking.

June 12   St. John of Facundo, Confessor.

June 13   St. Anthony of Padua, Confessor. This saint can help you find anything you may have lost.

June 15   Sts. Vitus, Modestus, Crescentia, Martyrs. Did I remember to tell you about the St. Vitus Dance?

June 18   St. Ephrem the Syrian, Deacon, Confessor.

June 19   St. Juliani Falconieri, Virgin. She miraculously received Viaticum (Holy Communion) at the time of her death.

June 20   St. Silverus, Pope, Martyr. This pope was exiled to the Island of Pontus by the Empress Theodosia.

June 21   St. Aloysius Gonzaga, Confessor. Hailed as "a veritable angel in the flesh" because of his purity.

June 22   St. Paulinus, Bishop, Confessor.

June 24   Nativity of St. John the Baptist.

June 25   St. William, Abbot.

June 28   St. Irenaeus, Bishop, Martyr.

June 29   Sts. Peter and Paul, Apostles. What a double-header. The two great ones on the same day!

July 1   The Most Precious Blood of our Lord Jesus Christ.

July 2   Visitation of our Blessed Lady. Mary's trip to see her cousin, St. Elizabeth, who recited to her a verse of the "Hail Mary."

July 3   St. Leo II, Pope, Confessor.

July 5   St. Anthony Mary Zaccaria, Confessor. This guy's middle name really was Mary. No one knows if he ever questioned his sexual identity. Come to think of it, a lot of male saints have Mary as their middle name.

July 10   The Seven Holy Brothers, Martyrs. The sons of St. Felicitas who preferred death rather than the renunciation of their Baptismal vows.

July 11   St. Pius I, Pope, Martyr.

July 12   St. John Gualbert, Abbot. He set out as an assassin and ended up in a monastery.

July 12   St. Anacletus, Pope, Martyr.

July 14   St. Bonaventure, Bishop, Confessor, Doctor. This guy is called the "Seraphic Doctor."

July 15   St. Henry, Emperor, Confessor. This remarkable King of Germany preserved virginity in marriage. His wife, some say, had buck teeth and bad breath.

July 16   Our Lady of Mt. Carmel. On this day in 1726, the Virgin Mary gave a scapular to St. Simon Stock.

July 17   St. Alexius, Confessor. The prince who became a pauper, long before Mark Twain came up with the story.

July 18   St. Camillus of Lellis, Confessor.

July 19   St. Vincent de Paul, Confessor. Founder of the Congregation of the Daughters of Charity.

July 21   St. Praxedes, Virgin,

July 22   St. Mary Magdalene, Penitent. Heaven's holy hooker.

July 23   St. Apollinaris, Bishop, Martyr.

July 23   St. Bridget, Widow. The Princess of Sweden, not the Irish Virgin.

July 24   St. Christina, Virgin, Martyr.

July 25   St. James, Apostle. This used to be the feast day for St. Christopher, before the incredible giant was exposed as a pious fraud.

July 26   St. Anne, Mother of Our Blessed Lady. Go to the novena in Scranton, PA, where her bones can cure what ails you.

July 27   St. Pantaleon, Martyr.

July 28   St. Victor I, Pope, Martyr; St. Innocent I, Pope. Confessor. More proof that Heaven is packed with popes.

July 29   St. Martha, Virgin. According to Catholic tradition, she was the sister of Lazarus and Mary Magdalene, who was not a virgin.

July 30   Sts. Abdon and Sennen, Martyrs.

July 31   St. Ignatius of Loyola, Confessor. The founder of the Jesuits.

Aug. 1   The Holy Machabees, Martyrs. Jews who got their own feast day. Proof that not all (just almost all) saints are Catholic.

Aug. 2   St. Alphonous Mary de Liguori. Another male Mary. This one founded the Redemptorists.

Aug. 9   St. John Mary Vianney, Confessor. This guy really was a confessor. He heard confessions 16 hours a day every day of his priestly life.

Aug. 6   The Transfiguration of our Lord Jesus Christ.

Aug. 8   St. Dominic, Confessor. Mary gave him the Rosary. He gave us the Inquisition.

Aug. 10   St. Lawrence, Martyr. This guy was roasted to death on a red-hot gridiron over a slow fire.

Aug. 11   St. Clare, Virgin. The patron saint of television.

Aug. 13   St. Pontus, Pope.

Aug. 15   The Assumption of the Blessed Virgin Mary.

Aug. 16   St. Joachim, Confessor. The Virgin Mary's father.

Aug. 17   St. Hyacinth, Confessor.

Aug. 18   St. Agapitus, Martyr.

Aug. 19   St. John Eudes, Confessor.

Aug. 20   St. Bernard, Abbot. He preached the Second Crusade, which was a complete disaster.

Aug. 21   St. Jane Francis de Chantal, Widow.

Aug. 22   The Feast of the Immaculate Heart of Mary.

Aug. 23   St. Rose of Lima, Virgin.

Aug. 24   St. Bartholomew, Apostle. This guy really got skinned.

Aug. 25   St. Louis, King, Confessor. The King of France who got crowned in Heaven.

Aug. 26   St. Zephyrinus, Pope, Martyr.

Aug, 28   St. Augustine, Bishop, Confessor, Doctor. This guy gave us the doctrine of original sin. Thank you very much.

Aug. 29   The Feast of the Beheading of St. John the Baptist. Three churches in the Middle Ages claimed to have possession of this great man's head.

Aug. 31   St. Raymund Nonnatus, Confessor.

Sept. 1   St. Giles, Abbot.

Sept. 2   St. Stephen, King, Confessor. The first Catholic King of Hungary.

Sept. 8   The Nativity of the Blessed Virgin Mary.

Sept. 9   St. Peter Claver, Confessor. The first Catholic abolitionist.

Sept. 10   St. Nicholas of Tolentine, Confessor. This saint prayed day and night to alleviate the suffering of souls in purgatory.

Sept. 12   The Most Holy Name of Mary.

Sept. 14   The Exaltation of the Holy Cross. This feast is a celebration of the recovery of the Holy Cross from the nasty King of Persia who stole it.

Sept. 15   The Seven Sorrows of the Blessed Virgin Mary.

Sept. 16   St. Cornelius, Pope; St. Cyprian, Bishop, Martyr.

Sept. 19   St. Januarius, Bishop, and His Companions, Martyrs. Every year, at a church in Naples, the powdery blood of St. Januarius turns into liquid and runs through plastic tubes. It's a real tourist attraction.

Sept. 20   St. Andrew Kim, Priest, St. Paul Chong, Lay Apostles, and Companions, Martyrs of Korea. Proof of Asians in the mostly Occidental Communion of Saints.

Sept. 21   St. Matthew, Apostle.

Sept. 22   St. Maurice and Companions, Martyrs. St. Maurice was the commander of 5,000 Roman soldiers who refused to make sacrifices to the pagan gods.

Sept. 23   St. Linus, Pope, Martyr. The guy who succeeded St. Peter as Pope.

Sept. 26   St. Isaac Jogues, St. Jean de Brebeuf, and Companions, Martyrs. Jesuits who really irritated the Iroquois Indians.

Sept. 27   Sts. Cosmas and Damian, Martyrs. Two brothers and physicians who were great faith healers.

Sept. 28   St. Wenceslaus, Martyr.

Sept. 30   St. Jerome, Priest, Doctor. The strictest of saints.

Oct. 1   St. Remigus, Bishop, Confessor.

Oct. 2   The Holy Guardian Angels. More proof that you don't have to be human to be a saint.

Oct. 3   St. Therese of the Child Jesus. She is known as the "Little Flower" because she died in the odor of sanctity.

Oct. 4   St. Francis of Assisi, Confessor. Our Lord "favored" him with the stigmata.

Oct. 5   St. Placidus and Companions, Martyrs.

Oct. 6   St. Bruno, Confessor.

Oct. 7   The Most Holy Rosary of the Blessed Virgin Mary.

Oct. 9   St. John Leonard, Confessor.

Oct. 10   St. Francis Borgia, Confessor. Yes, a member of the notorious Borgia family is a saint. His uncle was a pope.

Oct. 13   St. Edward, King, Confessor. The "model for Christian kings."

Oct. 14   St. Callistus, Pope, Martyr.

Oct. 15   St. Teresa of Avila, Virgin, Doctor.

Oct. 16   St. Margaret Mary Alacoque, Virgin. She revealed to the Christian world the devotion to the Sacred Heart of Jesus.

Oct. 18   St. Luke, Evangelist. He was also the artist who painted the "Black Madonna."

Oct. 19   St. Peter of Alacantara, Confessor.

Oct. 21   St. Ursula and Companions, Virgins, Martyrs.

Oct. 25   Sts. Chrysanthus and Daria, Martyrs. A husband and wife who were buried alive.

Oct. 26   St. Evaristus, Pope, Martyr. Are you poped out yet?

Oct. 28   Sts. Simon and Jude, Apostles. Jude's real name was Judas, but no one wants to think of Judas as a saint.

Nov. 1   The Feast of All Saints.

Nov. 2   The Feast of All Souls. These souls are still cooking in purgatory. Some won't be ready for the Messianic banquet for thousands of years.

Nov. 4   St. Charles Borromeo, Bishop, Confessor.

Nov. 8   The Four Holy Crowned Martyrs. Four brothers—Severus, Severian, Carpophorus and Victorinus—who were fed to Roman circus animals.

Nov. 9   St. Theodore, Martyr.

Nov. 10   St. Andrew Avellino, Confessor. This guy was a saintly lawyer. Sounds like an oxymoron to me.

Nov. 11   St. Martin, Bishop, Confessor.

Nov. 12   St. Martin, Pope, Martyr. Two Martins in a row or, in Latin, a Martini.

Nov. 12   St. Didacus, Confessor. He was known as being "simple-minded."

Nov. 14   St. Josaphat, Bishop, Martyr.

Nov. 15   St. Albert the Great. Teacher of St. Thomas Aquinas.

Nov. 16   St. Gertrude, Virgin.

Nov. 17   St. Gregory the Wonder Worker, Bishop, Confessor.

Nov. 19   St. Elizabeth, Widow.

Nov. 21   The Presentation of the Blessed Virgin Mary.

Nov. 22   St. Cecilia, Virgin, Martyr. Forced to marry a pagan, she converted him on their wedding night and made him vow to preserve her virginity.

Nov. 23   St. Clement, Pope, Martyr. The third successor of St. Peter to the papal throne.

Nov. 25   St. Catherine, Virgin, Martyr. An educated woman from Alexandria who lost her head but not her maidenhead.

Index

C

P

Pachomius, 118
  gift of tongues, 118
  monasteries, 118
pagans, attack on Christians
  with words, 94
  Celsus, 94-95
  Christian defense, 95-107
  Fronto, 97
  Lucian, 94
pardoners (papal emissaries
  who sold letters of indulgence), removal from purgatory, 22-23
parochial school system,
  St. Elizabeth Ann Seton,
  founder, 239
*Passion of Perpetua and
Felicitas, The*, 71
Patrick (Christian missionary), 136
  conversion of nation to
    Christianity, 136-137
  shamrock, 137
patron saints (and
  patronesses), 251-258
  Doctors of the Church,
    161-162
    St. Albert the Great,
      166
    St. Ambrose, 164
    St. Augustine, 164-165
    St. Jerome, 163-164
    St. Thomas Aquinas,
      165-167
  Mary Magdalene (prosti-
    tutes), 17
  places, 258-261
  St. Aldegund (cancer and
    childhood diseases), 221
  St. Andrew (fishermen,
    fishmongers, and
    sailors), 37-38
  St. Antony (basketweavers
    and brush makers), 117
  St. Barbara (all who han-
    dle explosives), 128
  St. Bartholomew (butch-
    ers, furriers, dyers,
    leather workers, shoe-
    makers), 38

St. Basil the Great (hospital administrators), 122
St. Bee (laborers), 220
St. Bernadette (shep-
  herds), 208
St. Boniface (Germany),
  143
St. Brigid (Ireland, New
  Zealand, milkmaids,
  fugitives, and poultry
  raisers), 138
St. Catherine of
  Alexandria (wheelrights,
  students, college professors), 104
St. Cecilia (music), 65
St. Christina the
  Astonishing (madness),
  222
St. Christopher (travelers,
  bachelors, bus drivers,
  ferryboat men, horse-
  men, police officers,
  skiers, and truck driv-
  ers), 224
St. Columba (poetry), 140
St. David (Wales), 185
St. Dorothy (brides,
  florists, and gardeners),
  127
St. Emillion (Spain), 185
St. Fiacre (cab drivers, gardeners, and needle
  makers), 145
St. Gabriel (telecommuni-
  cations industry),
  172-173
St. Homonbonus (tailors),
  217
St. James the Greater
  (chemists, apothecaries,
  druggists), 43
St. James the Less (dying),
  42-43
St. John (bookbinders,
  booksellers, publishers,
  and writers), 43-44
St. Jude (lost causes), 41
St. Justin Martyr (philosophers, philosophy, and
  apologists), 97
St. Marcarius (pastry
  chefs), 120

St. Martin (drunkards,
  innkeepers, and geese),
  218
St. Mary of Egypt (peni-
  tent women and
  reformed prostitutes),
  130
St. Matthew (bookkeep-
  ers, accountants,
  Church mission), 45
St. Matthias (alcoholics),
  46
St. Nicholas of Tolentino
  (souls in purgatory), 22
St. Paul (Protestants), 50
  appearance, 51
  disciples, 55-60
  legends, 52-53
  turn against Judaism,
    51
  undermining of St.
    Peter, 50
St. Pelagia (actresses),
  130-131
St. Peter (Heaven), 14
St. Peter (Rome and
  Catholic Church), 36
St. Philip (bread makers
  and pastry chefs), 46-47
St. Restituta (women in
  prison), 74-75
St. Roch (protection from
  plagues), 15
St. Scholastica (rain), 131
St. Sebastian (archers,
  athletes, ironmongers,
  soldiers, lace workers,
  and plague victims),
  88-90
St. Simeon (shepherds),
  121
St. Simon (saw men and
  curriers), 40
St. Teresa (Spain), 204
St. Therese (florists,
  France). 231
St. Thomas (architects,
  builders, and construc-
  tion workers), 39-40
symbols/emblems,
  261-264